25 stories

I would tell my Younger Self

by Dr. Julian Hosp

25 Stories I would tell my Younger Self

Copyright © 2015 by Dr. Julian Hosp

ISBN-13: 978-988-14850-0-7

Website: www.25stories.org

Give feedback on the book at:
www.facebook.com/25stories

Dedicated to my Mom,
as it was she who paved my way.

25 stories I would tell my Younger Self
by Dr. Julian Hosp

"How your seemingly small and unimportant decisions have a huge and often unexpected impact on your life."

PREFACE

"There's always room for a story that can transport people to another place." – J.K. Rowling

Making mistakes seems to be a given. But what if I told you that this is pure stupidity? "Why?" you might ask. What if you could have anticipated it being a mistake because you had the chance to know what could be the most likely outcome already in foresight? "Impossible!" you might think and of course, if you attempt something for the first time, chances are, you will most probably not get it right. But let me take you to a place in your early youth: Think of your very first bicycle ride - when your mom or dad put you on that bike and got you going for the first time! I would imagine that you did not get very far and fell over. But even though it was your first time, did something major happen to you? Most probably not, and the reason for that is quite simple: Your parents anticipated that you might fall. They had experienced it enough themselves and so just after they put you on your bike and gave you a push they were chasing after you ready to catch you if you fell. Most likely they even gave you a helmet… just in case… Yes, you might have fallen, but your parents where there to catch you and your helmet protected you, even though you probably weren't going very fast anyway. Eventually, pretty much all of us survived our first bike ride without many scratches.

So, what's my point here? Well, whenever I think of that story, that most of us experienced as children and then maybe even again as parents, it makes me wonder, why in that case did we prepare ourselves properly, but in so many other cases we don't? Like, for example, do you remember the first time you invested money into something? You lost it, didn't you? Your first love? Broke your heart? The first horror movie that made you afraid of clowns? The first time you had to speak in front of a group of people and you blushed and couldn't get a word out? You could have been well prepared, but you probably didn't wear your "helmet" or have your parents running after you to protect you. We do learn from these experiences through positive feedback: when something works out, we do it again. The same is true for negative outcomes: you get hurt and stop doing that activity afterwards. The examples I have been giving above are quite easy and straightforward ones, and I could elaborate on school choices, the sports you play, the job you work in, or the life partner you choose.

So why not improve the whole learning process like in the bicycle story? "What if there was a "helmet"? What if there was the possibility for people to avoid making all their mistakes by themselves over and over again, but they could instead learn from other people, who had already made these mistakes before?" The result would be that one would avoid crashing all together, or just trip, without serious injury. Crashing in that context is just a figure of speech, of course. So, how do we learn to "crash better"? There are around a million, "Self Development" books out there and even more articles on the Internet, such as for example, "The ten most important things to avoid as a teenager". I have read many of them, but probably just as it is with many other people, the points these books try to get across hardly ever stick. They are too factual and I can't relate to them well enough to remember them long term. Yes, a tip like: "Always save 10% of your income" sounds great, but you know what? The month after I read it, I am spending a 100% of my money again and nothing is left over. Feel the same way? Even though you have just read about something in one of these "Self Development" books the month before, it does not even stay with you after such a short time. So after some contemplating, I figured there must be a better way!

During my business development work for several companies we had one key lesson to increase sales: "Facts tell, Stories sell!" Customers would not buy the product you were selling directly, no matter how good it was. Rather, they were buying your story about the product and only through relating to that story would they actually buy the product afterwards. It always sounded a bit strange when we taught that to new sales people, but everyone knew it was working. Translating that into the problems I was facing (and probably millions of other people out there as well) it would mean that for me to actually learn and become more prepared for life, I had to tell a story about the problem, and explain the lessons I derived from that experience afterwards. Otherwise, it would not stick, and I would not be "wearing a helmet". Think about it! What was the last YouTube Video you watched, podcast you listened to or event you attended? What did you take away from it? It is probably a story that teaches a lesson, am I right? Take a second, and think back! It is not the fact itself; it is the attached story that gets you to remember it. Based on that idea I started giving little talks for the company I was working with. I started sharing stories and I gave tips based on what I had experienced. The feedback was great and these little talks turned into larger presentations and then even keynote speeches in many countries all over the world, such as Europe, the US, Hong Kong, Singapore, Thailand and several others. I began to realize how much a simple but well-structured story inspired people, as long as I included the lessons to take away from it afterwards. Just like myself, people started to better relate to what was being explained to them. The lessons started to stick, not because of the lessons themselves, but rather because of the stories that they could relate to and put themselves into.

Over the years I have given so many talks that I developed a list of all the stories that I had ever shared. This was very helpful because before an event I could speak to the organizer about the type of audience and content they expected. Then, in 40-45 minutes I could share the three to four stories that fit the best. This list had grown quite extensively and so at some point I wondered: "Wouldn't it be way more powerful if more people could listen to ALL of the stories rather than just a few during an event? Maybe a few people in the room would need to hear those three stories and someone else three others!" So, I created a final list of 25 of my most powerful and helpful stories that I would have loved to send to my younger self in a time capsule. This is how the book's title "25 stories I would tell my Younger Self" was born. While reading these 25 stories, you will see many parallels to things that have happened or will happen in your own life. You will realize that it is not about my story being so unique, but I want these stories to inspire you to take away the key messages and adapt them to your own stories. We all share many similar values, beliefs or merits and so, even though a story may be unique in itself to you or me, we can learn valuable insights by looking at the path other people have walked before us and where it eventually led them.

The book is not about trying to teach the reader how to avoid mistakes all together, because that would mean to stop attempting new things. Rather its intent is to increase the awareness about the experiences of others and how to learn the most from these events. The 25 stories are ranked chronologically as I experienced them in my own life. Some of them go on for longer periods or intertwine with each other. My teachers always complemented me on my ability to extemporize on all kinds of subjects, but scolded me on my ability to write proper English. So, when writing this book I wanted to make sure you are experiencing my stories in my own words and thinking. I am not using a ghostwriter and sometimes I will use words or sentences that might be slightly incorrect. But I feel it is crucial to get my points and feelings across so you can experience the true Julian Hosp, and not some altered one. Thank you Terry Teemley and Gillian Kew for their help with editing – no one could have done a better job leaving my style but putting it into proper English. Still, if you find a mistake, do understand this is the way I am, and keep the mistake :-)

Many people ask me, if I had been given this book from a Future Self, would I have made no mistakes afterwards? Of course not – I would have still made hundreds! I would have just learned faster from my mistakes or have been better prepared – that is really important to understand. It is not about NOT making mistakes; it is about understanding that every decision in life is a choice - whether you say "yes" or "no". And, each choice has consequences – many times unforeseeably huge ones. It is not about worrying which choice is the right one - it is just about understanding how to be prepared and make the most out of every choice. You might be experiencing different stories in your life, but that is not the point. It is about learning from my experiences, so you can implement them into yours. If I manage to achieve just one thing with this book, I would love the reader to understand this law of "cause and effect": if you want to end up where someone else ended up, take the same path! And if you want to end up somewhere else, take a different path! It is one of the simplest rules in life. But despite that simplicity, so few people actually follow it. In the next 25 stories I will show you many paths I took, and if you like the resulting outcomes, walk the same paths as well. If you don't want to end up where I ended up, choose different ones. This is the main lesson to take away.

Despite all the 25 stories being connected of course, each of them is closed in itself, and can therefore be read and used independently. While you are reading the book or listening to the audio, try to start and finish one story and not pause in between. That makes sure you get the full story and the attached lessons in one go. The stories are structured as an easy read anyways and are mostly only a few pages long, so that should not only make sense but also be very doable. If you want to get the most out of each story, do not only think about what lessons you are taking away, but more important, what action you will take based on what you just learned. So, have a notebook ready to mark down YOUR personal key takeaways – best: handwritten. Remember, you can treat this book or audio just like entertainment and it will do its job well, but the true power lies in adopting the key lessons into your own life and treating the book like a business asset – this will only happen through reflection followed by taking committed action! Some of the concepts and ideas will be new or challenging to you, so remember that your mind is like a parachute: It only works if it is open!

With this, have fun and enjoy the read.

Cheers, Julian Hosp

CONTENTS

INTRODUCING THE HOSPs

"The ones that are crazy enough to believe they can change the world - are the ones who do!" – Steve Jobs

I Julian Hosp, was born on February 3rd 1986 in the early afternoon in a small Austrian town called "Hall". My mom jokingly says I was already a problem child before even being born because I tricked her a couple of times that I was going to come out and then when I actually did, she didn't believe me anymore and almost arrived late at the hospital. How funny was I as an unborn already, right? At the hospital the nurse made a mistake and didn't clamp my naval cord properly. It made me lose a lot of blood, so during my first ten days in this world I lived in an incubator. I guess I loved challenges from day one already. My parents describe it as the toughest time during their parenthood – the second toughest one being when I entered puberty a bit over a decade later.

My dad, Laurin, was - and still is - a self-employed architect, and my mom, Anneliese, is a full-time mom with all the demanding tasks attached to that. Had she been working outside of the home as well, she would not have had the time to care for me as much as she did. This life-work balance was the best thing my parents could have given me. My dad's parents (my grand parents) are still alive and the reason I am pointing this out is that at over 90 years old they are still cycling, windsurfing and climbing mountains. If you don't believe it (which most people don't), go on my YouTube Channel and watch them being interviewed by our local TV station about their daily routines that most 60 year olds would be happy to be able to do. Despite having a quite average foundation, as you will see in these upcoming chapters, I must have a pretty good gene pool when it comes to longevity and energy. At least I hope so.

I can't remember much of my first couple of years, other than when I was around two years old, my parents "gave" me a younger sister, Simona. My parents' focus shifted completely to her while up until that point I had received my parents' sole attention. The resulting sibling rivalry instilled a drive of me constantly having to prove myself, which turned out to be quite important for some of my later achievements. Despite that, my sister and I got along quite well - most probably because I had this hunger for constantly being better than her to "win back my parents" and her not really caring about all that. We grew up in an average house in an average town called Mils. My family had an average income and with four people we were an average size family. Why am I telling you this? You can be totally ordinary to have extra-ordinary results. It is all about the action you take based on the choices you make. My sister and I went to the same Kindergarten; she was of course two years beneath me. Afterwards we went to the same Elementary School and Junior High School. In High School, I decided to spend time abroad in the US, while she stayed in Austria. I would not be the same person today had I stayed in Austria as well. Being in the US and away from my parents and my accustomed surroundings made me very open minded and gave me many other skills, which turned out to be crucial during my later years. I am not sure if becoming a professional basketball player or pro kite boarder would have happened the same way had I stayed in Austria. I might not have studied medicine or moved to Asia for business either. Many of the seeds were planted during this time with all the new experiences and impressions I received there.

Today, my sister is a successful therapist, my mom is totally dedicated to sports, and my dad is still working on his architecture projects. I run several successful online and offline businesses and I am passionate about sports as well.

My phone is full of productive podcasts, inspirational lessons, great audiobooks, and motivational pictures. I am based in Hong Kong, travelling most of the time for business and leisure. I consider planet earth my home, with my friends, business partners, and relations spread across the world. Still today I am jotting down new stories and lessons into my journal - so let's see; maybe we will see 25 more stories sometime in the future. I want to deeply thank my mom and dad for raising me the way they did. I did get to spend more time with my mom when growing up, but the times I got to spend with my dad are as precious as they could be. Looking back, we have had hundreds of discussions on mistakes made... But this is exactly what this book is about. 25 stories that we all would have loved to have before growing up! Thanks, mom and dad – I love you and you are the best parents possible! I also want to thank my sister Simona for living with all the "bullcrap" I gave her, and constantly challenging me to be the bigger brother. I also want to thank my best friend Daniel, for being the big brother to me that I never had. I will cherish the kiteboarding times and friendship forever. Last but not least, my girlfriend Bettina! I could have never gathered the energy and inspiration to write this book without her! I love you darling!

Ok, enough cheesy talk, let's get going. We've got 25 stories to share and valuable lessons to take away. Here we go!

1.

THE SWIMMING STORY –
ICE CREAM AS A REWARD

"The only love that I really believe in, is a mother's love for her children." – Karl Lagerfeld

My mom was born in the 1950s in the same town that I grew up in 30 years later. Her family lived in a worn down farmer's house with six children plus maids and workers. It was the remnants of the post-war era, so her childhood was quite rough. Especially being farmers, times weren't easy. While other children could go play or go swimming in the summer, my mom had to work in the fields from a young age to help harvest the crops that ensured the family's survival. Still today she talks about what a hard-working mindset the family always had. Her parents told her over and over however, that once she was older, she would reap the rewards and get back tenfold of what she had put in. They kept their word and when my mom got married 25 years later to my dad, her father gifted her enough land and money so that my parents could build a beautiful three-story house for the family. Shaped by her experience, she instilled the same mindset into me from a very early age. Luckily, I did not have to work hard on our family's farm (even though I helped out a few times), but whenever I wanted to get a treat or a small extra, she would make me work for it.

The memory that sticks out the most is from going to the public swimming pool close to where we live. My cousins, friends, and Elementary School teacher still tease me when going down memory lane. I was five or six years old, and after a few hours at the pool I asked, like most children at that age would, whether I could have an ice cream. I was well behaved and I had learned that if I smiled very nicely my chances of convincing someone would increase exponentially. I made the cutest puppy-dog face a six year old could make, while begging my mom for an ice cream (just for the record: it cost around one US$). My mom loved me smiling at her, so her face lit up and she replied: "Sure darling; remember, if you want something in life you have to go and get it. So first, you have to swim back and forth five times in the large pool. Then I will buy you the ice cream!" The first time this happened I could not believe what I had just heard. I had behaved well throughout the entire day at the pool, had played nicely with the other children and had just put on my magic smile – and still she would not get me an ice cream. I was not only tired, but all of my friends had already received at least one, if not two. "But mom, all my friends are eating ice cream already. They just got it from their parents and they didn't have to do anything for the ice cream either! Come on mom, it is just an ice cream! Plleeasseeeee!" She was firm in her decision.

Imagine a six-year-old boy begging without stopping! You were a child once – did you get an ice cream when you asked? Do you have children yourself? Would you give in and give it to them? "Why was my mom making such a big deal out of it?" I begged and pleaded, but she stayed firm. No chance in convincing her to say, "Yes" to an ice cream just like that. "Swim back and forth five times and I will buy you one. Come on darling, that is not much to ask for and you are a good swimmer," she kept on motivating me. I actually wasn't a good swimmer back then (how many six year old kids are?) and on top of that I felt a little cold, exhausted, and I didn't want to go back into the pool and swim five times back and forth (250m in total). This would take me around 15 or 20 minutes or even longer. I tested her, and just sat there crying, hoping she would change her mind. The pool closed and we had to leave – without ice cream! I kept crying the entire way home. I felt devastated and told my mom I didn't love her, because I was sure she didn't love me either, the way she was treating me. "All the other parents love their children way more than you do!" I yelled at her before I ran into my room. I don't have children of my own yet, but this must have been an extreme experience for her. It was not only that the other children were making fun of me, but also the other parents frowned at her about how strict she was with her six-year-old child. On top of that, I started yelling at her, denying that I loved her (I did love her of course). She did stay firm however, to teach me the lessons she was taught by her parents.

The next time we went to the pool and I asked for an ice cream, the same story repeated itself. I asked. I begged. I cried. But then I realized that I had to give in. She would not move one bit. So I started swimming: One time. Two times. Three times. Four times. I tried to cheat and only go for four, but she was smart enough to count and made me do my last round. After I had finished my five turns she did something amazing for me: Instead of buying me only one, she made up for the last time and I got two ice creams. I have to admit, they tasted like the best ice creams ever. I was exhausted, but I felt I had achieved something and I had earned it. Every time at the pool, we repeated this process. I wanted ice cream, I asked, I begged, I pleaded, I cried but then gave in, because she was firm as a rock. I was so aggravated! She kept telling me how I would thank her for this experience later and how my efforts would benefit me a lot later in life. "What did she mean? If I swam now I would get free ice cream in the future for all my life?" It made no sense to me because I had never seen anyone giving away free ice cream. The habit she was instilling in me would be giving me "free ice cream". It was not going to be in the way I could understand it at that age, and it was not literally ice cream, but my mom ended up being right. Yet, that did not really help me back then, and over and over again our argument about the meaningfulness of the process kept repeating itself. However, after a few times I was used to the extra swimming routine. Having to swim five times back and forth was simply how my day at the pool would end. Well, not quite!

After a few times my mom had realized how good a swimmer I had become and how easy it was for me to swim the five times back and forth. At first I thought that was her initial plan, to get me used to the swimming. Nope! One day when I was just about to get out of the pool after the fifth time, my mom smiled at me and said: "Great job darling, but since you are so good now, I want you to go six times back and forth for your ice cream!" WHAT? I couldn't believe it. She just raised the stakes for no apparent reason. That was so unfair! The deal had always been that I would do five times and not six. I fell into my old pattern: I cried, complained, pleaded and argued. But it didn't help. She was firm. I remembered the first day when I had to leave without an ice cream and I did not want the same thing happening today. I had been looking forward to a nice chocolate ice cream all day and so I gave in and went for the sixth back and forth. I did get my ice cream and I loved it. Soon she raised the limit to seven times, then to eight, then nine, and finally to ten. She never went higher than ten because it would take me almost half an hour of swimming and she did not want to wait that long either. I started to get used to her methods at the pool and when we went skiing, sleighing or mountain biking later on she used them as well. I only got a treat once I had achieved a certain task that she would come up with upfront. Yes, initially I complained and revolted, but I knew there was no point. She would not give in, and so instead of getting treats without much effort like many of my other friends did, I had become used to having to do something to earn them.

I was only a few years old back then but it is incredible what important lessons I got to learn at that age. I had not only become an excellent swimmer, which helped me tremendously to become a professional kitesurfer, but first and foremost I had learned that nothing in life that is worth something will come without giving something in return! The higher the

[handwritten in left margin: Transactional Thinking]

value, the bigger the effort needed. Now be careful here when you are reading this: I am NOT saying that you always have to pay money for something to get something else in return. It is possible to get something even without having to put in any money. The reason I am pointing this out so clearly, is that many people believe they need a lot of money to get something else, which is absolutely incorrect. There is pretty much always a way that you can get something without money, you just have to find out how. For me that one-dollar needed to buy the ice cream was a lot of money. It was more than I actually owned and was similar to many other people who would wish to get something that was beyond their capabilities at that very moment. I do not know your current situation, but maybe you want a nicer car, to pay off your mortgage, find a new partner, leave your existing one, get a different job, travel more, etc.... Whatever it is, it is like my ice cream. I did not have a dollar. And maybe you don't have the US$100,000 you would need. The first day when I wanted my ice cream I just said: "You know what, I am not putting in the extra effort. How mean is my mom for not giving me the ice cream just like that." But since my mom did not give in I had learned my lesson on the second day. I really wanted the ice cream, so I knew I had to swim back and forth. It was important to my mom for me to understand that nothing in life comes without having to give. That "something" can be money, but more often it can be time, can be effort, or can be actual work. Whatever it is, you have to understand the concept. You will see in later stories that it was very important for me to achieve big things, and I had learned at an early age that I could achieve many things as long as I was willing to give something to get something. Talking about your dream holidays, quitting your job, or becoming famous: it does NOT necessarily take money to do that. If you think that it will just come to you, think of my mom being completely firm and not giving me the ice cream. This is how the world will treat you. If you "swim", you will get it. Of course, the older you are the bigger the challenges become and the tougher the "swimming" will be. But guess what? That is how life is, and this book will help you not only understand exactly that, but will also show you ways how to get what you really want.

The second important take-away from this story is to be prepared for the stakes to rise without any apparent reason. The day before my mom raised the stakes, I would have been given the ice cream for swimming five times back and forth, but suddenly it rose to six times. You might think this never happens in our world, but au contraire! Every year, companies have to perform slightly better due to inflation. Housing prices continue to rise over a ten-year period of time. The prices of everyday goods increase a few percent every year. Your employer wants slightly more work done every year. Sport records keep getting beaten over and over again, and what was world class twenty years ago is now average. My mom saw me getting accustomed to swimming back and forth five times, so she increased it to six. She prepared me for the real world by constantly raising the bar. For you this means to not settle for yesterday's results. Be prepared for the challenges to get harder. Keep working on your skills and constantly strive to improve yourself. Winners live up to the challenge, while losers just give in. I was tempted to give in when she raised it to eight times. I thought she was nuts. But I knew that was the only way to get the ice cream, which I really wanted. In my business ventures later in life that fact became clearer and clearer: so many people were not prepared to grow. They gave in and settled for not getting what they actually wanted just because the stakes had risen. Remember: Winners accept the challenge. They live up to it and embrace it. It motivates and inspires them! This does not mean that if you get an insurmountable obstacle of a goal and you don't accept the challenge, that you are a loser. It means that winners love to be challenged every day as long as it is somehow doable. For some unexplained reason they love to go the extra mile, and you should learn to become such a winner.

The third lesson is to understand how to motivate people properly. I needed that in business so many times, and if you have children yourself, this might come very handy too. I truly believe that people love challenges, but only under certain conditions: First they need to clearly understand what the benefit is of winning and they need to want that benefit. Second, they need to be able to believe that they can achieve it (here many times they might need a coach or someone to motivate them to keep believing in it along the way). And third, if they achieve the challenge, they need to get the reward. When these three conditions fall in place, people easily strive for excellence and give it all. Let me point out the how these three conditions worked out in my story: Condition one: I wanted the ice cream, and it was clear what I had to do to get it. Condition two: My mom chose something for me to do that was not effortless, yet it was achievable. Had she chosen ten times back and forth right at the very beginning, I would not have bothered to even try and just become frustrated because the ten times would have seemed too much. Condition three: She kept her part of the deal and gave me my ice cream after I completed the swimming. In today's society I so often see that people are completely demotivated and lose their thirst for more. Why is that? It is exactly because of this important lesson: One or more of the three conditions are not met properly. Too often it is not clear what is the actual benefit of doing something. Or, the benefit is clear, but it is not properly shown what has to be done to get it. Other times the challenge seems way out of reach, and one does not have the confidence of actually being able to achieve it. I once worked together with an organization that made exactly these mistakes. What happened? People just stopped trying, which was very sad considering that most people actually would have loved to strive and work hard, but just got demotivated by the organization's mistakes.

Remember this important story and take away the three key lessons. At the end of every chapter, I want to inspire YOU to take action based on what you just read. You must take action to get results. Even though it is not about having the exact same experience I had, you might be in or get into a similar situation where you need to give in order to get something in return, and now you know how to play this game. Summing up, which single most important action will you take after reading this story? It might be related to money, relationships, health, etc. Or it might be teaching your children the same life lesson by not giving in to a treat until they have completed a task first. Whatever it is, take action now, or write it down as a task that you commit to doing right away.

SPACE FOR MY TAKE AWAYS

- Effort leads to benefits
- Have to want the benefit to give the effort.

"Nothing in life that is worth something will come without giving something in return."

↳ CU Command — For everything to be worthwhile, you must give something in return.

JH Giving in return may or may not involve money.

Receiving is giving; receiving without also giving something else is taking

JH There is pretty much a way to get something w/o money, you just have to find out how.

- You could decorate an apartment for free, but then where is the balance to avoid "taking" money well spent, time traded to others, effort in the search.

- Stakes will rise. because growth requires it; growth wants challenges, thrives, enthuses
  $gr. = $ Flow when within <u>Zone of Capability</u> (i.e. achieveable)
  <u>The "certain conditions" - Low</u>

Did I not challenge Theora enough as Ann had during the post years?

What lesson's did I teach about work, meeting challenges? Ask her? Survey her these lessons?

<u>4 Conditions</u>
  1) Want Benefit
  2) Believe can do it + 4) Within Time Horizon
  3) Receive reward

2.

THE TREE STORY – LEARNING DELAYED GRATIFICATION

Someone is sitting in the shade today because this someone planted a tree a long time ago. – Warren Buffett

Have you ever grown a tree? I am not talking about buying a tree and then replanting it in your own garden. No – I am talking about buying a seedling and growing it to become a beautiful two-meter tall tree. Well, believe it or not, I did - Duhhh, otherwise I wouldn't be sharing my second story, right? At the beginning of the first year of Elementary School (ages six to seven) our schoolteacher designed a project for each of the students. There were 27 of us in our class who would be working on it throughout the entire first year: We had to plant a seedling and grow it into a tree. I have always liked peaches so I decided to choose a peach-seedling. I don't know if you have ever seen one of these small and delicate things. It's difficult to imagine it can grow into a several meters high tree. You should definitely get one and try it out yourself. No, wait! Make it nine or ten seedlings and try it with those. I think you can already see what I am getting at. I got home with my precious seedling, and went into our garden to look for the perfect spot to grow my peach tree. Our teacher had told us that the planting area should be moist, so that the tree would always get enough water, sunny, to get energy, and neither too close, nor too far away from other trees, so the roots would not become entangled once the tree got bigger. Why not too far away? I cannot really remember anymore, but I think I had the feeling the tree shouldn't feel alone in our garden. Looking back this sounds kind of ridiculous, but I was convinced trees didn't like to be alone.

I took a little shovel and started digging a hole. When my dad saw me he completely freaked out as he thought I was messing up the garden while goofing around. Once I explained my task to him, he smiled and just let me be (I am sure he laughed inside about what a naïve little boy I was, thinking I could grow a peach tree). So, while I was digging, I remembered the instructions we were given in class: do not dig too deep, otherwise the sapling cannot grow out. Further, do not dig too shallow, otherwise it gets damaged easily. "Ok, but what was that supposed to mean? Not too deep? Not too shallow?" Anyway, I went with my gut feeling, and dug a hole around 15-20 centimeters deep. I had picked a pretty good spot: soft, moist soil with no stones or gravel. I put my seedling in the hole and covered it loosely with soil and dirt, careful not to press down too hard. The whole process took me around half an hour, with my dad watching. He actually helped me put a little wire around and on top of the spot, just in case I would forget where it was, and to keep animals away once the seedling sprouted. After I had finished, I went back in, totally excited. I had it all mapped out: I would water the tree, take lots of care and even use fertilizer, so it would grow, get extremely strong and provide many peaches later on. My mom could barely get me away from the window as I was staring at where I had planted the tree, hoping I could see it grow right away. But of course, nothing happened that day. This is where a naïve child got the timing totally wrong: I was not growing bamboo. I was growing a tree.

The next day, we all shared our experience with the rest of the class. We were all wildly excited about having picked the best spot or used a special strategy. You can imagine how seven-year-old children feel. After school I went straight into our garden, to have a look at the results. The box-shaped wire was still there, and guess what? I could see beneath it?

Nothing! The spot still looked like the day before. "Of course", I was thinking, "That makes sense. It is only day one and for the tree to actually come out it will take a little while!" I took the water hose and sprinkled the spot. I was totally excited. Nothing had happened yet, but so what? It was just day one! I knew a tree wouldn't grow over night. Day two was exactly the same and so were days three, four, five, six, and seven. But day eight was different. A week had passed and something had changed. Something BIG. When I arrived home after school you know what I saw at the place where I had planted the tree? Still nothing. What had changed dramatically however was my excitement and commitment. I had been watering the seedling and taking care of it every day since day one - but still not seeing any results had me not as excited anymore as I had been in the first few days. Our teacher had warned us it would take some time, but come on, a week had passed by now! I had put in quite some effort over the last several days, so I should be reaping some of the rewards, right? I tried to keep my head held high, but over the next days and weeks, I expected less and less when coming home from school. My excitement for the tree project started to fade more and more and other short-term school projects popped up and drew my attention. For example, we had to fit together wooden pieces for a birdhouse, which we would hang outside the classroom during the upcoming winter. I especially enjoyed that activity, as we all had lots of fun, and after a few days of fiddling and gluing it was completed. It reminded me of the swimming story (see the first story, if you have not already read it yet): If you do X, you will get Y afterwards. The birdhouse pieces would not go into place by themselves, but after a couple of days of consistent effort it looked wonderful and was ready to be hung outside. The tree project "sucked" in comparison. I was quite frustrated and since there was no apparent progress with the seedling I even started to skip watering it regularly.

The other children at school had a similar experience. Some even shared about how they would dig out the seedling, to make sure it was still there. Then they would replant it at a better spot and start over. The more I listened to them the more I started to wonder whether I should do that as well. Maybe my spot was not good? Or was it the seedling? Maybe I had made some mistakes? Did I water it too much? Too little? I started having serious doubts. It had been a couple of months now since I had planted it and I could not see any noticeable progress so far. Our teacher kept reminding us to keep going and keep taking care. It would all work out fine. But I was not convinced. When I got home that day I took the shovel, pushed the wire away, but just when I was about to start digging, my mom, who was watching from the window, shouted to get me to stop:

"What are you planning on doing?" she inquired decisively.

"I want to check on the seedling. I am not sure if I planted it correctly. I just want to be sure it is ok!" I replied truthfully. I told her about the birdhouse project at school and how much it reminded me of getting an ice cream once the "job" was done. I added that I was pretty upset that the tree growing was not working out as I had expected. I told her about the other children at school and that they advised me to take the seedling out to check on it and plant it somewhere else instead.

"What did your teacher tell you?" my mom asked.

"She told me to keep taking care of the tree and just keep going!" I answered.

"So why are you listening to the other children who are as clueless as you are and not your class teacher, who has been doing this exercise with hundreds of other children before you?"

I didn't really have an answer. My mom always knew how to get me to convince myself of something rather than her forcing it upon me.

"So, what should I do? I don't know if I did everything correct!" I challenged her.

"Let me tell you something about when I was your age", she started with a forceful voice: "Every spring, our entire family would plant the seeds for the crop. We would go out and put them all over the fields. We did that, knowing, that we did our best we could, and we would wait until after the summer, until all the vegetables, and potatoes and all the other fantastic things we had planted would come out, ready to be harvested in fall. You know what would have happened if a few months after we had planted them, we would have checked on them, just because we could not see anything growing yet?"

I didn't know what to reply, because this was basically the same situation I was in at that moment - so I said nothing and just kept listening.

So she continued: "We would have had nothing to harvest in fall, because we would have killed the crop!"

I looked at her and she smiled because I must have looked as if a light bulb had just switched on, right above my head!

"So, what am I supposed to do?" I wondered.

"Did you plant everything correctly?" she checked

"Yes, I did, at least I think so!" I nodded my head.

"Did you take care and make sure the tree had all it needed to grow?" she continued.

"Yes, I did!" I kept nodding.

"Well, then keep working hard at it, because what you need now is faith, that everything will work out fine!" she assured me.

I looked at my mom, not 100% sure whether I should agree or not. I was not convinced whether I had faith or not. I was only 99% sure I had done everything correctly, and so there was that 1% left that made me feel insecure.

My mom noticed that and so she added: "When getting your ice cream for swimming or when building the birdhouse you get an immediate reward. However, the large rewards will only come once you learn to really keep working on a project for a sustained period of time, while having the faith that it will all work out at the end. You don't know if it will actually work out – but if it does the reward is so much higher. Since you started off correctly and you have been taking care of the seedling properly, you must have faith, just like you had on the first day. You will see; the tree will grow out of the ground!" At school however, things started to get worse and the children kept talking to each other how the seedling project did not work. A few of them had even given up and quit entirely. When I spoke to my teacher about all this, she just smiled and said: "Julian, I have been doing this project every year with my students, and every time only a few students manage to grow the tree. It is not that it is so difficult to grow it, but you have to have patience and faith in order to make it work. That is what makes it so difficult." "How long will it take until the tree finally appears?" I asked her. "The reason I am not telling you is because I want you to learn, that for the best things in life, you have to work consistently, without seeing progress right away. The progress will happen, hidden beneath the surface, and will suddenly pop up. No one knows when, but suddenly it will!" "Ok, but what if the other children are right, and I killed the seedling?" I kept pondering. "You see Julian, this is very unlikely. Nature has its goal to make things happen. As long as you keep taking care, that seedling will find its way and as long as you don't actively destroy it, it will come out at some point. The universe wants it to work out, otherwise none of us would be here." Her points made sense, and so I followed her advice. My motivation was not at a record high, but I started to understand and love the process, rather than being too addicted to a fast result. It was the first time in my life that I had learned to delay gratification.

I kept taking care - sometimes a bit less motivated, sometimes a bit more. A few weeks later I came back home from school and my mom welcomed me with a bigger smile than usual. "Check your seedling!" she suggested. I ran into the garden, and guess what had happened? A tiny greenish, brownish tip peeked out of the ground. The tree finally made some progress. I was blown away and full of happiness. What a magical moment. All the hours of caring had finally paid off after more than half a year. Wow! It had been totally worth it. If we had mobile phones back then, I would have called all my friends in school, but back then I had to wait until the next day. I was so excited. I was sure all my other friends would be as excited and I couldn't wait to share my story with them. That day I took special care of the seedling. I asked my dad to help me strengthen the protection around the tip, so birds or other animals could not nibble on it. I also took a little doll from my sister, to act like a miniature scarecrow. My sister was not particularly amused about her doll's new profession, but I convinced her that this was absolutely necessary and so she gave in. I placed it next to the wire to keep my future tree extra safe.

At school the next day I immediately went to my teacher and told her about my success. She smiled at me and gave me a high five. I was so proud. Then, I shared my success with my friends. Shockingly, they didn't seem happy about what I was telling them. They brushed me off, declaring that either I must have been lucky or they were unlucky as their tree was not out yet. They asked me whether I had cheated by buying a little tree instead of a seedling. In the morning I had been totally fired up, but now I was sad listening to them putting me down. I did not understand their reaction. Why weren't they as excited as I had been? Just the week before we were joking and laughing about the silly tree project and now it seemed like I was the bad friend because I was the one who had managed to get the tree to grow out of the ground. During lunch break I did not want to spend time with them anymore, and so I ate my home-packed lunch alone. My mom had even included a little love-you note congratulating me for sticking it through with the tree. I threw the note away. I was angry and upset. I did not understand my friends' reactions. I went to our teacher and talked to her about what was happening with me and the other children. "Julian, the other children are frustrated. They went through the same process as you did. It was just as hard for everyone. It always seems easy when looking at others, but everyone has to undergo the same challenges. You managed to stay patient while they didn't. Now they are frustrated, because they also would love to get your result, but they were not willing to put in the effort. So instead of admitting they had done something wrong, they will try to make fun of you or accuse you of cheating." I was disappointed, but a few days later a few of my classmates also managed to grow their trees and we had some great times sharing our success stories together. The ones who had given up or kept changing their strategy all the time never managed to get it to grow out of the ground. They kept complaining that it was not their fault, but that we were either lucky, had been cheating, or they were simply unlucky. It took me quite some time to understand what my teacher had told me but at some point I managed to stop listening to them. I just hoped at some point the tree project would become the past and there would be other topics to talk about with them again.

Over the next weeks and months, I kept taking care of the tree and made sure nothing would disturb it. I had a couple of challenges to win before the tree finally became large and strong: One time a crow started to rip the wire apart and almost managed to get to my 30cm high tree. I got there just in time to scare the bird away. Another time, one of our neighbor's children, who I was also in the same class with, was so disappointed about him not succeeding, that he tried to rip my tree out of the ground. I managed to safeguard it last minute. It really upset me that he had tried to destroy my success, just because he had not been able to stick it through. Over the next months, the tree became bigger and stronger, and required less and less work. Fortunately it had been quite a mild winter that year without much snow, which helped to speed up the growing process. Almost a year from the time that I had planted the seedling, little branches and leaves started to appear. During the first few months no change had been visible, but now there was something new and exciting happening every time I checked on the tree. It was now holiday time, and it was the first time our family would be away from home for over a month since I had planted the seedling. I was quite anxious about leaving it, but when we came back home the tree was still there and had grown even more. Soon, the tree was becoming so big that I had to remove the wire. It really was not needed anymore anyways. The most amazing moment happened, however, when a couple of years later that tree started to grow peaches. Real peaches! I was in my last year of Elementary School when that happened and it made me extremely proud. The tree kept growing and growing, and aside of a bit of pruning I did literally nothing else other than harvesting the peaches in the fall. They are the best peaches you could possibly eat. Every bite reminds me of the persistence it took to grow the tree in its infant stages. Back then, it was vulnerable, but today, that tree is self-sufficient. My teacher and my Mom were right: The universe and nature want the best for all of us. We just have to work hard, have faith and learn to delay our gratification. Whenever I have a hard project ahead of me today, and I am about to give up, that tree reminds me that the big rewards come if I keep going.

You might not be interested in growing a tree, but this story should remind us of all the things we attempt to do that take time before we get to reap these rewards. When I was swimming for my ice cream in the first story, I got the ice cream right afterwards. That was quite easy to understand and so I swam again the next day. I am sure you also have these occurrences where you have to give and then you get the gratification quite fast after that. Delaying gratification is the key to getting larger rewards. Many things in real life are based on this concept. Putting in effort over time, without seeing immediate results, prepared me for what I would face over and over again in my life later on. In business I did not earn much in my first couple of years, but made good money once the business was off the ground. In studying for a degree at university, I did not see any earnings during the years of studying, but reaped the rewards afterwards. I am sure you can apply this concept to many examples in your own life. Any parents reading this should strongly consider preparing their children well for exactly that. In the 1960s and 1970s a Stanford Psychologist called Walter Mischel performed the Marshmallow Experiment[1] to test the effects of delayed gratification on children. The setup was fairly simple: A teacher and a child were in the room. The teacher would put a marshmallow on a plate in front of the child and explain that the child could either eat the marshmallow right away or, once the teacher would be back from a quick break, the child could have two – as long as the child would be able to wait. The teacher then got up and left the room. He would not leave for too long, only a couple of minutes. There are great videos on YouTube showing this experiment and it is fun watching the children in front of the marshmallow – a must see in my opinion. What happened then was quite foreseeable: some children managed to wait until the teacher returned, while most chose not to wait and ate the marshmallow straight away. This experiment might sound simple, but don't forget that the children were only three to five years old. Would you have managed to wait? The remarkable thing about the experiment however was that Dr. Mischel continued to track the future success of these children, to see how well they would do later in life. What he found was astonishing: if children were good at delaying gratification at an early age, they would be more successful later on in life. It absolutely makes sense, since the most rewarding things in life come

1 http://psycnet.apa.org/journals/psp/21/2/204/

only after long periods of work without any instant benefit. Growing the tree was a similar experience for me at an early stage and had gladly prepared me well for real life later on.

The second lesson is about reaching a "tipping point" in a venture. For me this was the point where I suddenly didn't have to take care of my tree anymore, but it still kept growing. Up to that point I had to water the tree for months, without seeing any actual results above the ground. Of course there was growth happening beneath the surface, but I did not see that for quite a long time. At some point a tip of the tree appeared, and from then on the tree's growth was also visible outside. This was the tipping point, as from then onwards the tree kept growing, even though I was gone on holidays and did not really take care of it anymore. The closer I got to that point, the more mental effort it took me to keep going, just because the same boring task of watering the tree had been going on without any apparent progress. I even wanted to give up several times. Then suddenly, in one snap, the benefit ratio flipped and I needed less and less mental effort to keep working, because I saw the tree growing and later could also harvest peaches. After the tipping point it was close to impossible to "fail", because everything was getting easier and easier while the rewards became higher and higher. The author Malcolm Gladwell talks about it in great detail in his book "The Tipping Point". Especially in processes that are about delaying gratification it is a topic that should be well understood in regards to the work-rewards ratio. The phenomenon sounds so simple, yet many people do not consider it when they work towards a challenging goal over a sustained period of time. Many times they give up, just before they would have reached the actual tipping point, because the mental stress has become too large and they stop pushing further. Picture a piece of wood, lying on top of a metal stand. Your goal is to hit it with a sharp tool until the piece of wood finally splits into two separate pieces. Let's assume it takes you ten hits and on the tenth one it breaks. Which one was the most important hit? Well, none of them; they are all equally important. But chances are, the last hit was the hardest, because you had to hit it nine times already before, without any apparent success. With every hit, it became more difficult, until the tipping point was reached. Doing the ten hits is probably quite doable, but in most situations you would need to have to do an unknown amount of hits until the wood finally breaks. You would not know if it breaks after ten, fifty or one thousand hits. Would you have stopped hitting or gone all the way? This is how our world actually works, and this uncertainty factor is, what makes it so tricky for people to delay gratification. We don't know when the tipping point is reached. We just know one thing for sure: It will be reached at some point, and so as long as you push through all the way in anything you do, you will "see your tree grow".

The third lesson I learned was to understand the behavior of other people in regards to such delayed gratification processes. Most people are not able to stick it through. They prefer to give up and get instant gratification at something else. The reasoning of the children in school was the same as the reasoning adults have when they give up on things: "Maybe it is not meant to work. It is broken. I am sure the other person is cheating. No wonder it works for you, but for me this would never work." These are all comments we hear when we manage to delay gratification but others don't. Most people will lack patience to wait for delayed gratification and fall for this trap of blaming something or someone else. It is then also very common for those people that do not manage to make it to show jealousy and even hatred towards those that make it, even though they could have achieved it as well. In my example, the children pulled me down, discouraged me and one even tried to destroy my tree. I have never been really good at dealing with this behavior from other people and you will see me struggling a lot with that in other stories. Even though I think it is unfair how people react, this is how society behaves, so I learned to get used to it – and so should you.

Now, I would like to challenge you to ask yourself a few questions: "Where in your life are you "growing a tree"? Are you thinking about quitting because it is hard to push through? Are you ready to achieve a lot more by reaching that tipping point? What single action will you take right now, based on the information you just received?" Whatever it is, do it now or write it down as a TO DO, and take the required action. Remember, only taking action will give you your desired results.

SPACE FOR MY TAKE AWAYS

3.

THE GYMNASTICS STORY - FINISH WHAT YOU START

"Winners never quit and quitters never win."
– Vince Lombardi

From an early age on I have always loved sports and our family would go cycling, hiking or skiing any time possible. I especially enjoyed doing sports outside, which also led me to become a professional kitesurfer later in life. Since the weather in Austria was not always suited for outdoor activity all year round, I decided to sign up for indoor sports as well during my years in Elementary School. I tried out for badminton and table tennis, but neither one of them got me hooked. One day I watched people on television doing flips and jumps and I found out they were involved in gymnastics. That looked mind-blowing and so I wanted to learn that as well. My mom was not so happy, not because of the sport itself, but because she would have to chauffeur me back and forth to the local gymnastic club three times per week and it was a twenty-minute ride each way. So you can imagine her reluctance.

I convinced my friend Chris to join me. He had also tried several other sports, including Judo, but had not liked them either. I believed it would be easier to convince my mom if Chris and I went together and (of course) it was tons more fun being there with a friend. So every Monday, Wednesday, and Friday we would have a 90- minute gymnastics course. I made a deal with my mom that in return for her taking us back and forth I would commit to doing an entire year and not quit half way. She did not like it if I started something but then did not finish it. In gymnastics she said it would be a waste of her time if she took us three times a week but then we would quit shortly after. So I promised her I would at least do the whole year and then reevaluate afterwards. The first time Chris and I arrived at the gym we expected to learn straight away how to do flips, rotations, jumps or loops. To our disappointment, we did none of those. Rather, once we arrived, we warmed up for ten to fifteen minutes and then stretched for sixty more. Sixty minutes of stretching, non-stop. We stretched every single muscle in our body - from our little toes to the muscles behind our ears. I couldn't believe it. What a disappointment. I was expecting to have so much fun, and all we did was sit around for a whole hour to stretch. On top of that, we had a Hungarian trainer, whose name was Attila, just like the warrior, and that is what he was like. He didn't really speak German too well and he constantly yelled at us when we didn't have proper posture. He would scream something about keeping our muscles flexed and not "soften up" – whatever that meant. I was never quite sure what he wanted me to do so I just kept my head bent slightly downwards hoping he would not pick on me. Since that naturally meant I was not standing up straight, he would come over, raise my chin and tap my arms and legs to make sure I was keeping them firm and flexed. He was a nightmare of a trainer (at least I thought so) and the gymnastic lessons were as exciting as watching paint dry.

When my mom picked us up afterwards she asked how it went. Both of us expressed our disappointment, so she tried to cheer us up: "Come on guys, this was just the first day. It will get better the next time, you will see. You have to prepare your bodies for the hard hits that you will be getting from jumping and flipping!" It did make sense what she was saying and so Chris and I committed to trying out a second time. When we got there two days later for our second session the ninety minutes of stretching torture just repeated itself:

Attila made us do the same thing as on day one: Warm-up, stretch, stretch, stretch some more, stretch even more, finish stretching, cool down. Wow, how exciting – NOT! I was a hyperactive eight-year-old boy and now I was forced to stand still, stretch and keep my posture for what seemed like an eternity. Chris was not very excited either, but afterwards in the car my mom managed to convince us to go again. She claimed that she had heard that the second week would get better and be more fun. Gullible as we were, we believed her. But believe me, it was not more fun. The second week was just as boring as the first week. The standing still and stretching just repeated itself and thinking about this being only the second of upcoming 40 weeks until the summer holidays I did not know how I would stick this through and keep my promise. I was glad that Chris and I would be going through this together… at least I thought so.

He had made the same promise to his parents about going until the end of the school year, but after the third week he convinced them to let him quit. Initially his parents tried to make him go but after he kept complaining about the lessons over and over again, they eventually gave in. In exchange for the gymnastic lessons, he decided to take ice hockey lessons. He tried to convince me to join him but I wanted to keep my promise. Every day in school he kept going on about how much fun ice hockey was, how great the trainer was and how exciting the skating and bumping with the other children was. Chris really made me feel bad, as I realized how much I would be missing out while being stuck in boring gymnastic classes. Moreover I was disappointed in him, as both of us had committed to go to the gymnastic lessons together and I would never break that promise. He did break it however and was now trying to get me into Ice Hockey, and kept pushing me to just convince my mom to stop gymnastics. At home, I confronted her about the idea of changing. She was already prepared for the argument, and instead of going in to it she asked me:

"Julian, son, listen. Did you promise to stick through the whole year when I asked you a couple of times?"

"Yes mam!" I replied. She would have made a great lawyer as she basically made me close my own case.

"If you break your promise by quitting in the middle, do you think I will ever believe you again?" she asked?

"But mom, I really don't like the lessons and by the way it is not even in the middle, it is still at the start of…"

"Julian!" she cut me off, "I don't care, "We made the deal of you sticking with it through the entire year, and I did not raise a quitter! You will keep going to the gymnastic lessons even if I have to drag you there myself!"

So that's what she did. I tried to hide and make us get there late a couple of times, since there was a rule that if you were five minutes late, the door would be locked and you couldn't join the class. My mom had anticipated me trying to delay and so she scheduled in some extra time. My plan actually backfired because it resulted in us arriving there even earlier than before. As a quick side note, I want to point out that the door-locking-strategy left an impression on me, as I would use the same technique once I got older when I needed to get people to arrive on time for presentations or workshops. Airlines or trains do the same thing – they just leave if you are late. But for a presentation or movie people can still get in no matter if they are late. To avoid that, I use the same strategy that Attila used for the gymnastic sessions: I simply lock the door five minutes after starting, and latecomers cannot participate anymore. Pretty much like a train that has left the station. At first people complain, but then they learn the rule to arrive on time. You can try this yourself if you struggle with late starts on events.

The sessions did not get much better, and months two and three were just as boring. One thing I did notice however, was how flexible I was becoming. No wonder, I had been stretching for at least three hours every week – and I am talking about hardcore stretching. I could do the splits in any thinkable way and even twist my legs inside out or upside down and still lie comfortable on the gym floor. I even got used to Attila's bad accent and I felt like my Hungarian was becoming fluent – or at least whatever language he was throwing at us when he got upset if we didn't instantly understand what he wanted us to do. I had made friends with some really nice children: Florian, Dominic, Markus, and Christian. It was also at that point that I met a guy called Daniel for the very first time. Back then the two-year age difference was too big for us to click, but ten years later we became best friends and still are. I am still amazed how early life made us cross paths. As time moved on Chris stopped mentioning ice hockey and to my surprise started asking me about the gymnastic lessons again. I told him that they were better now. Actually they were still the same as at the beginning, but I was now used to them. On top of that I had tons of fun with the other children before and after the lessons playing in the huge pool of soft, fluffy balls that we were not allowed to use at the beginning of the year. Normally the older gymnasts used the fluffy-ball-pool to train for new jumps without getting hurt. The other children and I would arrive thirty minutes early or stay thirty minutes late and goof around in the pool. It was hilarious and a lot of fun, and made up for the long hours of stretching. Chris did not seem all too delighted about what I was telling him. I found out later that he had also quit ice hockey after a few weeks because he got bumped too hard a few times. Afterwards he had tried a couple more sports and quit within just a few weeks. It seemed he never really learned to stick it through to get good at any of them.

Through mid-year, Attila suddenly started to shake up the ninety-minute lessons. We would still warm up for fifteen minutes as usual but instead of the long stretching afterwards, we now only stretched for ten to fifteen minutes. Then we did different exercises built on top of each other. The movements became harder and harder from session to session. We started with basic rotations and moved forward to flips and twists, step by step. This was getting super exciting and exactly what I had signed up for at the beginning of the year. We also used the fluffy-ball-pool not only for goofing around, but also for actual training and we assisted each other while attempting new tricks. We had a lot of fun when other children crashed a jump but of course did not get hurt. Now I understood Attila's plan: We would never have been able to do these difficult things straight away, because our bodies were not ready for them yet. Attila made us do the stretching and warm-ups so that every fiber in our bodies was ready for the strenuous jumps and figures he would be teaching us now. It was working. I learned all the flips and jumps that I had dreamed of before. Attila had given us a great base, and we could build from there. One of the reasons none of us would get injured, was the flexibility and strength we obtained during those early training sessions that I still benefitted from even in later years, Not only did I stick to my promise with my mom to finish the year, but I kept doing gymnastics throughout the entire time I was in Elementary School. I even went to the Austrian Championships in Vienna. I did not win, but the experience was still wonderful.

The foundation I received has helped my career in sports up to this day. When playing Basketball in Junior High and High School, many of the other children sprained their ankles or twisted a knee and in kitesurfing, many friends strained their shoulders. Thanks to my gymnastic lessons, I could always rely on my flexible and fit body. On top of that, I built some great friendships and learned some very powerful things that would stick with me all through my life. Not only the physical aspect such as the body control that helped me in sports every single time later on, or the extreme flexibility that kept me fit – but just as in the swimming and tree story I took away some valuable life lessons that shape me to this day and help me make the right decisions when needed. We talked about not giving up in the story about growing a tree, so the three lessons from this story are entirely new ones:

The first lesson is to pick your team well whenever you start something new. It wasn't that Chris and I were on a common team, but I had felt we were in this together. I had made a strong commitment to my mom and I felt obliged to go all the way. For him, this was not as important. I learned my lesson here, and in many future projects I became very careful with whom I would partner up. The questions I always asked were whether we had the same goals and objectives and what our commitment were towards our goals. Many times this has proven to be a great lesson learned early in life, but there were times when I did not stick to it – and then messed up. You will read this in the Brazil Story, for example, where I did not choose my team wisely and therefore messed up big time. In the gymnastic classes I met a "great team" through the other new friends I got to know there. They had the same goals and interests. There is a great story and book that I read later in my life about Ernest Shackleton[2], who was a celebrated Antarctic explorer. Even though he chose to explore the most dangerous and seemingly impossible terrain, he managed to keep his crew together and became notorious as a leader for that reason; and even received the nickname "The Boss". When asked how he did it, he bluntly replied that he had made it clear in advance what the circumstances would be throughout the trip, and what he was expecting from each and every person on the journey. If problems arose, he would remind the men about their commitments and make sure that they would stick to them. A smart man this Ernest Shackleton!

Lesson Two: Most things you start from scratch won't be a lot of fun until you get good at them. This sounds like such a no-brainer concept, but this is what breaks most people's

---

2   http://en.wikipedia.org/wiki/Ernest_Shackleton

spirit when learning or trying new things. Many people would love to learn to surf, or would love to be a great skier, but they underestimate the level of difficulty and give up because they are not prepared to put in the effort to get the reward. This leads to many people going for a few attempts to learn these sports but very few of these become proficient. Malcolm Gladwell wrote an excellent book called "The Outliers"[3] where he says that "talent" is totally overrated. He states that talent is the ability to do something really well based on an innate ability. In many studies, however, he shows how skill is the actual ability one has to develop. Skill is only learned through hours and hours of practicing or training. He quantifies that it takes 10,000 hours of intense practice to become a true expert in a specific skill – be it programming, playing an instrument, or sports etc. If you do 100 hours, you start seeing significant improvements, and once you have done 1,000 hours, you will be among some of the best. With 10,000 hours you are world-class. In our gymnastic courses we did around five hours per week, so after around half a year, we had stretched quite a lot and were ready for more. That was the point everything started to be fun and get easier. Later in my life when I learned to play basketball, this pattern repeated. In kitesurfing it was the same thing. Many of my friends tried to learn new things but gave up too early. They never understood this principle properly and gave up before the actual fun would start.

Lesson three (and to me personally, a really important lesson) was to always keep a promise you had made – be it big or small. I had made a deal with my mom and it was clear to me, she would stick to it, as long as I would stick to my part. She would drive me, as long as I would not quit the next day. I promised her I would re-evaluate my decision after the first year, but not earlier. Breaking that promise would not have been that big of a deal at that age, but it would have hurt my credibility for future promises. I would have felt

---

3 http://gladwell.com/outliers/

hurt as well if my mom had suddenly changed her mind and stopped driving me to the classes. Any of my partners that I am working with today know that my word counts like a signature. If I say I will – I will, but if I say I won't – be sure I won't. Set yourself timelines when you reevaluate your decision and stick to them. Some people confuse keeping a promise with dreaming small, meaning that you should not have big goals and dreams, so you can always keep and not miss them. You will see in one of the later chapters that this is absolute garbage. There is a clear distinction between making a promise that you should keep, and a vision or dream that you want others to buy into. Such a dream or vision has to be huge and most likely the actual result will be a bit beneath. That is absolutely ok and actually intended in these cases. But remember if you ever deal with someone that breaks a clear promise - walk away – and remind yourself not to pass this feeling of being let down on to others by breaking a promise yourself. Do business with honest and respectful people. It will make you successful in your business and personal life as well.

You may have experienced something similar in your own life. So, before moving on to the next chapter, let me ask you this: What single most important action are you going to take RIGHT NOW based on what you have just read? What commitment are you going to make to stick through? What are your key criteria for selecting partners for your next business- or personal-venture? Write down your commitment (your promise to yourself) and do it now. Otherwise, you will most probably never do it!

SPACE FOR MY TAKE AWAYS

4.

THE BASKETBALL STORY -
"I CAN'T" DOES NOT EXIST

*"Whether you think you can, or you think you can't
- you will be right." – Henry Ford*

In my first story I had learned a great deal about understanding that I had to give in order to get. In the second story I learned that most things wouldn't be fruitful unless you stick it through and do not quit. And in the third story I learned that many things you start are difficult until you get good at them. I was now just slightly older than 10 years and I was entering Junior High School. I had been very committed to gymnastics up to that point and the upper-body-strength, body control and speed I had developed would help me a lot in many other sports later on. My new school was quite far away from the gym and so I started to struggle more and more to balance the logistics of school and sports. Since my hyperactive nature required me to work out on a daily basis I started looking into other sports. The other kids in my gymnastic group had similar experiences as well, and were also looking into alternatives. Some of them entered a soccer club but I never really liked soccer, even though it is one the most popular sports in Austria. Some of them started performing in winter sports. I was a good skier, but just because we would go skiing often from a very young age, not because I really enjoyed doing it (Malcolm Gladwell's 'hour principle' came into play again here). Initially I wasn't very sure what to do, but then three friends of mine from school, Lukas, Peter, and Nicolas decided they would try out basketball.

Until that point I had only heard of basketball but had not actually played it, nor seen it being played. I was curious about the sport so I went to the school library. I had always been an autodidact and loved to self-teach by reading and learning about many topics. Books quenched that thirst to a certain degree, which lead me to finish the entire school's library in Elementary School. People started to catch on and they gave me dictionaries as birthday presents. Any other kid would have probably hated that, but I was the happiest boy ever. There was a series of books called "What is…" and the authors would write in simple language about various topics like science, psychology, and astronomy, for example. I could sit around for hours learning about things, from airplanes to spacecraft, to how the human body worked. Our Junior High School library was pretty extensive, as the school had been collecting books for over a century. Remember, this was at a time where CDs were just about to appear and long before the Internet age. They also had videotapes one could borrow and watch right there at a video console. I asked the librarian whether they had something about basketball. After checking she told me they had only one tape and no one ever watches it – basketball was just not popular in Austria. "Excellent", I thought and she guided me to the aisle where I could watch it. It's incredible to realize that less than ten years later we could just watch all that on YouTube (or maybe by the time you are reading there is already something new). Amazing!

The video playing showed an unknown (to me) Afro-American player. At that point I wasn't even sure whether he was any good or not. His name was Michael Jordan. Today I know he is the best basketball player of all time, but back then I was just listening in and sucking up all the information. The video was translated into German and he would speak about how he had been kicked out of his High School's team because he had not been good enough. He then talked about winning the NCAA college title at North Carolina University and about his (back then) three championships with the Chicago Bulls. They showed him doing amazing things and it seemed as if he could fly through the air when going for something that I later found out was called a "dunk" (which is basically a very powerful play because the player pushes the ball through the rim from above and chances of missing are very slim if you do it properly) This tape of Michael Jordan totally inspired me to give basketball a try. It looked extremely fast-paced, strategic, and fun. The video (today I know it is called Air Time – and is available on YouTube if you want to watch it) had me totally fired up to find out more. So that same Wednesday afternoon I joined my friends for my first ever basketball training session.

In gymnastics we would never wear shoes but to my surprise most of the other kids were wearing some sort of fancy sneakers when playing basketball. I must have looked like a total geek by playing barefoot. Our coach, Mr. Freytag, split us into three groups, depending on how good a player he thought each of us would be. He put my friends Nicolas and Peter into the middle group. Lukas was put into the best group because he had been playing with his older brother for some time already. I was put into the last group, which really hurt my feelings. I knew I had not even held a basketball up to that point, but when I was put into that group I swore to myself that I would never ever go into a "beginners group" in my life again. The first thing Coach Freytag made us do was to hold a basketball. But not just hold it, rather position us properly, learn to pass, learn to catch and understand the basic rules of the game. It was a total "first" for me and it reminded me of the first weeks at gymnastics: It was as boring as hell but I was convinced I would undergo the same learning process when trying something new. After my first basketball practice, I told my mom that I would stick with it and begged her to buy me some proper gear. She had secretly hoped that I would not like basketball, as she rather wanted me to play volleyball, like she did at my age. When she saw how excited I was she agreed to buy me my first pair of Air-Jordan shoes and my first "Silver Spalding" basketball. I was so proud to be well prepared and immediately went in front of our house to practice so I could improve my ball dribbling skills. I remember to this day how long it would take me to finally being able to dribble the ball in-between my legs: weeks! Today, it is as natural as breathing.

The first group practiced three times a week, but because I was not in the first group yet, I only had one session a week. In order to get faster progress I asked Lukas, who was already in the first group, what they had done during the training. As soon as I got home I would try the same moves and dribble around in our parking lot. I easily practiced for 6 hours a day, despite not having an actual basket and clue how to shoot the ball yet. This was a defining moment, not only for me, but also for my parents and neighbors. From September 1996 onwards, they would hear non-stop basketball dribbling and shooting, from the time school finished all the way until the sun set. A couple of times the neighbors called the police, as they argued that I was disturbing their Sunday 7am sleep. All that did not keep me from training hard. I wanted to play on the actual team and have a significant impact during the upcoming season. For that I had to get a good basic basketball foundation which included knowing how to catch the ball, dribble, and pass, without making any mistakes. Had people watched me playing an imaginary game in our parking lot without actual baskets I am pretty sure they would have thought I am crazy. Despite being quite short, I could still jump high and sprint up and down the court faster than most of the other kids. I was working hard on my ball handling skills in order to get promoted into the middle group soon and play with better kids. Coach Freytag immediately saw my hustle and after a couple of trainings promoted me into group number One, skipping the middle group. I could now play with some of the best kids in our school.

Now I was in a completely new world. These kids not only handled the ball well, they could also shoot it. Up to that point I had maybe tried to score a basket nine or ten times ever. First of all I had no basket at home and during the trainings in the lowest group we would focus on the basic skills and not on shooting. If I wanted to keep up with these kids, I had to get in a lot of practice. So after the training session, I begged my dad to buy me a basket and set it up with me in front of our house. So now on top of the non-stop dribbling I added hours of shooting to my daily practice routine. In order to get more shots in during the same time I convinced my sister to pass the ball back to me after the rebound. In return, I helped her with her math (one of my strengths that I was happy to share so that we could both improve). The hundreds of hours of practicing increased my skills drastically. I also convinced my dad to install a couple of bright lights in our parking lot so I could play during the "daylight-saving" time months. My neighbors hated it as it was almost like living next to an extremely bright sports stadium. I owe my dad a lot for helping me with that as it allowed me to play until late at night after the sunset at 5pm. Even though I did not get to spend so much time with him during my early years when he was extremely busy working, my dad was always there for me when I really needed him. Although he had to deal with all the neighbors who were now seriously complaining, he knew the lights would help me a lot and he wanted me to succeed. During the winter when it was snowing, I wore gloves and a jacket in order to continue training. One good thing that my parents loved was that I was taking care of the parking lot by making sure it would be free of snow and ice. I had my first 1,000 training hours logged in probably after around half a year and I started reading basketball magazines to learn about the actual game mechanics. Most of them were in English, so my mom was happy to pay for them, as it would boost my English skills at the same time. Always go for the Win – Win!

My hard training paid off and I "made the cut" and got on to the main team. Coach Freytag put me in the "Point Guard" position, which was also called the "playmaker" position. Since I was quite short (today I am only 5-10/178cm tall), talked a lot, and loved giving orders that position was well suited to me. I loved dribbling the ball down the court and directing the play. I started to learn to read the game and started to understand when to score myself and when to pass on the ball to someone in a better position. The bad thing about being the Point Guard was, that whenever we won a game, it was not the point guard getting the credit, but the shooters or centers, as they were the ones scoring most of the points. If we lost however, it was mostly the point guard's fault, as he had failed to direct the game properly. It was ok for me though, as it taught me a lot about taking the blame for losses and giving credit to others when winning. We won the championship that year and the year after. It was a great experience and in those years I put into action a lot of the lessons I learned about sticking it through at the beginning and that smart work pays off. At the end of Junior High, Lukas was still playing, but Peter and Nicolas were not as committed anymore. However, I had met three new friends and we had become very close: Felix, who was a shooting guard, Dominic who was a small forward, and Andi, who played the center position. Many times we skipped school to meet and play at a playground for hours and hours. That is where my online nickname, "play-grounder" is from, which I still use in blogs or social media sites. Andi and Felix were playing for a different team, which was not organized by a school, but through a professional club. They convinced me to switch over, together with Dominic, as this would improve our chances of entering the professional league later on. Our dreams were to enter the NBA, which is the best basketball league in the world. Well, none of us made it there, but I got to play professional basketball in our local team in Innsbruck.

It was the fall of 2001, I remember it that well, because of the 9-11 terrorist attack happening during one of our basketball trainings that season. Our team's coach was Barney, who was known to be one of the toughest trainers out there. Everyone was scared of how tough his trainings would be and how mean he could get if players were screwing up. It was my first training with him and the entire team was starting training for the new season. I had trained especially hard over the summer on the playground, and I considered myself as fit as I had ever been. I was 15 years old, could almost dunk even though being quite short, had quick and safe ball handling skills and had been running and conditioning my entire body to the max. My hustle seemed to be paying off as I was being considered as one of the players for the under-sixteen national team. So despite hearing all these horror stories about Barney, I felt prepared for the upcoming 2½ hours training that day. Well, that was before the training… Barney loved training drills where the entire team had to work as one unit in order to succeed. It worked like this: All of the players, except one, lined up on one side of the court. The best free-throw shooter would take a shot from the free throw line, which is around five meter from the basket. If he scored it was the next person's turn. If a player missed, the entire team had to run a series of sprints within a given amount of time. We were twenty players in total that day, and chances were high that not everyone was going to score. Running four or five of these sprints was not a big deal, but after that it got problematic because people would get tired and not be able to stay under the time limit anymore. A vicious circle started: the more tired people were, the fewer times they scored, which resulted in even more sprints which made the players even more exhausted. So the usual strategy was to let the good shooters start first and hopefully score and then the worst shooters could try at the end, when it did not matter as much anymore if we had to run. That day however turned into a disaster.

Despite some warnings of my friends, I had hit the gym before the training. Therefore I was quite worn out already before starting the actual basketball training with Barney. As I was an excellent shooter I was usually one of the first players to take the shot. That day I missed my free throw, beginning a practice that turned into a sprinting marathon. Only two of the first ten players scored and it was unlikely that any of the ten upcoming players could make it. My body started to wear out and on top of that, I hadn't eaten or drank much before the training. Basically, it was a disaster in the making. After the tenth sprint I already felt slightly dizzy. The others were doing a bit better, but once I could not stay under the time limits for the sprints, Barney would make me re-run the sprints over and over again until I would make it. Next player was up to shoot – miss. Next sprint. I didn't make the mark again. Everything was spinning – I was close to exhaustion. Barney looked at me and barked out: "Ready, set, GO!" He pressed the timer.

I looked at him and just blew out a few words: "Coach, I can't run anymore, I am totally exhausted!" Barney's facial expression didn't change one bit. He looked at me, and came slightly towards me. It was the first time I was at his training, and he didn't even know my name. I was just a random player to him who was exhausted and didn't want to run anymore. He bent down to me, put his arm around and in a friendly manner he said the sentence that still hollows in my ears today: "Son, only when you lie puking on the floor, not being able to move anymore, your muscles don't function properly and you are passed out in your own vomit, until then you tell me you "can't" do something. Until that point son, until that point it is you DON'T WANT TO! You don't want to run, because you are lazy - because you are a sissy. Because you give me some wimpy kid excuses. Admit it! Admit you don't want to run anymore. I don't need these kinds of players. I need players who want it. Players who want it bad! Players who want to win - not players who don't want to and come up with the sissy excuse of "can't"! Son, with that attitude you will not achieve anything in your life. The moment you say you "can't" there will be hundreds of others who push through because they want it more than you do."

He straightened back up, looked at the rest of the group and shouted: "Get that loser out of my training. I need people who want it so bad, they don't even know what the word "can't" means!"

I looked at him, not really sure what I just heard. My brain was not functioning properly. My mind was drowsy and I thought I had not understood him properly. But the next words I heard clearly:

"You either run these sprints until you puke, or otherwise get out of my training, because I do not train losers who don't want it bad!" he drilled his these words into my mind. I definitely did not want to be a loser and so I took all the energy I still had left inside of me and ran. I didn't make the first mark. Not the second either. I was close to passing out. Barney just replied with a dry voice: "You are not finished. You can still stand straight. I don't care if you crawl, you can still go!" I looked at him in utter disbelief. He looked like one of those monsters in movies, which enjoyed torturing people. Then I looked at my team – I could not let them down. So I sprinted again – and, I made the mark and finished. As soon as I reached the finish line I collapsed on the floor from exhaustion. My head started spinning, my hands got tingly and my vision started to blur. I felt an incredible pressure inside my stomach and next I was lying on the floor puking my guts out. My body was as exhausted and finished as it possibly could be. Two of my team members brought towels and water over to me. Barney looked at me, bent down and told me softly: "You see son, remember this feeling for the rest of your life, because only now you would be allowed to say I CAN'T!"

I could barely comprehend his words, I was totally knocked out and just lying on the floor trying to get my things together. It was one of the toughest days in my life, but as with any of such experiences, they also taught me a lot. The seed Barney had planted in my mind that day would change the strength of my mind forever. You see, most people let their emotions or body dictate their actions, but it is actually the mind that decides. When you set an alarm at 6am and your body tells you it is too early – it is your strong mind that says I CAN and you still get up. When you are tired from studying, and your brain hurts, it is your mind that says KEEP GOING. There are thousands of examples like that, and any successful athlete, entrepreneur or artist will tell you the same thing: "The mind must be stronger than the body – otherwise you will always give in once it gets tough!" I was fortunate enough to learn this during that training. Barney was one of the best coaches I had the honor to play for, and we actually became good friends in addition to our basketball relationship. He taught me the basics about mindset, proper playing tactics and leadership skills. Without him I would have never been able to help our team win that many games, play in the professional basketball "Bundesliga" and have all the success I had in that sport. The lessons I learned, especially through that one incident, despite being embarrassed and disappointed at that moment, are priceless!

So many people use the words "I CAN'T", even though what they really mean is I DON'T WANT TO. "I can't join you guys. I can't learn this language. I can't do math. I can't work 70 hours a week. I can't accept this challenge. I can't write a book…" Think about all the times you say I CAN'T and replace it with I DON'T WANT TO. Remember, the thoughts you think will often dictate your actions. The actions you take will bring the desired results. Try it out – I challenge you to stop saying or thinking the word I CAN'T for just a week. Either replace it with I DON'T WANT TO or even better, ask: HOW CAN I? "I don't want to get up at 6am, but how can I make it happen? I don't know how to write a book, but how can I learn to do so? I don't want to work long hours, but what if I still need to do it? I don't want to learn this new thing, but what if I still do it? How can I push myself to the next level?"

The second important lesson I took away from that basketball training was that you will only replace the phrase, "I can't" if you have a strong enough reason WHY to push through. When I was playing basketball, my so-called WHY was extremely strong. I had a commitment to my team members and more important to myself. I could not let them or myself down. I would go all the way. Whatever action you are about to take, you will likely come up with excuses why you "CAN'T" do it. This, aptly coined "excusitis" is a litany of excuses that keeps them from achieving greatness. The reason people come up with excuses is, because they seem to work and offer an easy way out. If you tell yourself you CAN'T get up at 6am because you would have only 5 hours of sleep and be too tired the whole day – sure, it makes sense - and it works. So your mind says: ok, great, I can sleep in until 9am. It worked. But you didn't get anything done. You had an excuse. "I can't make the meeting, because I have to take care of my cat." You are right - it works. But is it really that you can't, or do you just not want to come to the meeting? How does this sound: "I don't want to come to the meeting, because I have to take care of my cat." You have to find a strong enough reason why you want to overcome the obstacles and still deliver. If you are willing to work hard for it, you will stop making excuses, just like staying in bed at 6am. Everyone's WHY is different. Some of you want to stop smoking; others want to lose weight, while others want to earn a million dollars. Whatever it is, you need to understand that you will not reach your goal without giving something in return, as we talked about in the prior chapters. You have to replace the words "I can't" with "I don't want to" or "How can I?" but you will only do that if you have defined a clear reason why. Remember that: Whenever you are willing you make an excuse for not doing something, it is because your reason to "find a way to do it" is not strong enough. If that sounds weird to you, take a minute and let it sink in. I would probably feel the same way, had Barney not embarrassed me in front of all my teammates that day.

     This brings me to my third lesson of the story: You need coaches and mentors in your life if you really want to achieve new heights. Many people think coaches and mentors are only for top athletes or performers. Actually, everyone should have a coach or mentor for things they take seriously. If you want to stop smoking, get a coach who will support you and help make you stop. You want to lose weight? Get with a fitness trainer or dietician who will help you lose it. Why am I saying that? I would have never run that extra sprint, had Barney not pushed me to my limits and beyond. Many times the mind is not strong enough and it needs outside help to overcome the body's resistance. A good coach or mentor will help you to go beyond your perceived limits, so you can achieve what you could not do on your own. Since then, I have worked with mentors, coaches, or accountability buddies in many areas of my life that I took seriously. Every successful person I know is doing that, and so should you. Start with one area and go from there. Grow beyond what you thought was possible and become powerful beyond measure.

Remember, you cannot change other people, but you can change yourself. Stop saying "I can't" and replace it with "I DON'T WANT TO" and "HOW CAN I?" Simply by thinking different thoughts, you will start taking different actions. Find your WHY and get a coach to help you achieve it! So, let me ask you, based on what you have read in this chapter, what is the single most important action you will take right here and now? TAKE ACTION NOW and stop using I CAN'T! Because "You Can".

SPACE FOR MY TAKE AWAYS

5.

THE SANDWICH STORY - OUTSELLING THE SCHOOL CAFETERIA

"Why join the Navy if you can be a pirate?" – Steve Jobs

Throughout the previous pages I have shared some mindset stories with you, wherein my mom had a big influence on me. Also, sports do indoctrinate a tough mental culture into athletes, which benefitted me a lot. However neither my parents nor the people around me at that age were very business savvy or entrepreneurial. I am not sure where I got these ambitions from, but already at an early age I wanted to travel to new horizons, experience new adventures and try out new things. I hated fitting into the "norm". In the next couple of stories I will share how, during my adolescence, this drive grew and expanded. You will see the stories changing from mindset lessons to gaining experience as I attempted many exciting new things at this young age.

Just like most other children in Junior High School, I didn't have much pocket money. The money I received from my parents was used mostly for school lunch. I didn't really need much more, as my parents bought my basketball gear when we went shopping and I had a school ticket for the bus. Mobile phones weren't really very common yet (It was 1997 and I was only 11 years old), and other than school, lunch and sports I was at home doing homework or playing basketball outside. My parents wouldn't give me more than a few Euros a day. They were not poor, but what more did I need other than a sandwich and a drink for lunch at the school's cafeteria? During that time I became really good friends with Peter (my first basketball buddy, as you may remember from Chapter Four) and together we spent lots of time studying or playing basketball.

One day, we sat in Peter's room, playing with a little toy basketball and trying to hit a little hoop that he had screwed to a wall above his bed. We were talking about school and basketball, and at one point, the topic of money came up. My family was never very keen to talk about money, not because my family thought money was bad, but just because they thought there were better topics to discuss, such as my performance at school. Peter and I started to chat about how much pocket money would be great to earn. After some discussion I asked the magical question, "Ok, so how can we actually do it?" We started to brainstorm. We didn't have any way of earning money; we just received our monthly allowance, and in order to get that we both had to do basic chores such as taking out the trash, cutting grass in the summer, or cleaning the driveway in the winter. Being only 11 years old we were too young to look for a part time job, as the legal working age is at least 15 years. We kept shooting the little toy basketball, when an idea crossed my mind: We were already receiving some pocket money, which we were spending on lunch every day. Lots of our schoolmates had already thought about buying lunch outside of school, which would have been slightly cheaper, but as long as it was only one sandwich or so, the savings did not make the extra hassle worthwhile. I kept shooting the basketball, running back and forth, picking it up from underneath the basket. I had always been highly mentally productive while either standing or walking around. I could never be creative while sitting or lying. My brain was working and pondering at full speed. What if we used the money we had, and bought bread, ham and cheese at the local supermarket in bulk? What if we bought enough food for ten sandwiches, sold them a bit cheaper than the cafeteria did, and used the profits to get our two sandwiches for free? We could save up our lunch money that way and earn additional profits on top. Peter and I were excited. We did the math, and it would work out fine. That was the day we started our own first business together.

We didn't have any written contract, but we had made an agreement that we would share the profits, 50/50. Ok, but how to get started? It might sound ridiculous, but both of us were lacking the funds to prepay the ten sandwiches, which would be more than our entire week's pocket money allowance. I didn't know the terminology back then, but what we basically did at school the next day was to raise money. There were 25 children in our class, and all of them had to buy lunch at the cafeteria just as Peter and I did. There were only a small percentage of children who either brought lunch from home or bought it at the supermarket themselves. The benefit of buying it outside school was just not enough for the individual, having to go all the way to the supermarket, waiting in line and then storing a soggy sandwich and warm drink until lunch break, a few hours later. All that for a few cents! In order to raise the necessary funds I asked every child whether they would like to only pay 99 cents instead of EUR 1.5 at the cafeteria for their next day's sandwich. I told the children we were getting a special deal if we got at least ten people together. After initial skepticism I managed to convince them to be part of our first ever business plan. The 99 cents sounded like a total bargain to them, as they would save over half a Euro compared to the cafeteria. I guaranteed that we would offer the same if not better quality and so it made no difference for the children to buy the sandwich there or from us. They would, however, be saving quite a bit. I showed them how our side of the business worked (without revealing how much profit we were actually making – I just wanted them to understand we were not stealing their money) and so they agreed. None of them told their parents of course, because the children knew that that way they could save a few Euros a week. It was a WIN-WIN situation and within two hours we had 14 children wanting a sandwich from us the next day.

They all gave us either 99-cent or some didn't care about the extra cent and gave us a full Euro. Why not make it a Euro in the first place you might wonder? Well, I just copied what all the supermarkets were doing and I realized that 99 cents sounded a lot cheaper than one Euro. We ended up having a budget of roughly EUR 14 (plus a small amount from Peter's and my pocket money) at the end of the day. That same afternoon I prepared a knife and cutting plate at home. Peter and I planned on meeting at a supermarket early the next morning. I realized why the other children would never do that: I had to take an earlier bus to make it in time and none of the children wanted to do that for just a few cents. We walked down the supermarket aisles and calculated what we needed. Both of us knew we would only have long term buyers if our quality was the same, if not better than the cafeteria's sandwiches. We needed at least 14 plus two for ourselves, which would be 16 sandwiches in total. There was a special bulk sale of 25 bread rolls for only EUR 2. I convinced Peter to take a gamble and go for it: "We will get other children to buy one as well, you will see!" He agreed. He found a special deal for some excellent ham and also cheese. Total: EUR 13. I had an idea: "Lets add pickles! How awesome would the sandwiches be with pickles? The cafeteria is not doing that, so it would make our sandwiches so much better!" A jar would be EUR 3, which was slightly above what we had, but the jar would last for days. It was one of the best buying decisions we made. The pickles became our unique selling point, paired with an unbeatable price.

Armed with enough "raw material" for at least 25 sandwiches, we went to our classroom. We stored it in the back of the room in a cupboard and used every break to prepare fresh sandwiches on-demand. Soon, the entire classroom smelled like fresh cheese, ham and pickles. Imagine the teachers looking around when entering the room looking

for where the strong smell was coming from. It was hilarious!
I was right: the children loved the sandwiches! After we had
handed out the 14 that we had presold the day before, Peter
and I took each one, so we only had nine left. Word spread
like wild fire when the first happy customers shared with
others how awesome our sandwiches were. We had so much
demand for the last nine sandwiches that we ended up selling
them for the same price as the cafeteria was selling them. We
did not have to compete by price anymore; moreover we were
competing through better quality. People simply loved the
pickles! Think about it: If you ever ate a delicious sandwich,
pickles are a must, right?

Peter and I had a net profit of roughly EUR 10 that day,
and on top of that our own sandwiches were free. Children
started asking already about the next days – and "pre-orders"
started coming in. To keep the marketing strategy simple we
had the preorder running at the same price of 99 cents, but
stated that the same day price would be EUR 1.5. I wanted to
get all the orders in upfront. It would not only help our cash
flow massively but also give us a more predictable way to plan
our purchase. The children loved the offer and once children
from other classrooms heard about what was going on, we
had over 30 pre-orders for the next day. Our entire school had
around 1,000 students – keep that number in mind down the
road when we started to expand to other floors. Peter did all
the accounting, collecting the money and handing out of the
sandwiches while I was in charge of purchasing raw material
at the supermarket, preparing sandwiches and negotiating
with new children. At the age of eleven I learned two of the
key skills in life: selling and negotiating with others. Business
was booming. By the end of the week we had 50 regular
customers and net profits of roughly EUR 30 per day. We
could now buy the largest bulk orders at the supermarket.
A few days later the supermarket I normally went to became
too small and I had to get up even earlier to take a different
bus to a wholesale store further away. This would allow us to
cut down costs even more and gave us tremendous profits.

Within ten days our total net profit was roughly EUR 200. In order to grow further we had to scale the business. The main issue was manpower: We didn't have enough time during the breaks in between classes to prepare all the sandwiches fresh. One sandwich would take around one minute including cutting it up and putting everything in. I probably could have entered the sandwich making world championship as for over an hour (split over three breaks) I was doing nothing else than cutting and preparing them. I did not want to pre-make them in the morning, as I knew the children loved the fresh, non-soggy sandwiches. We could not accept more than 70-80 orders a day due to the time constraints of making the sandwiches and Peter was being bombarded with children's pre-orders for the next day. The only solution: we had to take on our first employee. We recruited a friend of ours who would receive two free sandwiches per day in return for helping to prepare them. That would free me up so that I could grow the business by getting more customers. Soon we grew to 120 orders per day, which served our entire school complex. In order to grow further we would have to move to the other complexes. This was not as easy, as children coming from the same complex, which we had been doing so far. I wanted to grow our sales, but I was not sure how we could tackle expanding to the other parts of the school.

During one of our "business meetings" after school, in a café close by, we were discussing how to grow our business without adding too much logistical work. I came up with an idea: "We already have over a 100 customers. What if we add a second product?" We had thought about offering drinks before, but their weight made it a nightmare to buy them in bulk. I continued: "What do almost all children love? Bread with Nutella[4] on it!" It was delicious, cheap to get and easy to carry in the jars it was sold in. They agreed and so the next day I bought the largest jar of Nutella the supermarket offered. Liquidity of money was not an issue at all anymore. Within a

---

4   Nutella is a chocolate, hazelnut spread

month we had made net profits of over EUR 500 and we had daily revenues of over EUR 150. The Nutella breads were a hit. We could sell them for the same price as the sandwiches, but the cost of the raw materials was less than 20 cents each. Even more important was that we were buying bread already, and adding the Nutella to our shopping list was simple and not much strain on the logistics. Since most of the children saved a couple of Euros per week by buying our sandwiches, they now treated themselves to a Nutella bread, two or three times a week with the extra money. Soon we were selling over 200 breads a day and I felt that we had to another one or two "employees". They wouldn't really cost us much, but we definitely needed them. Peter and I decided to have "job applications" to see who would be qualified, as by that time many kids wanted to work for us and get two free sandwiches a day. We had now earned over EUR 1,000 in just a couple of weeks and business seemed to be going through the roof. Peter and I started dreaming of expanding to the other school's complexes and making tens of thousands of Euros a month. We felt we were on top of the world, but whenever you think nothing can stop you, you will find your master.

The next morning I was arriving with two large bags, each with 100 breads inside. We had a lot to do with preparing the sandwiches and teaching the two new employees what to do. I was already in full work mode when I saw Peter sitting quietly at his desk. "Come on, stop being lazy – we need to work!" I yelled at him. He should have helped me unpacking and preparing the breads. He just looked up quietly and said, "The principal just left! He wants to see us now!" "Does he also want to buy sandwiches and Nutella bread from us?" I joked, smiling. But Peter did not smile one bit: Yikes, now I was worried as well. I dropped the bread and both of us walked over to the principal's office. Our heads were bowed. Most of the children passing us knew and greeted us. Usually we would respond in a cheerful way, but not today. We entered the principal's office. He sat there, together with our main-classroom-teacher, our school advisors and the cafeteria owner. When I saw the cafeteria owner sitting there I had a bad feeling about what had happened: Since over 20% of the children were now buying from us he was taking massive revenue hit. It had never crossed our minds that by us gaining all these customers we were taking them away from someone else: in that case, him. And of course, that did not make him very happy, as the cafeteria was his main income. The atmosphere was dead serious. "Sit down please", the principal ordered. For over an hour Peter and I had to listen to what a bad example we were, how bad this was for our reputation and how much we had infringed the school's rules. Our parents were informed about this and we would get a suspension warning. Should anything similar ever happen again we would be expelled from school.

After the one-hour lecture, Peter and I were quite devastated. We didn't mean any harm and the other children had loved it. Today I understand the politics within the school: the principal had to protect the cafeteria. Later I found out that during those six weeks the cafeteria almost went out of business due to the loss in revenue. Even though my parents had known that we were doing something, they didn't know the exact details. When they received a call from the school principal, they grounded me for a week. Today they admit it was one of the funniest things ever – I am pretty sure the principal would say the same, looking back. After the initial shock of what had happened, Peter and I recovered and things started going back to normal. We still had taken away some massive profits, since both of us had earned over EUR 500 each in just a few weeks. Normally we would not even receive that kind of money within a year. A few months later we almost started our second business venture during our Junior High School years with a similar model selling ice cream. However, after we caught some tractions and word started spreading like wild fire again, we immediately cancelled operations. Both of us were too scared of being expelled from school. This experience in business however laid the groundwork of my entrepreneurial thinking for the years to come, and made me prone to running businesses myself, rather than wanting to work for someone else. Our sandwich business was my very first business and I call it quite a success. Yes, we were shut down just a few weeks after starting, but it taught me the key business lessons in a very practical way:

First, if you want to start your own business or create a company, the best way to do so is to spot a need in the market place. Chances are if you experience a problem, others experience it as well. If you manage to come up with a solution to that problem, and you offer a good solution to others, you can earn money from it. Any great business concept starts this way. Facebook came out of Mark Zuckerberg's and his co-founders' capitalization on the need for college students to exchange information." Steve Jobs and Steve Wozniak started Apple to bring the computer to the masses. These are only a few of many examples, but they all have one common denominator: They all spotted a need in the market and built a solution or product to cater for that need. At my young age, I was not able to spot large problems, because I did not really have any. But it was clear to Peter and I that the lunch situation was not resolved in the best way and that there was need for improvement. What I have taken away for myself is that it makes sense to try finding five to ten problems every day. I jot the problems down and try to come up with reasonable solutions. This is the key concept. Spotting a problem is sometimes not so hard, even though this is already a challenge for most people who are used to living their lives without opening their eyes to the world around them. The true magic lies in finding a solution to a problem. For most problems, I cannot come up with a good solution, but every once in a while I notice a great opportunity, and then I go for it. This is something everyone can do. Look and be open to the challenges around you, and look for ways to challenge the status quo by offering a different approach to these challenges. Take notes on paper, or your phone, and think about them. You will be amazed how many problems in life are waiting for solutions, and maybe you are the person that comes up with the next Google, Facebook, or iPhone!

It is important to note here that having only an idea is pretty much worthless. You need to take massive action and be prepared to work hard, non-stop. Many other children had the idea of making a small sandwich business in our school, but only Peter and I actually did it. Some tried, but they didn't like getting up two hours earlier to have everything done before school started. Peter and I were willing to do all that, and we executed it really well. Some people might be hesitant to get started on their idea due to lack of funding. Peter and I had no money either, but there is a very popular saying: "If the opportunity is good, the money will come!" It means if you can show people who actually have the money how good the opportunity is, they will invest their money into that opportunity. If they don't want to give you their money, chances are it is because the opportunity is really not good. I drew up a pretty good business plan for what we needed, and it allowed Peter and me to raise enough money from buyers to get started. Today, anyone who is committed to get something off the ground will be able to do so through online crowd funding platforms or pitch events. Where there is a will, there is a way!

The second thing I learned was that in business there should always be a WIN-WIN. The sum of the parts is greater than the parts themselves, but in nearly all cases you are taking market share or diminishing growth opportunity from another business. For Apple this meant that profits for IBM, Microsoft, and / or Samsung would be negatively affected. For Google this meant that AltaVista, Yahoo, or both would have to give up market share. In my case, the school Cafeteria was losing its market-share to Peter and me. I did not really understand this at that time. I just thought: "Great, we have dozens of customers every day, how awesome is that?" Well, I then learned that someone was missing revenue because of us selling sandwiches and Nutella-breads. From that day on, whenever I started a business or venture, I would ask myself: "Who will benefit from what I am about to do, and who will lose out because of that?" Best is to create a WIN-WIN-WIN situation, where not only you and your customer are winning, but the competition as well. This is more difficult to achieve, but such ventures are very long lasting. An example for that is Apple, who is producing its iPhones using some components made by Samsung. Here Apple, the customer and Samsung are winning, making it a triple WIN. Looking back, I should have made some deal with the cafeteria owner, which he probably would not have accepted anyway. It would have gotten us less profit initially, but would have allowed us to stay in business much longer.

The third lesson was an obvious one: expect the unexpected! Even though it is clear to the reader that the cafeteria would have us shut down, it was absolutely not clear to Peter and I back then. I was convinced we would be selling sandwiches all year long. When asked, most business owners would tell you they did not "see it coming". To an outsider that event was quite inevitable, but not to the person inside. A clear sign could have been our massive growth. Whenever something expands so massively, there tends to be a drop back to the norm. Ok, for us that meant we got closed down, but in normal life this happens every day on the stock or property market. Be aware of these fast growth phenomena, as the figures will likely drop back to their averages. From that incident onwards, I would create the habit of asking myself: "Am I missing something? What am I not expecting?" Do not misunderstand; it does not mean I am looking for the speck of dust on a marble bust. It just means that I hope for the best, but expect the worst. And I will be prepared for it. So many business owners or investors use calculation models based on assumptions and great numbers without ever contemplating that these perfect-world values might not be applicable in the real world, where things can go south very quickly.

So, what will you take away from this story? And most important, which immediate action will you take right now? Will you take action on a deep-rooted idea of yours? Do you see how to raise money for your idea? Will you prepare your own note-taking list to jot down ideas that come up during the day? Or, will you go through your numbers again and put in a safety margin? Whatever it is, take a minute and do it right now!

SPACE FOR MY TAKE AWAYS

6.

THE SAVING STORY -
MONOPOLY IN REAL LIFE

"Yessss! First time I played Monopoly and managed to finish the game without kicking over the board or slapping the cheating banker." – Unknown

As you read in the introduction, my sister and I got along quite well as children. Even though we were not the closest brother and sister one can imagine, we did complement each other nicely. A passion both of us shared was playing board games. There was one in particular called DKT. It means "Das Kaufmaennische Talent" which was the German version of Monopoly and simply meant "The Talented Businessman". The two of us spent many weekends playing that game, and we would often team up to play imaginary third players. The game taught us how to collect money from all kinds of income streams, build little houses, earn on the profits and interest rates and eventually, build a hotel. If you have never played Monopoly or DKT you should definitely do so. Today you can even download the game as an app to your phone or tablet, so there are no excuses. Of course we won every time, since we left the third player no chance! Besides having fun playing, the game taught us at an early age how to manage income and expenses in an easy and simple way. Moreover it also inspired me to establish good money habits outside of the game world.

After Peter's and my sandwich business burn, we were both too scared to start something new at school, remembering the risk of being expelled. I was looking into what else I could do to make some money. I had saved up most of what I had earned from the sandwich business but other than my parent's pocket money, which mostly went for daily lunches, there was no new money coming in. Sometimes my grandparents gave me a little when they came for a visit, or one of the neighbors paid me for mowing their lawn or helping to clean their driveway in the winter. But that did not happen very often. Monopoly was very similar, just on a larger scale: As a player you never had enough money; most of the time you were just getting by. Many times you would have to take up loans to finance a property, or bargain with others to get better deals. So, many times I was sitting on the bus to or from school thinking about how I could extrapolate the game into real life. I was too young to buy any apartments or build hotels, and with my little savings I would not get very far. Just as I had done when learning how to play basketball, I went to our school library and asked for the best book on how to make money. The librarian looked at me, puzzled, and was not sure how to reply. She took me to an aisle that had the books on economics. "These are all the books we have about that for our students", she claimed.

I started browsing through the books, but for most of them I did not even understand their titles: Words like Macroeconomics and Microeconomics sounded totally foreign to me. The books had tables of numbers and even more complicated words in them. I just wanted to learn how to make money, and was not interested about how to jot down tables of numbers. I kept looking. Most of the books were quite thick with hundreds of pages. Suddenly, I stopped; I spotted a tiny book, with maybe 80 pages. It had a paperback cover, not a hard one like the others. I pulled it from the shelf and was immediately delighted. It read: "The richest man of Babylon!"[5] I had heard of Babylon only once, and I could only remember it was about a huge tower. Even though not

---

5 http://en.wikipedia.org/wiki/The_Richest_Man_in_Babylon_(book)

really clear what this book would be about, I loved the title simply because I could understand it. I sat down on the floor and started reading. It was not written in easy language, but rather older style words. I did understand what it was about: A man in Babylon talked about the lessons he had learned on how to earn, and more importantly, keep money. One of them especially stuck with me: "Gold cometh gladly and in increasing quantity to any man who will put by not less than one-tenth of his earnings to create an estate for his future and that of his family." It meant that whatever I would earn I should put away 10% in savings. Wow, I could never do that I thought. How am I supposed to survive on that? I was spending every single penny I earned on lunch and food. My parents had budgeted my pocket money exactly on what they assumed I would need. The extras I was making I was using for any other small expenses, so nothing was left over to save. After a short, inner debate I decided to follow the book's tips to become rich as well.

Initially, I did not fully comprehend how I could take away 10% of my "gold", in my case money, if there was no money left over at the end of the month. I soon realized that the book had taken that into account and was teaching its reader to put the 10% away "before" even receiving that "gold". For me that meant I had to "put away" 10% as soon as I received the lunch money or the allowance for doing chores. It seemed absurd; I was convinced I would not survive on the remaining 90%. My entire spending was set for 100% and I did not see any way to cut my costs. I talked myself into trying it for a couple of days and to my amazement I realized that I indeed could live on only 90%. I started to become more frugal on my spending behavior and quite fast I had my new behavior dialed in. During lunch I would cut a drink every other day and when I received some money when playing basketball, I took away some of it immediately, so I could not spend all of it. I have no idea how I did it, but in my first month I had saved EUR 15 without really having to suffer from missing out on much. It doesn't sound like a lot of money, but this was really a lot compared to how much I was "earning" at that age. I could not believe that from one month to the other I could live on EUR 15 less, when just the month before it had seemed impossible to save just even one Euro. It was all about the "trick" to put away 10% straight away at the beginning of a month. There had never been anything left over, simply because I would spend everything that I had. Once I started to put away 10% I still spent everything, but that was now only 90%. I had tricked myself into saving money while believing I was still spending everything.

My expenses were now under control, but I had to increase my income if I wanted to increase my net value. In Monopoly I could increase my income by stacking up houses until I was able to build a hotel. Then I would use this money to buy other houses and build even more hotels and so on. I tried to translate that into real life. A new basketball store had opened in Munich, which was around a two-hour drive from where I was living. Our whole team needed new gear on a regular basis: new shoes, jerseys, basketballs, and so on. Normally, each one of us would individually buy all those things in a local store, which from an economic point of view, was not the smartest option. Since the store had very little competition it was higher priced than those in Munich's more competitive market. It would have made sense to buy jerseys or shoes in bulk and get a better deal compared to our local store. However, that was not possible since we didn't have money at the same time to buy together. So, we each bought when we really needed it. To go to Germany to the cheaper stores was another option, but to go just for one person would not save money because of the travel expenses. Online Shopping was just starting off, and there was a minimum order value of EUR 500 for free shipping, which none of us could achieve.

Then it dawned on me: Neither one of us could achieve it alone, but if we pooled the orders together, we could get the cheaper price and have free shipping. The idea was great but the challenge was to find enough friends who had the money to buy their essential basketball gear at the same time. The only way to make it work was to take the orders in advance, upfront the money for those that could not pay immediately, and then collect it later. At first I thought there was some risk involved, but then I realized that even if one friend would not end up paying, someone else would buy the order from me and I would at least break even. In order to avoid similar issues to those of the school cafeteria incident, I planned on keeping it a small operation, offering no competition to the local store. I ended up doing only two orders of around EUR 550 each that year and so I am quite sure the local store did not even notice that my friends and I ordering online from Munich and not from him.

What was my profit out of the arrangement? My first benefit was that I needed to buy basketball gear anyway, and by ordering from Germany and I saved over 30% on my own purchases. That was massive compared to the year before. I was only able to do that because of the other people who had joined and bulk ordered. Therefore I offered them the same price that I was paying as long as they gave me the money straight away. Not everyone was able to do that and for around half the people I had to upfront the money. Those children still paid a slightly discounted price compared to our local shop, so we agreed on splitting the savings. It was a win-win for both sides: The children got their gear slightly cheaper while I had around 15% profits, which was pretty good interest on my upfront capital, which was my second benefit of the deal. The third benefit for me was that I was a front-runner in Online Shopping. The store in Munich had only around one to two online orders a week. Amazon was not really known yet in Germany or Austria and so paying money over the Internet in the hope of getting goods later was something completely new for most people. The store was so happy with my two orders, that they added free shorts and shirts on top of it. I kept those for myself, adding it to my benefits. Comparing that to "grown-up revenue" it sounds like not much profit, but it is the same as in Monopoly. You start with one house, and then go to two and so on. For me making all that profit at such a young age was quite good. Moreover I learned the techniques and skills that would allow me to sell kites while I was a professional kitesurfer, flights when I was into flying, or apartments today. The core principles stayed the same, just the amounts increased – I kept buying "houses" till I earned enough to buy the "hotels".

During the basketball-investment I was making nice profit without having to spend any time on it. It was literally the first time in my life that I saw my money working for me. None of the other children could have done the bulk order, because they were lacking the funds. I had tapped into the power of earning through smart investing: money generating more money. With lots of time involvement I could have scaled the bulk orders and grown by expanding to other areas in sports and reaching more people, making it an actual business, but I was happy with the profits I had made and the entire team had benefitted from it too. Many people lose money on their first investment, but I made a good profit. It had nothing to do with luck, but with two of the most important rules about investing that I was applying unintentionally and that I will talk intensively about in one of the last chapters: Know your product, and make money on the "Buy". Comparing that to Monopoly, it meant that chances for me to lose money were very low: I got a good deal when buying the "house (gear)" and I was an expert on the "product". I was buying the gear 30% below market value plus I was very knowledgeable about basketball gear. Imagine buying a totally overpriced street in Monopoly and not knowing what it could bring you in rent or actual value? You would never buy it. Ever. Well, guess what? In real life most people invest into different things every day, even though they have no idea about "the product" and whether is overpriced or not. Then they are surprised when they lose money on their investments. Spoiler alert: you will see in upcoming stories that I will not learn these lessons properly until I lose tens of thousands of Euros exactly because of making these same mistakes.

Including all incomes and savings, minus expenses, I netted a profit of over EUR 1,000 that year. Simply through getting my money to work for me and understanding how to save 10% of my income. It might not seem a lot, but it certainly was to me back then and for some this might seem totally out of reach even today. I was extremely proud about having made so much money that year and so I went to my dad to exchange the EUR 1,000 from smaller notes into two EUR 500 notes. Until that day I had never held such a note in my own hands. It was kind of like celebrating a victory! I had a taste of how powerful "money working for you" was and now I was looking for more ways to do this. Just like Monopoly, I knew about interest rates when you put money in the bank. As a disclaimer: I don't like leaving my money in a Savings Account at all as I believe there are dozens of better ways to get your money to work. But being only 13 years old, a Savings Account was one of the best options I had for my money, especially as back then I received 6% interest through a special promotion. In Austria, banks organized annual savings events. Children could take their little piggy banks and put their money into a savings account, where they would get a special savings deal in return. Only people under the age of 18 and up to a maximum amount were allowed to use that deal. I qualified and wanted to put all my money in the account.

My mom took my sister and me to the bank. I had my piggy bank with my accounting booklet with me. Still today I am extremely detailed about doing accounting. I never liked doing it but I know it is important, so even though I am outsourcing it to an accountant or my personal assistant, I still keep a good overview. Getting into the bank, there were quite a lot of people. Most parents with their children used the opportunity to get the special promotions. My sister and I were waiting in line and when it was our turn, I opened my piggy bank and proudly displayed my EUR 1,000 to the bank clerk. He didn't seem so impressed, as he probably saw hundreds of people with a lot of money. My mom on the other hand was extremely surprised. She had expected me to have around EUR 100 saved up. The bank issued a receipt of a little bit over EUR 1,000 and now it was my sister's turn. She opened her piggy bank and not more than EUR 20 fell out, just like it had for me the year before. Now the clerk was also surprised and my mom was in utter shock. Coming out of the same family with similar pocket money neither one of them expected me to have that much more than her. My sister was never keen on saving or earning money and so she just saved what was left after she had spent the rest – which was not much. I would say most people treat money that way. I, on the other hand, had been really dedicated by using the 10% trick and had saved a lot that year.

In total shock my mom did something that deeply hurt me at that moment and I have remembered it for the rest of my life: She opened her wallet and added EUR 400 to my sisters' piggy bank. She probably would have added more, but that was all she had in her wallet at that moment. I still feel deeply hurt thinking back of that moment. I had worked so hard to save that money but my mom tried to level the playing field by "cheating" to help my sister. I didn't tell her at that time how hurt I was, but still today we have discussions about what happened that day. The entire event turned out to have ambivalent effects on me: On one hand, I was very disappointed because I had worked so hard to get my EUR 1,000, but my sister benefitted by EUR 400 without putting in any effort. On the other hand, it motivated me to earn so much more the next year that my mom could not afford to give my sister the same amount of money. She had taught me to live up to any challenge and that was what I did. I worked harder and harder to build my net worth and only five years later I had saved over EUR 10,000. This allowed me to spend part of my High School time in the U.S., as I had to pay for half of all the travel and tuition myself. At that young age I had learned how to save money in such a short time with extremely limited income. Even though earning EUR 1,000 or US$ per month some people never manage to save more than a few dollars or Euros a year because they feel they do not make enough. I felt the same way once, but then I learned how to save money properly. Saving EUR 10,000 within five years with very limited income as a teenager is absolutely possible by applying the simple 10% rule. Just imagine what a grownup with a US$1,000 monthly salary would be capable of, doing the same thing.

The lessons for life came just at the right time. Playing Monopoly with my sister laid the groundwork for my interest in finances. No matter whether you have children or not, or if you are or still feel like a child, you should play Monopoly and learn the principles of money. Robert Kiyosaki built a special game called the Cashflow Game[6] – a pity I could not play that when I was younger - but it is definitely a great game no matter how old you are. It will teach you all these principles in a fun way! Monopoly inspired me to take the lessons from the game into real life, plus I learned the principle of saving 10% of your money before you start spending a single dollar. An interesting point is that the same principle can also be applied to carving out time in your calendar. One thing I am taking away from this now that I am running several businesses, is that time is a very precious commodity that you have to budget properly. So if you have the feeling that you do not have enough money to save, or you do not have enough time to do something, remember this principle: Carve out the 10% at the very beginning. Talking about time, this means to budget the time needed for an important thing at the beginning of the week. If not, other things will eat up your time, and you will end up "not having enough time" for what you originally planned on doing.

---

6 http://www.richdad.com/apps-games/cashflow-classic

The second lesson was an unintentional one: Whenever you invest you have to make the money in the "Buy". I already elaborated on that briefly in the story. The best investment is if you get to buy a dollar for only 70 cents. Think about it: If someone would sell you dollar notes for 70 cents you would buy as many as you could, wouldn't you? That was exactly what was happening for me. I knew that I got 30% off the price that people were willing to pay, plus I had very limited risk. Would you pay 70 cents for something that is worth only 60 cents? How about paying 70 cents for something you do not know the actual value of? These questions sound strange, but this is what people do on a daily basis: They invest into stocks they cannot evaluate. They buy apartments without knowing what they are actually worth. And then people are surprised that they lose money on their investment. I have to admit that I was lucky on my first ever investment; I did not understand that principle, yet I applied it properly. I did know a lot about basketball gear; shoes, shirts, balls and so on. Whenever you find investments, where you consider yourself quite well read on the topic, and you find a bargain where you get to "buy a dollar for 70 cents", you should invest as much as you can. Sadly, two times in my life after that I got "ripped off" big time by other people when I did not follow this rule. It happened once when buying property in Brazil from a guy called Ralf and the second time when I invested into a Model Agency in Hong Kong with a girl called Laura –stories you will read about later on in this book.

If you ever played Monopoly, and you know the game well, you understand that there is a lot of math behind winning, just as there is in real life. There are properties on the board where it is statistically more likely that people land, and so it makes more sense to buy these rather than others. The statistics behind Monopoly are quite fascinating and you can find them on Google if you are interested. So what is the third lesson here; the moral of the story? Just like Monopoly, in real life there are events that are totally unexpected and against the odds that set you back a lot without any prior warning. It was a small thing for my mother to help my sister out moneywise while I had been very careful with my money and saved a lot the entire year. In Monopoly this could happen as well, and while you are on track to win it all, you might land in prison or the other person may hit the "jackpot" when picking up a random card. It is great to play the money game with a good plan, but you have to be prepared for pitfalls. At the bank, my mom had hurt me unintentionally but at the same time it motivated me even more afterwards.

I hope this story of my first investments inspired you to think about what you have done right or wrong when dealing with money. The important thing now is not what you have learned from reading this, but what action you will take based upon what you just learned. What will it be? Putting away that extra time at the beginning of a week for your important tasks? Saving 10% of your income at the beginning of the month? Learning to get your money to work for you? Yes, I know it sounds scary, but believe, me, it will turn out fine as long as you learn to make the money on the "buy". Invest money wisely, and learn that it is not about how much you make, but how much you keep! TAKE ACTION NOW!

SPACE FOR MY TAKE AWAYS

7.

THE AMERICA STORY -
EXPANDING MY HORIZONS

"One way to define insanity is by doing the same thing over and over and still expecting different results." – attributed to Albert Einstein and Benjamin Franklin

I did not particularly like school, as I found that I was not interested in what was being taught. I had always been an avid reader and very good at teaching myself. I really loved math and science though, so I tried to skip as many of the other classes and played basketball with friends instead. My dream was to play in the U.S., and so I trained hard every day. I hit puberty in Junior High School and my parents realized that I had started to become even more intolerable and rebellious than previously. In order to motivate me for school they made a deal with me: if I had good grades and would save enough to pay for the trip, they would support me in fulfilling my dream by enabling me to go to the U.S. So I studied hard to pass every year with "excellence" and live up to the requirements my parents had set for me. Once I was 15 years old I confronted my parents to cash in on their commitment. I had saved enough money myself and I had been one of the best in my class every year, despite also being one of the students with the most missed classes. My parents had secretly hoped I would either change my mind at some point or would not be able to keep my side of the promise. But I was allowed to fill out my application to be transferred to a U.S. High School and play basketball there. A host family in Nashville, Tennessee accepted my application and so my dream became reality. I will be forever thankful to both my parents in Austria, but also to my host parents in the US. Had either one of them not stepped up to help me, I am not sure if, at the age of 16, I could have left my home to explore new frontiers.

I did not think saying good-bye to my parents would be that hard, but it was. I was pretty much crying the entire flight. Of course I couldn't tell my parents that – they would have just tried even harder to convince me to stay. This was at a time that emails and basic cell phones had just started to become popular, but in order to login to the Internet you needed to use a slow, dial-in modem. The only contact I would have with my parents was a once a month phone conversation. It was the first time I had ever flown on an airplane and it was pretty much the worst trip of my life: all three connecting flights had massive delays and on the 2nd one we even had a bomb threat. What a great start into my first year away from home. Arriving in the U.S. was nothing like I had ever imagined it to be. I knew the U.S. only from movies and the image I had created my own imagination. I had pictured it as a perfect world: Everybody happy, supportive with endless opportunities. Oh boy, what a cultural shock it was. I arrived there right after 9-11, and the US was about to go to war with Iraq. People were quite offensive towards foreigners, and being from Austria they constantly asked whether I was a Nazi. What an odd question, I always thought, since all that had happened over 60 years earlier. On top of that I barely understood what people were saying, as I could not decipher the southern slang. Rules at school were very different as well. Once, a fellow student told the teacher that I was cheating, when actually I didn't understand a question. The Principal immediately put me into ISS (in-school-suspension). This also went on my school record and lead to serious explaining in every college application later on. Looking back, the first couple of weeks and even months were a complete nightmare. It was no one's fault other than my own, as I had arrived with completely wrong expectations. Many times I felt like picking up the phone and asking my parents to get me back to Austria. Fortunately, as mentioned above phone calls were really expensive and online communications were not common yet. I was stuck and had to make the best out of it.

My host family was great and it soon started to feel less like a "host family" and more like a "real family". Originally I was supposed to enter as a High School junior (second to last year before graduating) but since I could manage the classes easily I was allowed to go straight to the senior level. This meant that I had to do some extra activities, but also that I could graduate from a U.S. school. I was extremely excited. Also, remembering why I went to the US in the first place, cheered me up a lot: basketball. I played every minute I could, before school, during lunch, and in the evenings. The rules for High School athletes in the U.S. are very strict, and students may only train with a coach during certain periods of the year. The rest of the time we were allowed to play for ourselves but not in any organized training sessions. In Austria I was training with the team all year round, so this seemed very strange to me at first. I soon saw the benefit of it however as doing it this way I had hundreds of hours to fine-tune my shooting and dribbling. Most of the school infrastructure in the US is built around sports and athletes. As long as I had excellent grades (which I did because I studied quite hard to qualify for graduation) my teachers actually encouraged me to train hard to help our school win games. Our school was not very large, but it had a team of coaches, medical staff, and physical trainers that most professional teams in Europe cannot afford. Within a few weeks, I was in the best shape of my life, thanks to my detailed workout regimen. Considering all this it is no surprise to me today that athletes from the U.S. are so dominant in many sports.

After the initial cultural shock, I started to get used to the true America. I bonded with some great friends during these years, especially Chris and Jay, who I am still in touch with. We played together on the team and spent a lot of time together on and off the court, and we basically would "ride together and die together". In school we helped each other out and on the basketball court we pushed each other to the limit. We were too young to drink, but since Chris and Jay each had a car, we were able to get around and have fun. In Austria, where school and sports were organized independently this was a bit harder, but in the U.S. the school campuses were basically designed for close friendship and bonding. In retrospect, it was interesting to see how some "friends" who were superficially friendly when I first arrived dropped away over time. Others had been a bit more reserved initially, but once they realized that the stranger from overseas was really friendly, they opened up. I learned a lot about making friends during that time, which has helped me throughout my entire life so far, considering how many places I have travelled. Most people stay in the same place their entire lives. They never learn to adapt to a new environment or different people. Then suddenly a change happens and their lives seem to fall apart. It reminds me about new technologies today. I truly believe I could not be so open-minded had I not been thrown into the cold water when I went to the U.S. at the age of 15. The first few months were really tough, but the longer I stayed, the more I learned to adapt quickly and the better my time became.

During the time I was there the U.S. went to war with Iraq. No matter whether you were for or against the Iraq war, literally all of my friends and "family" knew or had someone close who left to fight overseas. This was particularly hard for me as I felt I was caught in-between. I never liked violence and particularly hated war, but knowing that my friends had family there who were actually risking their lives was a very scary feeling. I had never cared much about politics or the news, but both were extremely important in our daily lives in the U.S. Two or three times a day we would pledge allegiance to the American flag at school. If something like that would be done in Austria or Germany, we would be called Nazis and reminded about World War 2. It was so interesting to see how different our cultures were. Their patriotism left an everlasting impression on me, and actually helped me to create great team cultures later on. I did not use the same tactics the U.S. was using on their people, but I realized how important it was to work towards a common goal within an organization. Steve Jobs used similar tactics within Apple by creating an enemy that Apple had to beat. At the beginning it was IBM, then Microsoft and today it is Google or Samsung.

Time flew by and in the middle of the year I switched host families in order to be closer to school and to be with the people who had become very close friends. I moved in with my new host family: Chris and his sister Ashley, and their parents, Paulette and George. The first time I went to their house, George asked me: "So, you are Julian from Austria. Let me ask you this: Have you ever been to the birth place of Adolf Hitler?" I was pretty much in shock and just stood there, not knowing what to answer. My host sister Ashley and host brother Chris pulled me away and told me he was just joking. I am pretty sure he wasn't. Today it is a great running joke whenever we see each other, but back then I thought: "What a weird man!" Nevertheless, George was great and I learned a lot from him. First of all he introduced me to the Starbucks concept. I could not believe when I found out that people were willing to pay up to US$5 for a single cup of coffee. I realized back then that the most important thing for people was and still is how you make them feel. If the feeling was good they were happy to pay almost any price without complaining. I am pretty sure you can relate to that by asking you a quick question: What would you rather have, US$5 or a beautiful flower? Chances are you would pick the flower despite it being worth less than the US$5 in monetary terms. The reason is that money by itself does not directly make you feel good. A beautiful flower on the other hand warms your heart, no matter whether it is cheaper to buy than US$5. Starbucks has mastered this concept and I owe it to George for understanding it. I used the same principle for my own businesses later on. I knew people were happy to pay a lot more for a service as long as its quality was superior and they felt good about it. You might be reading this and saying: "So what... What's so special about that?" Well, if that was clear to everyone on our planet, we might not have such poor service in so many places. I had always been quite committed on delivering excellence and my experience with Starbucks reinforced that drive even more.

Besides spending a lot of time at Starbucks, George also loved going to the library. It was like a dream come true. Most of my friends hated books, but George loved reading just as much as I did. So besides basketball, school and Starbucks, I spent a lot of time with him going to the library. He would be reading history books while I was totally immersed in Astronomy and Quantum Physics. I had always dreamed of going into space and flying around the moon. One day he asked me a question totally out of the blue: "So what will you study after High School?" I had asked myself the same thing before, but had never really come up with an answer. Most of my friends in school had decided about their studies already but I had believed I had a year longer to decide. Now that I skipped a year it was only a few months until I would enter college. Time really flew by. I was interested in many things, especially science, economics and psychology. "What do you think I should go for?" I asked, trying to push the question back to him. "Well, if you want to make me proud you either become a lawyer or a medical doctor" he replied straight away. I stood there, not knowing what to say. I had neither relatives nor friends who were in either of those professions and so I was extremely insecure as to whether this was really the path to go. Yes, I was definitely interested in studying law or medicine, but I had never contemplated that thought in detail. George stayed persistent and said: "Julian, I want you to make up your mind because time is running down. Here are two great books; one is about being a lawyer and the other one about being a medical doctor. Read them this week and then give me your decision afterwards". I was stunned. He really thought I was going to make up my mind. To my own amazement I did.

During my time in the U.S., I had learned an approach to tackling new challenges, and I had hundreds of them every week. Most teenagers have a certain stability and predictability in their life. Their school might change, but their family stays the same. Their friends might change when they switch from one sport to another, but then maybe they stay at the same school. Think about your own time when you were or still are a teenager. There is a certain stability that you tend to keep, and around that you change things once in a while. Well, for me I felt there was zero predictability. Everything changed from language, culture, family, school, friends, habits, etc. I was struggling with that for the first few months and it almost made me go back home. Over time, I adopted an approach that allowed me to let change happen easily, without worrying about what it meant. I started to embrace change, while for most people they strongly dislike it. I had no choice. Whenever someone offered something new to me and I was not sure whether I should go for it or not, nor how I would be able to actually achieve it I started to work on a three step plan:

1. I said YES first, even though not being really sure.

2. Then I would tell people around me that I would do it, thereby building up   internal pressure so that I really had to follow through.

3. I worked out the plan along the way

I needed to work this way because otherwise I would have moved forward very slowly. That's what got me stuck in the first few weeks. It was not the change per se - it was I trying to figure out what it all meant and which way I should go. Unintentionally I had used the same approach even before going to the U.S. I did have some doubts, but I really wanted to go. I told everyone I was going to go but I had no idea how to make it happen or what would happen once I arrived there. The nice thing about the universe (I just call it universe, you might call it your god, or energy) is that there are so many opportunities, and all you need to do is set your mind to it with a firm decision and it will happen. Many people do it the opposite way, and that is why they get stuck. Think about the last new thing you did or had to choose: Changed jobs? Planned a trip? Started a side business? Whatever it is, how did you move forward? Did you love the idea, committed to it first and figured it out afterwards, or did you try to figure everything out first before you committed? At the beginning of my trip to the U.S. I used the latter approach and it never got me anywhere. Along the way I changed and in order to make it easier on me I used additional social pressure by telling people that I was going to do it. Try it out for yourself the next time. You will see; it will all work out like magic even though it might look incredibly scary at first.

While reading George's two books I knew I had to make up my mind, and then just go for it. Living in the U.S. had taught me how to listen to my gut feeling and make decisions with limited information. I think it is one of the skills I am the most thankful for, and I learned it when millions of new things started hitting me and I have to filter the few important ones to make my decision. I truly believe you cannot develop a good gut feeling if you have too much information. So while reading the books I realized quite fast that becoming a lawyer would not be an option for me: I did not enjoy boring legal texts and was way too hyperactive to sit still. I had always preferred math, science and sports and so my gut feeling was to go for medicine straight away. At the end of the week I told George that I would study medicine. He was the first person to know. I had said YES, and now it was time to tell the others to make myself commit to it. I called up my parents, and they were skeptical at first. None of us had a medical background they pointed out. That was normal about telling others; they tend to tell you the dangers or negatives about an option. I was firm. I would study medicine. I just had no idea where and how. That was the third step: to figure it out just as I had done all the other times.

Looking back, my time in the U.S. was one of the most important times in my life. Not all parts were great, but I learned many valuable lessons. The first key lesson is: if you have the opportunity to go abroad at an early stage, DO IT! Say "Yes" now and figure it out later! If you are a parent or future parent, have your children go abroad at an early age. It is the best thing you can do for them. Say "Yes" and figure it out later. I would credit a lot of my later successes to that time I spent in the U.S. going to High School. The independence I had to foster to overcome skepticism from other children in school, to adapt to a completely new environment, and to develop a completely new perspective of things, are all life lessons I gained because of going abroad. Many of my political and religious views were formed in ways I would have never imagined. And of course my skills in basketball improved a lot during this time, which allowed me to play at a much higher level when I went back to Europe. When thinking about whether you should move abroad, or if you are a parent reading this thinking about your child, then don't think about all the things that could go wrong, but trust that many things will go right. I cannot tell you how scared I was or how worried my parents were. I am sure they could not sleep the first couple of nights. You know why I think that? Because I could not sleep either.

If you want amazing results compared to others, by definition you have to make different decisions. You will keep getting the same results over and over if you keep going the same route that others have been going. This is the message of the quote at the beginning of the chapter. People are scared to choose a different route because it is the unknown. So what to do? Use the 1-2-3 strategy described above. Whenever people look at my CV, one of the things that stick out the most is I moving away from home at the age of 16. That touches many people because it is not ordinary. Take this as lesson number two from this chapter. You want to have extraordinary results? It is not about you being extraordinary, it is about making different decisions than other people would make in the same situation. Learn to be a contrarian and stand up for your opinion.

Lesson Number three was developing a "gut feeling". Today I can make up my mind about something or someone within seconds. I read a lot of books about gut feeling in recent years, and they all describe it similarly: Being good at going with your gut feeling is the ability to making decisions based on a very limited amount of information. Most people think that decisions based on a lot of information are mostly the better decisions, but studies show the clear opposite. True experts in any field develop a lot of experience and know what to look for to make a decision within a few seconds. Think about a sport you play. I am sure if you watch someone play that sport for just a few seconds you have a feeling how good that person actually is. In basketball for example I can judge a person simply based on how he or she is holding the ball. How their fingertips touch the leather gives me some important cues. This can be true for anything; mostly we just don't have enough practice. So how did I develop my gut feeling towards people or things to pursue? From one day to another when I arrived in the U.S. I had to meet hundreds of new people for the first time. I had to do so many new things that I had never tried and so I obtained a vast amount of experience dealing with new people or things. I developed a sense of learning who to trust and who not to trust. How would people behave who wanted to cheat me, and how people would behave who wanted the best for me? Many leaders in business and politics will tell you that having a good gut feeling and then learning to listen to it, is one of the most important tools they use. A gut feeling is not an innate talent; it is a skill that can be learned just like anything else. But just like anything else, it needs the right circumstances to be learned properly. I believe the best way to do that is to put yourself in a completely new environment where you need to improve your instincts and develop a good gut feeling, and learn to listen to it. Most people just never put themselves into a situation like that and therefore struggle with listening to their inner voice their entire life.

The next chapter will show you whether my gut feeling about medicine was right, and if so, how it all worked out for me. But first, I would love for you to ask yourself: what are you taking away from this story? Is it that you will go somewhere new to push your own limits? Maybe it is just for a weekend or so. Will you send your own children abroad if you have any? Go and work on your gut feeling? Whatever it is, the most important question will be: What action will you take NOW? Trust me, say "YES", TELL other people, and FIGURE OUT the details along the way,

SPACE FOR MY TAKE AWAYS

8.

THE SAT STORY -
STUDYING THE DICTIONARY

*"Education is important, because without education
you can't be a leader" – Nelson Mandela*

It was the beginning of 2003 and I had just made the decision to study medicine. My plan was to graduate from High School that year in the U.S. and apply to a college so I was on track to becoming a medical doctor. I had absolutely no idea how I could actually do that, and I had no doctor friends or relatives to ask for advice. My host dad, George, just kept telling me that I was a smart boy and with my good grades I would figure it out. Well, I can testify that having good grades has nothing to do with actually having a plan about life, because at that point I had literally no clue how I would actually get into college. None of my fellow students were going to study medicine, but they told me that the local college was an excellent medical institution. I went to our school's student advisor to understand how to apply. When I asked her for the forms she looked at me in disbelief: "Do you actually know what it takes to go there?" "No", I affirmed - I had absolutely no idea. I was committed to do it and would figure out the details later. "Have you already taken your SAT?" she asked me. "What was an SAT?" I asked. I had no clue. "Oh darling; and you want to study medicine?" she said with a condescending smile. This would not be the last time that people laughed at what I wanted to do, but I never really cared. Moreover it motivated me to prove to them that I could do it.

At home I asked my host brother Chris what the SAT was. He was an excellent student and would be able to help me. Chris explained to me that the Standardized Assessed Test was a test that most High School students in the U.S. take if they want to go to college. As the name suggests, everything about the test is standardized: Time, number of questions, kind of questions, duration, etc. Back then the scores ranged from 0 – 800 for English and for Math (today there are three categories so the maximum score is now 2,400, where back then it was a total of 1,600). The English questions are comprised of vocabulary, reading, and comprehension. In math, they ask you logical thinking questions, basic math calculations as well as speed calculations. Everything has to be done under time pressure with approximately one minute per question. The next exam was in either three or seven weeks, I could choose. Chris suggested I should take the one in seven weeks so I could study and prepare for the exam properly. "Prepare?" I asked. "Yes, prepare" he replied with a smile. Chris explained to me that I needed some serious vocabulary improvements and work on some of the math examples. He gave me a small booklet that he had used for his SAT training. He had achieved around 1300 points in total, which was excellent. I was committed to achieve at least the same.

I went to work the same day and started reading through the book. The first chapter was about expanding ones capabilities to connect and understand words. Some of these words I had never even heard in my life. Now I started to understand why people had told me that being a non-native English speaker I would face some massive challenges. I took a trial exam in the booklet to have a better understanding of where I was. In the English section I had zero out of ten questions correct. I could not believe it. Even though I had considered myself well read I had never heard some of the words before. The math part was a lot easier and I scored eight out of 10. However, I had to get used to the time pressure if I wanted to score higher in math. English was a total different matter. Here I had to step up my game by 1,000%. So, besides the daily basketball training in the morning, lunch and evening, I added two vocabulary lessons and one math session of 30 min each a day. I had seven weeks to go, and I wanted to do well. I spoke to George about my plan and he came up with a crazy idea: "Why don't you just study the dictionary at the library? You would learn all the vocabulary words there are." I looked at him in disbelief. "Study the dictionary? You are kidding, right?" I frowned. "No, think about it Julian. You are a good reader, so you will do well in the reading section, but they will ask you hundreds of word definitions and your English vocabulary range is somewhat limited. These SAT training books are made for native speakers. You need to start from scratch!" I seriously thought he was kidding, but the more I thought about it I realized he was right.

I went to the library with him. The biggest challenge was to choose the right dictionary. There are over 200,000 words in the English language and it was going to be impossible for me to learn all of them. Moreover, many of them where either obsolete or not necessary. I picked a dictionary for students that had around 30,000 words in it. I would know many already of course, but I figured 30,000 would be a good number to know. I had a little over 50 days to go till the exam and the dictionary had around 500 pages in total. While flipping through it I noticed that some entries were very similar and I would not end up having to study 30,000 different words, but probably a lot less. The plan was to work through ten pages a day, rehearse the words from the day before and have a small safety margin of time in case anything unplanned popped in. At the same time I wanted to do work on two to three pages of math examples a day. I did not need to improve my math but had to improve the speed and accuracy. After only two days I realized that I was too slow and I did not know enough words. If you want to experience what I mean for yourself, open a dictionary and start on its first page with A and see how many words you actually know. I had to learn many just on the first couple of pages. I figured it would get easier once

I knew more words, but if I didn't get more study time in or increase the amount of words I could learn, I would never get through the dictionary. I just was not efficient enough at memorizing the words.

When I was in my first year of Junior High School back in Austria, my mom had made me write flash cards to learn vocabulary when I started learning English. I wrote the word in German on one side and its definition on the other. It took me a bit longer to write the cards, but afterwards I knew the words inside out. Additionally, this allowed me to study on the bus and to organize the cards in a way that I could repeat those that I did not know so well yet. I made the decision to do the exactly same thing again for the SAT. I calculated that I had to write around 100 vocabulary cards a day, and work through the pile afterwards. That would take a bit longer than just studying the words, but I would know the words by heart afterwards. During the seven weeks I could easily learn 5,000 new words that way, which would get me close to know most of the English words that would get tested in the SAT. There were no statistics about how many words one needed to know but I assumed that 5,000 words would get me close. So every day I would work through around ten pages in the dictionary, writing down the word on one side of the flash card and a brief definition, synonyms and antonyms on the other side. It would take me about one minute per card, so I normally spent the entire morning doing my card writing and over lunch I tested my morning words and repeated some words from the days before that had been giving me problems. In the evening I worked on math and more vocabulary testing. The strategy seemed to work well, especially during the first few weeks. It did take a long time to write the cards, but since I had to think about each word when I wrote it, I was able to remember them afterwards.

After two weeks I had over 1,000 flashcards and that was when I realized a new challenge: I had to remember too many words! The 1,000 cards filled up a lot of space, so I needed to store the in boxes so they were organized and I could keep track of what I had reviewed and the words that were more difficult. After some thinking I came up with a solution for the boxes: I started to spread them out over different locations in the school, so that I did not have to carry them around all the time. I started to study different boxes at different locations throughout our campus. For example I spoke to my American History teacher, and stored the box with the cards from A - C there. The D – G box went to my English class and so on. I figured that the time during the morning or lunch was not enough and so I started studying during class. Most teachers did not notice what I was doing, but once my math teacher asked me why I was reading vocabulary cards in the math class. I tried to explain myself by saying that some words in his class were too difficult for me and so I wanted to write them down and look them up afterwards. He came over and looked at the card I had in my hand: It said "telesthesia⁷". He looked at me quizzically. I am not really sure whether he believed me, or he just let it slip to avoid being embarrassed not knowing the word himself. He just smiled and said: "That is so great Julian, keep doing that!" He basically gave me his official OK to study during his class. I was an A+ student in Math anyways, so it did not really matter.

Storing the boxes in various locations did not solve another problem however: There were simply too many words to learn in too short of a time. I don't know if you've ever tried to memorize 100 new words a day. That might go well for one or two days, but after three or four weeks you would have close to 3,000 words to remember. I was reaching my mental capacity. I had to adopt another strategy or otherwise I would be forgetting the older words while trying to memorize the new ones. By coincidence I learned about memory championships through a fellow student. I had never heard about them, but was very curious how they worked.

---

7   Sensation or perception received at a distance without the normal operation of the recognized sense organs.

He explained to me that memorizing decks of cards, random faces or various objects was not very difficult as long as you knew the right techniques. I was very interested, as that could help me speed up my own vocabulary studying. I do not want to bore you with the details, but how it worked was that I would be using so called *memory palaces* in combination with the words I was studying. These memory palaces were familiar places created in my mind, like my school, my room, my house, etc. Every new word I studied, I connected to that place. That helped me remember words not only faster, but also for longer. The reason for this phenomenon is that our brains have an easier job remembering things tied to a location, rather than just randomly remembering them. So I started running through the school from room to room creating more and more mental memory palaces to store the 5,000 words in those places. Believe it or not, but I will always remember "telesthesia", the word from before, being "located" in math class, because I connect it to the television the room with a cup of tea on top of it which gave me a warm tingling sensation, which is exactly what the word means. Yes, I know, that makes no sense but you will see: this memory palace will also help you to remember this word for a lifetime. Television – tea – tingling feeling = telesthesia. Of course I had thousands more of these connections for the other words. If you want more information on using such memory palaces just go on Google and you get many tips on how to use them.

After seven weeks of full on studying it was time for the exams. I was quite nervous, but I had given it my best and I hoped for good results. I knew this would be very important for my future. The exam lasted the entire morning with alternating parts of math and English. After I finished in the early afternoon I was exhausted from the exam but I felt relieved from the intense pressure. The last few days before the event had been insane. I had been walking through hundreds of memory palaces to remember all the words. This resulted in massive headaches during the night, probably because my brain was not used to processing so much new information. I also had written over 5,000 flashcards, which I stored at those memory palaces, most of which I still remember today. After the exam the pressure dropped. No more running around with 25 packs of cards. No more wandering through various rooms in the school to walk off my memory palaces. If there was a fine line between genius and insanity, I was sure I had been right on it. My teachers and friends thought I was crazy when they saw the effort I put in. Now I needed to wait for one week to get the test results. It was nerve wracking and I could barely sleep at night. If I got a good result on this test, it would be easy to apply to medical institutions - but, if I had screwed up, then it would be almost impossible. It's unbelievable how much is on the line for any U.S. High School student going through that process. The morning my results came in, I was almost sick. I had not eaten properly for the entire week, even though I had tried to distract myself by playing basketball. I opened the login to the website for my test score: I had a 780 out of 800 in Math, which was a near perfect score. Awesome. I kept scrolling down for English. I got a 730 out of 800! I only missed a few points in reading and my vocabulary work was near perfect. This was absolutely exciting and I realized it had been totally worth my efforts. Considering I was non-native, my results were some of the best in the country and even comparing them to native English speakers, I was in the top 1%. Straight away I started filing my applications but then something else happened that I had not expected: My results had been mailed to other colleges automatically and so I was amazed that over 20 of the top institutions wrote to me proactively to offer me a scholarship, especially for my math results. I was totally blown away – the hard work had really paid off. Instead of having to pick from just one school, I could choose from over two-dozen different ones all over the country. I applied to seven of them, mainly because of their good medical programs but also because of their locations. But my main target was to stay close to Nashville so I could stay close to my host family.

What a great two years in the U.S. it was. We had played extremely good basketball and I had improved my skills a lot. I met amazing people that I would stay in touch until today. I studied a dictionary in seven weeks and passed the SAT exam with one of the best scores in the country. The things I learned and the experiences I had were so much more than I could ever have imagined. My dream to go to the U.S. had become a reality and I had made the best out of it. A few weeks later in June of 2003 I graduated from High School with honors. My dad, grandmother and auntie came to visit and we spent a full week in New York as a present for my efforts. It was awesome. I enjoyed the time with them so much, and I think it was quite tough for my dad to see me become so mature in just a year. The plan was to go back to Austria over the summer and then return in September to start my medical studies at one of the colleges. What I did not know yet was that this summer would mess up all of these ideas.

So what did I take away from my experience preparing for the SAT? I learned something really important: a strategy for how to study. If I had known that a lot earlier in my life, then I would have been way more efficient in my Elementary School or Junior High School in Austria. I never realized that students could have a study strategy, simply because school does not teach you HOW to study, only WHAT. I learned many things very early in life, but it took me 17 years until I realized how important it was to find my right studying strategy. I'm glad I learned this before I started to study medicine; otherwise it would not have been possible for me to organize my learning for all of my courses, as you will see later. My story is not intended to give you the one definite strategy; there are so many others out there. I just want to raise your awareness about the importance of a strategy if you want to be more time efficient and improve your long-term memory. Your "take-away" here should be to find YOUR best way to study or learn. Are you simply a reader or do you like to work through the content actively? What time during the day do you study well, is it morning, evening or night? Do you need to have it quiet or do you like music while studying? Do you prefer reading a book, listening to an audiobook or watching a video or seminar? These are all questions you should consider. My personal preference today is to work or study around other people. It has to be rather quiet and I love listening to classical music. I also noticed it is important whether you love to sit or stand while doing mentally challenging work. Some people prefer to sit, while others love to walk around or stand up when concentrating or needing to memorize something. For example I am listening to Mozart right now while writing this book and I am in a coffee shop in Hong Kong, standing at a table.

That brings me to my second lesson: Study for the long run whenever possible. What I mean is that while sometimes you just need to pass a test and you can forget the content straight afterwards, in most cases it makes a lot more sense to actually learn for life. Many studying techniques for the SAT were about passing the SAT with good grades, which of course made sense. I wanted to have both though: Good results AND a vast knowledge of the English language. For that you have to find ways to remember what you study. If you have to study a book of a hundred pages, first figure out the best way for you to study it. If you have a week's time then you should understand the strategy that works best for you. The memory palaces I was using were designed for me; you probably need different ones. The connections I was making between the words and the places in the palaces were great for me, but maybe no one else. Do you still remember the word in the math Session? Maybe you do, maybe you don't. But the television connection with the tea was a perfect reminder for me. Later, when studying medicine I would write down all the diseases on flashcards. It took me quite some time for each disease. But in return, I would know everything after that and most important, I remembered it for weeks and months. There is a saying: "If you want to cut a tree in five hours, sharpen you saw for four!" It basically means, preparing and planning is extremely important if you want to be efficient. Did it take me a long time to write all the cards? Heck yes! Most people could have studied many other things in the meantime. However, once my strategy was in place, I was faster than the others because I did not have to rehearse as much, using my more efficient technique. I studied for the long run, to learn for life.

My third take-away is also an important tip: I would encourage everyone to learn at least one, or better yet, two foreign languages. All the words I learned during that time not only helped me get great SAT scores, but also helped me so much throughout my career. Languages are one of the most important tools you need in daily life. My favorite top three languages would be English, Spanish, and Mandarin. Up to the point I was studying for the SAT, I had only learned German (my mother-tongue) and English. I had also taken a few French lessons, but did not take it very seriously. After that, even while studying medicine, I also learned Spanish – a move for which I am thankful up to this day. So if you have the chance, learn a new language or two. You will be able to touch a person's heart by speaking in their own language, which will help you tremendously in business and personal life. Your future self will thank you for it.

Before telling you why and how my plans had to be changed, I want you to take five minutes to consider: what is your take-away from this? Which study strategy will you apply? Which part of the story inspired you the most? And even more importantly, what immediate action will you take, based on what you just read and learned? Sharpen your saw right now, so you can cut the next tree ten times faster!

SPACE FOR MY TAKE AWAYS

9.

THE KITESURFING STORY - NAYSAYERS SAY, "NAY"

"I can accept failure, everyone fails at something. But I can't accept not trying. " – Michael Jordan

After arriving back in Austria from the U.S., the plan was to stay the summer and then continue my studies back in the U.S. My family and friends gave me a great welcome-back party. I had not seen them in over a year and it was incredible to see how much everyone had grown and changed. My parents took me to Italy for a holiday so that I could rest and relax a bit from all the excitement. It would get extremely busy afterwards and so I wanted to use the few weeks I had to chill. While staying in Italy I learned about a sport that got me hooked instantly: kitesurfing. Until then, I had only known about windsurfing, where you put a sail onto a large board and then use the power of the wind to glide along. Kitesurfing is a combination of flying a kite in the air and using a wakeboard-like surfboard to fly over the water. The addicting thing about kitesurfing is that it allows you to do amazing jumps without waves, simply on flat water. By sending the kite backwards it will rip you off the water and let you fly for a couple of seconds through the air. It was a fascinating sport and even though I had never tried it, I was sure I would love it from day one.

Back in 2003, the sport was still extremely young. Even though it was invented quite some time before, it never caught any traction until the new millennium. Around 2000, early adopters in the watersport community such as Robby Naish switched from windsurfing to kitesurfing and saw the new sport as a great mainstream opportunity. One of the major issues kitesurfing had back then was that it was quite dangerous. In order to become suitable for the masses, better safety features had to be developed. That did not bother me as I was totally thrilled by its possibilities and decided to try it out at Lake Garda, a popular lake in the north of Italy. From the very first moment, I totally connected with the sport. I could combine everything I had learned from my gymnastics, the bit I knew from skiing and snowboarding, and my upper body strength from the gym in basketball. I knew this was the part-time sport I wanted to pursue besides college and basketball. What I did not know that early summer weekend was that this sport would stop me from going back to the U.S. and would become my main activity just eight weeks later.

I convinced my dad to keep going back to Lake Garda every weekend of the summer. He had always liked windsurfing himself, so it was an easy "sale". Since I was now old enough to drive, I was able to get to a local lake near our home in Austria all by myself throughout the week. I spent every hour possible kiting on the water. When there was no wind, I learned more about the sport by reading magazines or watching the first DVDs that had just started to be published. As soon as the wind started to be strong enough, I would be out on the water until after sunset. I would try any trick I had just seen in a magazine or even figure out new ones. I connected with the local kitesurf community and one of the kitesurfers there became my best friend (and remains so to this day). His name is Daniel – yep, the same Daniel I had already met in gymnastics ten years earlier. An incredible coincidence? I don't think so - it was definitely fate. He had also just started to learn to kitesurf back then and the two of us clicked immediately. We would go on to do many trips together as you will see in later chapters.

One day in Italy while I was learning an extremely hard new trick called the Handle Pass, a brand ambassador from a local kitesurf brand was there and saw me riding. He came up to me after the seven hours I had been out on the water and asked me how long I had been kitesurfing. I told him, I was just here for the summer and that I had just learned how to kitesurf a few weeks ago. Being totally fascinated by my fast progress he offered me to use his brand's material for free until I was leaving to go back to the U.S. All I would have to do in return was to promote the kites and boards and talk about how great they were. I was totally stoked. Up to that point I could only afford one board and kite. I could barely believe that I could use all the kites and boards for free now from one of the best brands in the market. I gladly accepted and was now well equipped to train even harder. There was only one month left before I would leave again and I wanted to make the most out of it.

The Austrian Championships were held at the end of the summer, the week before my scheduled flight to go back to the U.S. I wanted to participate to see how good I had actually become. My entire life I had always been extremely competitive and I embraced the opportunity to measure myself against other Austrian kitesurfers. I knew I had not been kiting for too long, but I was determined to go and show off my best. Many of my local kitesurfing friends tried to discourage me from going: "Julian, you are not good enough yet. You have no experience in competing and you will discredit yourself." Most of the things they said were absolutely correct but it did not bother me at all. I was not competing against anyone else - I was competing against myself. Every time I went kitesurfing I forgot the world around me. The water splashing by, jumping into the air, cruising and having fun… all things that I enjoyed. But nothing gave me a bigger kick than stomping a new trick or throwing a new roll that no one at the lake had been doing before. I was determined to go to the competition, and even though I was just a beginner in the sport, I would give it my best.

To cut a long story short, my friends who had discouraged me were right: I was not ready for the competition. But they were wrong about me not going. Looking back, this was the most important kitesurfing competition of my life. Over that weekend I met some other kitesurfers who were paid to travel the world and kitesurf at the best places in the world. I wanted the same thing. I wanted to get paid to go where "normal" people spent their holidays. I had totally messed up the competition as I did not know the rules and I had used wrong kite sizes. My friends at home had told me that this would happen, but they totally misjudged the power of me getting hooked to the sport and the opportunity to become a professional kitesurfer. My friends had tried to keep me from going because they thought they would protect me from having my feelings hurt. Whatever you do, you will have people who try to hold you back into their group "norm". They try to protect you and so they try to talk you out of it by giving you all kinds of excuses and reasons why you should not do it. Do not let them; otherwise you will never succeed at anything. Had I listened to the naysayers before going to the U.S., I would have heard all the downsides of spending so much money or all the risks that were involved. Had I listened to the naysayers before going to the national kitesurfing championships, I would have stayed at home and missed out on ten years of paid, non-stop holidays and some of the best times of my life. You never know the huge effects that seemingly small decisions might have on your life. Never forget that in anything you decide to do. I will talk more about haters and naysayers in later chapters but at this stage I already realized how hard it was to push out of the norm to achieve something outstanding – you have to stand out from the crowd to do so.

The event got me hooked, and I could see the possibilities of the sport by watching what other people were already doing. I realized that kitesurfing was extremely small back then, but would have the potential of becoming huge. I wanted to be part of it and weighed my options of where to study medicine: If I went to college in the U.S., I would never be able to travel the world, as I would need to stay at school. In Austria I would have more freedom and I could travel as much as I wanted as long as my grades were good enough. The decision to cancel everything in the U.S. and totally reverse my plans was one of the hardest decisions I have made in my life so far. Once again, many people discouraged me and tried to point out all the downsides of my new plan. The sad thing is that these naysayers are mostly close friends or family members. They try to protect you and they mean well, but eventually you need to push through in order to succeed. I just thought: "Who in their right mind would not want to travel the world kitesurfing and having the time of their life?" So, I called my brand ambassador and told him about my plans to cancel my trip to the US and stay in Austria to pursue medicine and kitesurfing at the same time. We agreed on a promotional budget that I could use for travelling and competing, while in return I would make videos, a blog, and promote the brand. I was basically paid to have the life others were dreaming about. I could travel to places like Venezuela, Brazil, Mauritius, Spain, Australia, and New Zealand. All my expenses were paid and all I had to do in return was to kitesurf at these places and have fun.

Some of you might be reading this thinking: "What a crazy goof-ball – just in the story before he was talking about how hard he had worked for the SAT and now he studied medicine in Austria where the SAT was not even needed!" You might not connect the dots looking forward, but looking backwards I realized how much studying was about to come up in medicine. None of this would have been possible had I not studied for the SAT. I am no longer talking about 5,000 vocabulary words: I am talking about thousands of pages of diseases, body parts, drugs, and treatments. As I was travelling most of the time, I would have maybe 20% of the time to study compared to my fellow students. All the great strategies I had developed during the SAT studies were now paying off. I could just implement them again. My SAT study strategy had prepared me to being able to combine kitesurfing and studying medicine. And remember: Learning for life should be the primary goal.

Thanks to the warm temperatures that year I was able to kitesurf long into autumn and it allowed me to progress a lot with my trick level. Over the winter however, when all the lakes were frozen, obviously I could not kitesurf. In order to stay as close to the sport as possible I simply switched to snowkiting, which as the name suggests is kiting with skis or a snowboard on the snow. Despite sounding similar to kitesurfing at first, I soon realized that it was very different to kiting on water. Riding on frozen water was way more dangerous especially when crashing. While I could just let go of the control bar on the water, on snow this meant that I could get injured severely, and so I learned to control the kite in a perfect manner after just a few days in the new terrain. While most other kitesurfers trained exclusively on water, riding on snow not only broadened my array of tricks, but also actually paved the foundation for my kitesurfing success by improving my level of riding security. Back then snowkiting was even less well known than kitesurfing on water but today snowkiting is just as popular. That winter one of the first ever snowkiting championships was held and I decided to compete. I have to admit there were not many other good riders and so even though I had only been kiting for a few months I came in 3rd worldwide. It was a nice affirmation that I was on the right track after weeks and months of training, even though people kept discouraging me, saying that my path was the wrong one.

After my winter of training, I applied to compete in the kitesurf world cup, which would start in spring. Up to that point, I had only seen the world cup competitors in online movie clips and I was really excited to actually have the opportunity to compete against them. In my favor, the first event of the entire tour was in Austria at the same place where the Austrian championships had been held the year before.

Just like the year before, I had people around me telling me I should not go. They said I had just been lucky at the snowkite competition and that I would probably not even make the trials to enter the main event. The trials were used to rank kitesurfers and determine who was good enough to compete in the main event. Losing in the trials would have been quite disappointing for me, and the naysayers not only knew that, but kept pointing out that fact. But this time, I was well prepared. I could have gone through the trials, but I contacted the organizer in advance and sent them my kitesurfing resume and the results from the snowkiting competition. They had two wildcards, which they could award to any rider of their choice, which then guaranteed that rider a place in the main event. I knew one of the wildcards would go to the Austrian champion from the previous year, who was my good friend Michael. I wanted to get the second one. Eventually the decision went in my favor and so I had a guaranteed seat at my first kitesurf world championship. Naturally many of my friends claimed I was just lucky, but I knew that I could have made the main event even without the wildcards and also I had learned from my past event: Learn the rules and arrive prepared – to save energy for when it counts.

In the main event the world's top 32 riders were randomly seeded against each other and two riders would compete at the same time. In order to win one had to perform more difficult tricks at a faster speed and greater height than the opponent. A panel of judges decided who would advance into the next round and eventually reach the final, or get knocked out. My first heat was against someone from Holland. I did really well, landing some of my best tricks ever. Four out five judges ruled in my favor and I advanced. 16 riders were left. Next I was up against someone from the UK, who was normally better than me. Both Holland and the UK are famous for having great kitesurfers, thanks to the favorable conditions in these countries. On the water I soon realized that my opponent was struggling with the cold water and air, and the wind was quite gusty and unpredictable. While he could not perform at his best level, I on the other hand was completely used to the conditions from my training in the winter and could show my usual array of tricks. The results were close but I advanced in a three to two ruling. Wow! There were now only eight of us left. I was completely stoked, as I had dreamed of it but never expected the dream to become reality. The other seven riders left were all not only clearly better than me, but also a lot more experienced and so I lost the two next heats, which eventually put me in 9th place. This meant, I would get very good prize money and was now ranked in the top ten in the world after just my first event. I was totally excited and called all of my kitesurfing friends to share my great news. As in the tree story, some were excited for me, others told me I just got lucky. I used the prize money to pay for the next world cup event in Italy a few weeks later. I proved the naysayers wrong and came in Top Ten again. Maybe I just 'got lucky' twice in a row? After the event I was featured in several kitesurf magazines in the UK, Germany, and the U.S. Only one year before I was reading and learning from these magazines and now these same magazines were doing features about me! Had I listened to the Naysayers, I would have never been the one that they were now reading about in the magazines. It was one of the first times in my life that I realized I really had achieved something and I was really proud of myself.

The rest of the season I competed on the entire tour and, despite a few pitfalls, I had great results. At the end of the year I signed a deal with a French kiteboarding company, with whom I would be working with for a long time afterwards. It was the start of the life that many people just dream of, but never dare to try. I am convinced that so many other people would have the chance to do the same, but they let other people pull them down. I can't even count how many times through all the years that something I wanted to do was not possible: "You cannot become a professional kitesurfer because you do not live close to the sea. You cannot get a professional kitesurfing contract because no one knows you. You cannot compete at the world cup because you are not good enough. You cannot study medicine and kitesurf at the same time because it would be too hard to combine the two." Whenever someone is telling you that something cannot be done, the person is telling you that he or she cannot do it, and reflects this on to you. Do not listen to the noise around you – PROVE THE NAYSAYERS WRONG AND GO ALL OUT FOR YOUR DREAMS!

Many people did not understand why I gave up all that I had worked for in the U.S., but I followed my passion and that made me extremely happy. Everything I achieved in the U.S. was the foundation for what was possible afterwards. If you ever want to follow a passion yourself – DO IT! Listen to your heart and do not let others scare you off. Let me tell you one important thing however: as soon as you make a decision, be prepared for the universe to test you! When I said I wanted to become a professional kiteboarder and I went to my first competition, I failed miserably. While I was looking for my first company outside of the kitesurf industry to sponsor me, it took me dozens of emails and calls until I found a clothing, sunglass and even car company to finally support me in my vision. There were many times I had booked a flight to a competition without having the money for the return trip. I had to get a good result to make enough prize money to pay for my ticket home. So once you make a decision, it is a "given" that the universe will test you. If you ever watched the movie "The Truman Show" with Jim Carrey, you will see how Christof, the creator of Truman's world, tested Truman over and over again after Truman had decided that he wanted to find out the truth. The reason I am bringing this up is that real life works the same way and I remind myself many times about these scenes when facing challenges in my own life. If you are not strong enough, you will give in and let the naysayers win.

Besides the two lessons of ignoring the naysayers when following your passion and being prepared for the universe to test you, the third thing I learned was to distinguish between skill and talent, as I have never done before. For many people those two things are basically the same thing, but that is far from reality. I have just scratched the surface of this concept in earlier chapters but to be really clear you must understand that talent is innate and comes naturally to people, whereas skill is learned through practicing countless hours over and over again. Many people confuse practicing with simply doing something, rather than actual training. In kiteboarding this concept struck me harder than ever. I realized extremely early on in my kiteboarding career that my skill level would dramatically increase with every hour I spent on the water. But this is where I realized an important factor: average kitesurfers go out and regard their sport as a hobby. People who look at something as a hobby do it basically for fun, and avoid things that are difficult or painful, because it would no longer be fun. The reason a good tennis player is so good is because he serves 500 tennis balls a day without playing one actual game. The reason a professional golfer is a pro and not an amateur is not because he runs across the 18 holes that much, but because he practices those boring shots out of every possible situation for ten hours a day. Professional basketball players rarely play five on five during practice, as they would in an actual game. Instead, they run through the same shooting motions, moving drills and game calls over and over again. My point is that skill is not learned by just spending time doing something you like, but rather by training hard for hours and hours with an intensity that the amateur simply chooses not to do.

In kiteboarding this meant not just going out and kiting but to have a clear plan on what I was training on for the 90 minutes out on the water. At the beginning it was basic tricks, such as back or front rolls. As I mastered each trick, I moved on to new and more difficult tricks. Someone watching me on the water would think I looked like a total idiot, sometimes even a beginner. Why? Because I was crashing 99% of my jumps. You would hardly ever see me land a trick, because as soon as I was comfortable landing a trick, I knew I had to push harder for the next one, and BAM, I was crashing all over again. Amateurs love to show off their basic tricks over and over again, knowing they will land them. They are uncomfortable trying something new and most probably crashing. Crashing hurts and it is not enjoyable. Actual training is not as much fun as free riding. Playing one on one in basketball or tennis is so much more fun than actually practicing basic drills. Doing an 18 hole round of golf with your buddies is a lot more fun than being alone on the green working on your putting. But professionals are willing to put in the effort because they know the hard work will pay off, and instead of having a hobby, they have a profession. My hard work and constant training was the reason I could go pro and actually make a living out of my passion. If you want to see my crashes yourself, go on to YouTube and search for "Julian Hosp kitesurfing". You will find countless training videos of myself, where I not only show tricks I land but also all the crashes. One famous quote by Rocky Balboa, the fictional boxer in Sylvester Stallone's "Rocky" series is, "It is not how hard YOU can hit, it is about how hard you can GET HIT and still move forward." I reminded myself of this every time I crashed super hard and wanted to quit the session. In my kitesurfing videos I always wanted to pass this knowledge on to other kitesurfers. The experts do not train what comes easy, but what comes hard. Pushing yourself forward, not only in sports, moreover in whatever you are about to do right now, is the key to your success. Along the way to the top you will crash and you will get hurt, but only those that keep pushing and keep getting up will actually reach their goal.

I was a professional kitesurfer for almost ten years, travelling the world from age 17 to 27. I was paid for doing things that other people dreamed of, and I met not only amazing friends but the experiences enriched my life in an incredible and indefinable way. Many of the upcoming stories that you will now read about happened during my kitesurfing career and shaped almost one third of my life up to this point today. Personally, this story is one of the most important stories in my life, because it was so incredibly hard to commit to certain decisions that often made no rational sense at the time when I took them. Looking back, they were the best decisions of my life, but when taking them I was not always 100% sure. I learned that there are no right or wrong decisions; only those that you take or do not take. It all depends on what you make of it! I am sure, I would have made something good out of sticking to my decision to go and study medicine in the US, but I felt I would be better off with the decision I actually made. Many other people did not see it that way back then, but of course they see it today. It was a radical decision, but probably the best one of my life.

As always as the end of a chapter, I challenge you to think about what you are taking away from this story and to take immediate action upon that. Which passion of yours would you love to follow? Is the universe challenging you and are you about to give in, even though you know you should not? Do you have naysayers around you that try to pull you down? Remember, crashing is a given. Winners never quit. Quitters never win!

SPACE FOR MY TAKE AWAYS

10.

THE MEDICINE STORY - A DOER BEATS A THINKER

"A journey of a thousand miles begins with a single step." – Confucius

I told you in chapter nine that despite all the crazy kitesurfing action I was still determined to pursue my medical studies. In this chapter I want to share about this journey and tell you the lessons I took away. At the Medical University of Innsbruck around 1,000 people apply every year to study medicine, including students from Germany, Italy, and - of course - Austria. Due to the limited size of laboratories and other facilities, only about 250 people are accepted. The selection process lasts for the entire year. Six weeks into the first year there is a small exam, which weeds out around one third of the applicants. At the end of the first year there is a large exam that ranks the top 250 students who can then proceed. If you don't make the cut, you either have to wait a year and try again, or study something else. The limited seating causes a fierce struggle for seats within the auditoria among students every morning when classes start. Once those are filled, the rest of the students need to stay outside. Class starts at 8am, but in order to get a seat inside, one has to be there way in advance and wait for doors to open. This process moves earlier and earlier, and at around five weeks into the year, one has to get there at 5am in order to get a seat. Many of the students cannot handle the long hours and peer pressure, so they drop out even before the first exam is over. Looking back, I have to admit that it was kind of nuts, but I loved the competition. I was not really fond of spending any time at university, as I preferred to go kitesurfing and travel to great kite spots, but since I had absolutely zero idea about medicine, I figured the best decision was to completely immerse myself into the matter at the beginning. After the first exam was over I could ease off and go back to studying on the road while kitesurfing.

In order to get a seat I had to arrive at 5am as well. It was not until three hours later at 8:00am that morning class actually began and lasted until 12:00. We had two hours lunch break and then the afternoon sessions were held from 2:00pm until 6:00pm. After I got back home, I did some studying, then fell into bed and got up at four am to do the same thing. Many students complained about these circumstances and they even made it into the newspaper, describing the craziness. Initially I thought it was entirely mental as well but after a few days I realized one great benefit from this schedule. Since I got up that early, I had so much more time to get things done. Yes, initially I was extremely tired but over time my body and mind adapted to being sleep-deprived. To make the most of my morning, I arrived at 5:00 am, studied for one hour and then went to the gym next door for one hour. I noticed that people either rushed into the room at 5:00am when the doors opened or tried to sneak a place before class started at 8:00am. From 6:00 to 7:00am however there was almost no "traffic". So as long as I was back at 7:00am I had no problems getting the seat back that I had taken at 5:00am already. Most of the other students where simply sleeping on the tables waiting for class to begin, and so it was no issue getting my seat again and studying for another hour. I committed to spending around 14 hours every day at the university for just over a month. In order to pass my first year in medicine however, I needed to have a basic Latin test. Since I never studied Latin in school I had to take some classes, even though Latin is hardly used nowadays. Initially it felt like a burden, but just like getting up so early, I found a way to make it valuable: All the different diseases, classifications, and titles could be memorized easier with my techniques once I understood their deeper meanings and relations. Latin helped a great deal there.

The upcoming exam was not very difficult. The content was mainly a few basic medical terminologies, some science, and basic anatomy. If you went through the content once or twice it would not be too hard to pass. However, for some students, just reading the 500 pages within six weeks was too much. I decided that I would not write flashcards or use memory palaces. There were many topics, but they were quite superficial. After reading through the 500 pages twice, I passed the first exam easily and came in near the top of the class. Initially I thought that was great, but then I realized that would put my name on the map and people would be looking out for me during the rest of the year. I didn't want that, because I had planned on not going to classes for the entire second part so that I could kitesurf while studying. When the professors were passing out the honor cards to the top ten students, I asked a friend of mine to pick it up, so no one would have a clue who I was. It worked, and together with around 700 of the other 1,000 students I moved onwards to work towards the year one final exams without anyone paying attention to whether I was there or not. It soon became clear that the final exam was of a higher caliber and I planned on getting back to my study card strategy, using memory palaces. Additionally, I planned on audio recording myself when reading the content out loud. That way I could listen and rehearse while being on the road. I started cutting down university time step by step and at around Christmas time I was only there the basic minimum of just a few hours a week. I preferred studying on my own so that I could go kitesurfing. My mom knew my plans for the year and she was worried that I would become distracted with all the kite-surf related partying and travelling, and would not continue my medical degree. Perhaps she had forgotten that I was no longer a young boy begging to quit gym class. She had taught me well: I would never give up on anything once I had made a promise to myself to finish it.

El Coche in Venezuela, Cumbuco in Brazil, Mauritius or Australia… I travelled to the most glorious places on our planet to kitesurf… and to study! While other people were out partying and drinking I was so determined to get my medical degree that you would always see me with study cards and medical books. I knew I had to get at least 20 hours of studying in every week to make it, and I managed to reach this goal pretty much the entire year. On top of that, I had some of the most magnificent memory palaces. For example while studying "bones" I was on the Maldives. So I connected the names and parts of all the bones to little islands and places on this beautiful atoll. I felt that if I wanted to score in the top of the class that year, I had to walk the extra mile without needing to physically be there. I looked through my options and applied for two weeks of work at the hospital to sign up for some practical work. When talking to the secretary, she thought I was out of my mind. She asked me whether I was sure that I wanted to work for no pay, knowing I was only allowed to do basic tasks, as I had not much education yet. Normally students would do such non-paid internships after two to three years into their studies but not after their first semester. I felt that learning by doing would help me ten times more than just studying the theory, and that I could apply that real time learning when I was studying theory. After convincing the secretary that this is what I really wanted, she finally granted me a position at the surgery station.

I was not allowed to see any patients without an actual medical doctor present and I was supervised during every step I took. In order to avoid staff looking down at me, I told them I was in my third year of medical school (even though I was not). I had absolutely no clue about most of the things that were going on. I had read a crash course book about the station where I was working, but that did not help much either. The leading doctor of the station regularly picked on students. The two other students there were already in their fifth year. The surgeon bombarded me every day with questions I could not answer. The few instances I managed to answer one, he asked me more. He took me to see patients and embarrassed me in front of them by asking me to do things that I was not capable of doing. Of course, he was under the impression that I was a third year student, so was probably shocked that I could not do some of the things he asked of me! I must have appeared incompetent to him, and he treated me accordingly, making the two weeks I spent with him absolutely horrible. I do have to thank him for one thing however: the days of torture and being asked questions that I could not answer, prepared me for many medical endeavors afterwards and I am thankful for that. Saying that makes me sound like a masochist, but instead of actually teaching and training me he embarrassed me over and over again. I actually would have loved to stab him with my scalpel a couple of times. Coming back to the theoretical studies after those two weeks, I noticed a leapfrog change in my knowledge because it not only motivated me to get better throughout the practice, but also, it made sure I would not repeat those mistakes ever again in the future. I met him again at the end of my medical studies around five years later. He remembered me, and after I told him that what had actually happened he said: "I was sure you would give up after your experience with me, but now it actually makes sense. I am sure you will become a fabulous doctor!"

I had learned so many more things and I was so much more experienced just because of those two weeks. I was amazed what a huge impact doing actual work was, versus just studying the theory. I wondered why so few other students did not do this early like me. It dawned on me it was because most people need to have everything figured out first before they actually do it. Or, they are scared to do it until they have completely learned it. They do not want to be embarrassed or appear as if they do not know something. Many others could have taken the same short cut as I did, but they preferred to look and sound "book" knowledgeable rather than have actual experience. I had no other option and had to take drastic measures in order to combine medicine and kitesurfing. After those two weeks of practical work I flew to Cape Verde and Venezuela with my best friend Daniel to train for the upcoming world cup. Every day I studied relentlessly before and after the kitesurfing sessions. I had my study cards out, wrote new ones and rehearsed the older ones in my memory palaces. I probably would not have been able to study so effectively had I not completed the practical experience before. Had I done it vice versa and studied first with the practical work afterwards I probably would not have made it as fast. My work paid off and I finished at the top of the class, even though I was hardly ever physically present.

Since I had always been involved in sports, becoming a surgeon excited me the most, After the first year, we had an anatomy course with corpses and I decided not only to do the course myself but also to become a tutor straight afterwards to get even more hands-on experience. Most other tutors were normally in their 4th or 5th year, but I thought once again that it was better to achieve 100% competency through 30% knowledge and 70% experience. Most people think it should be 90% knowledge and very little experience, but I have never been "most people". Mark this as an important note: Your true value does not come simply from what you know, but how you apply what you know and from the experience you already have. Since I wanted to travel over half of the year, plus kitesurf on our local lake while in Austria, this endeavor of doing the anatomy courses proved to be quite challenging. The only solution was to spend days back to back in the anatomy center to get everything done in a single week's time, that other students would normally need a month to complete. I made friends with one of the janitors and he let me into the lab, whenever, and for how long I wanted, as he thought it was awesome that I was combining medicine and kitesurfing. Trust me, one of the scariest things in life is to be in an anatomy lab with 200 dead bodies at 3:00am all by yourself. Any horror movie you have ever watched will come back to full memory. Sometimes I managed to convince some friends to join me, but that was the exception rather than the norm, as they were just as horrified as I was. Sometimes my professor scared the living crap out of me by popping in to check on me in the middle of the night to see if I was actually doing my work. I had never been fond of "haunted houses" in theme parks, and here I was right in the middle of one.

The professor's grading was mainly based on two factors: first, how well you would be able to prepare the corpse and secondly, how accurate was your anatomy knowledge. Preparing a corpse meant that I had to cut away the fatty tissue with a scalpel so that the nerves, arteries and veins were visible. My knowledge in anatomy was great, thanks to my practical work in the hospital. I managed to combine the eight required exams into three exam sessions, doing three exams after a couple of weeks, then another two a bit later and then three just before Christmas. If everything went well, I could be part of the summer course as a tutor, which would allow me to get even more practical knowledge and make me a better surgeon later on. Throughout the semester I drove my professor crazy, as pretty much the only way we communicated was via email. I was out kitesurfing during the day and only in the lab in late afternoon or night. I studied and worked extremely hard, earning straight A's in both the oral as well as the practical exams. After I had completed the course, I applied to become a tutor. My professor thought I was kidding and asked me in disbelief: "How in the world can you be a tutor if you are gone all the time?" But I was prepared for that question and my idea was, that there were other students who would love to work late evenings or early mornings as well – so, as long as I could get just six or seven students, my tutoring group would be filled. He told me that I had one week to find such a group and to my professor's surprise I found my students quite easily. Many of them had day jobs or children, and were happy that I would work with them during the night. In addition to the knowledge benefit I would get being a tutor, it had some other advantages that would help me in both the short and long term. First of all, I received a small monthly salary, which I needed to pay for my kitesurfing travels. Second, I had to become expert about any medical topic we would be discussing within the group. Since I wanted to be a "picture-perfect-tutor" I stepped up my game to make sure that I could provide value to my group. I don't know if you have ever been in a teaching role, but this was the first time for me and it pushed my knowledge to a whole new level. That experience helped me so much when running kite camps or leading a business team in the future and made me understand that you will not fully comprehend something until you can teach it to someone else. Third and most important, was all the additional practical experience I gained about anatomy, special training courses and access to all the medical facilities. Other students preferred to study theory while I went kitesurfing during that time and took a rather more practical approach.

The rest of my studies were quite similar. I tried to spend as little time as possible on theory, got involved in practice and travelled the world kitesurfing. I finished my medical studies with honors at the age of 25. Initially I did not even want to participate in the graduation ceremony as I believed it was a waste of money and time, but then I understood that it would be the finish of something important, not only for myself, but for my family, grandparents and close friends, who had witnessed and supported all my efforts. Many amazing things happened to me during those six years of med school, and just like with my life as a kitesurfer, my medical years played a huge part during my life as well (At the time of writing this book, it is only four years since my graduation). Many of the future stories in this book happened during my time while studying but I wanted to keep this chapter for what I took away the most. My six years in medicine could not have been more different than any other medical student. It is not that I am special; it was just that I decided to always take action first rather than sit in a classroom to learn theoretical knowledge that would not help me much in my career as a medical doctor. I am sure that I studied just as hard as most of the other medical students, I just budgeted my time differently. On top of that, I used my proven study techniques to help me memorize anything quite fast and long lasting. I think I wrote over 10,000 different study cards during those six years – I am not sure if my mom still has some of them, but she always said: "No one is going to believe how crazy you are, so better let me keep the cards so I have proof!"

In the next stories I will share many more lessons from my time at university, but in this story I wanted to share the three most important overall lessons that I learned. The first one is my call for action. I remind you at the end of each chapter anyway, but I cannot stress enough how important it is to take action and gain experience rather than just learn the theory. Many of my fellow students were hesitant to do hands-on work early in their studies as they always wanted to learn everything first and then apply the knowledge step by step afterwards. I took a very contrarian approach: I always said, "Yes" first, took massive action and learned through actually doing. I made many mistakes and was humiliated by others over and over again. In a hospital, medical students are only allowed to do very minor tasks under supervision, such as helping with drawing blood, assisting the surgeon or joining the daily patient visits. We could not mess anything up. So what could have been the worst-case scenario? Literally nothing. The up side of it was however that this allowed me to achieve faster and better results than all the others. In any future endeavor I took the same approach: Take action straight away, stop pondering about what if, or what if not. Learn along the way – don't worry, it will all work out fine!

The second thing I took away was, once again, to think long term. When going to college, do not study a subject just to study and pass an exam. Learn for life! Take with you not only the information but also a deeper meaning. Connect with new people, learn a new language, a new skill or relocate to a new place. When I did my SAT cards or studied medicine, it was not only about the studying - it was also about a much deeper meaning. Today many people ask me why I studied medicine. Most students do so for a good cause, to help people or to make the world a better place. I studied medicine because I was and still am interested in it. I find it fascinating to understand the human body and mind, how it works, connects and why it does what it does. I am still in touch today with many of the people I met during those years and they have become some of my closest friends. Even though I never cared much about having a medical degree, I have come to realize how much other people do care about it. They read my business card, and just because I have a degree, they view me differently. Investors give me a few minutes of their time to pitch my idea, just because I appear different than most other people asking for their time. Airlines upgrade me into Business or even First Class, just because of a title in front of my name. One thing however that is actually extremely important to me is that it makes my mom and dad proud that their son has a medical degree, and that makes me happy. Therefore, if you are reading this, thinking about whether you should continue your studies or not, I can surely tell you one thing: Whatever you are studying may not really help you directly in your real life job, as the theoretical studies are often so distant and removed, no matter whether it is business, law, medicine or computer engineering. BUT, and this is a big but, you want to finish your degree. It will prove others that you are capable of getting things done. Also, it will connect you to people that are great to know in the future. So, do not study, just to study. Study to learn for life!

Last but not least, whenever you get the chance to work as a tutor or teach others, take the opportunity to do it. Being a tutor in medicine allowed me to learn more than I could have ever have learned by myself or through books. The questions I was asked challenged me to reach new levels of knowledge. Being a tutor looked great on my report card as well, because hospitals know how well educated are tutors with practical experience. Later, in kitesurfing and business, these concepts proved to be true over and over again, which you will see in the last chapters. This book would probably never have been written had I not been speaking publicly back then, which evolved into me presenting business plans. I had to put in so many extra hours to get to my best level possible for my students. I put in 100-hour weeks of studying, working and teaching on a regular basis. Many people complemented me on my work ethic later on and were surprised at how I could effectively perform with such intensity for such long hours. It was simply the same blueprint that I was going through in medicine already and I was primed to follow that workflow successfully.

Now, I want to challenge you to take action based on the new insights you just gained. Will you reconsider finishing your studies or taking up new ones? Will you stop thinking about figuring out all the details first but take action and get going? Could you tutor someone else in your field of expertise to help not only them but also you get even better? Remember, never stay solely in the theoretical – you need to take action to win.

SPACE FOR MY TAKE AWAYS

11.

THE PAUL STORY -
THE FIVE PEOPLE AROUND YOU

"In order to get more, you need to become more." – Jim Rohn

Many people are surprised about the extremely different ventures I have been pursuing in my life: professional basketball player, moving to America, studying medicine, kitesurfing professional and many others that you will hear about in later stories. One thing I realized is that every time my interests shifted and I became involved in something new, was that my circle of friends shifted as well. This might be easier to understand when I compare it to moving from High School to college: Most of your friends will either go to a different college, or simply not pursue college. Some will attend the same college as you but you may not hang around with them because you (and your old friends, too) are busy making new friends. In such situations it is natural that as we adopt new goals in life, our circle of friends shifts as well. In these cases the shift happens almost by default, due to the physical separation and distance between schools or institutions. It is just not as easy to spend the same amount of time with people if they suddenly are a lot further away and you no longer see them every day.

In my case most of the different stages in my life happened in different locations. This resulted in different friends associated with each new stage I entered. In situations where there are no geographic changes but where new skills changed the path I was taking in life, some of my old friends were left behind, or chose to stay behind, as we had less and less in common. Early on in my life it was my mom, who had a huge effect on my passion for sports and competiveness. When playing basketball it was my Junior High School friends that I hung around with. For kitesurfing, I could not have done it had it not been my dad, who loves the water just as much and enabled me to get all the training time I needed. Later on it was my best friend Daniel and my girlfriend Bettina who kept me motivated and challenged me to push the limits. In the U.S., during High School, it was my host dad George, who influenced me to start studying medicine and provided the right environment. So when people ask how is it possible for me to have such a broad spectrum of interests and such a diverse life, I would answer that it is because of the wide array of people I know in each field. The people around us affect us a lot more than we would imagine in pretty much all the areas of our lives. You don't believe me? Let's try an experiment: What is your monthly net income? Write it on a piece of paper. Next, jot down the five people you spend the most time with weekly. This should probably be your wife, husband, girlfriend or boyfriend - then maybe your parents and children. Co-workers? Best friends? Who else? Put the five names on a piece of paper. Next, write down their monthly net income. If you don't know it, guess it. Now add their incomes together, and then divide this number by five. How far is that average away from what you are making a month? Chances are, it is extremely close. Jim Rohn, a business leader and motivational speaker, said, "You are the average of the five people around you!" And if you think this only applies to one specific topic, you are mistaken. It is applicable to all areas of your life, including your health, your fitness, your job, your income, the way you spend your free time, and pretty much anything else.

The people around us, or our peer group, have such a deep impact on us that anyone of us will be pulled back to our peers' "average". A simple example to explain that in another context would be that of smoking. Imagine you are a smoker and you would like to quit smoking. During any break from work, or while having a coffee or when going out in the evenings, you are tempted to smoke. Now just picture yourself being around all those of your friends who also smoke, sharing cigarettes. It will be quite tough for you to give up the habit under these circumstances. Most often, after just a few attempts you will give in and return into the same old habit. And that brings me to the most important point of the upcoming story – a point that I will stress again and again: It is nearly impossible to increase the average of the five people around you, the only thing you can do is to change the five people! To use my examples from above, my mum could not help me in basketball, neither could have my host-dad in the U.S. helped me for kitesurfing. I needed different people around me every time and since I had been moving around I affected a natural change to these five people through geography. For most people who do not move around, this will be a lot harder and therefore even more important. It all comes down to one thing: If you want your average to change, either the five people have to change themselves (very unlikely) or you exchange the five people. If these five people are your closest friends or family, this might hurt a lot, and I am not suggesting you should get a divorce or never see your parents anymore. You have to be aware of this concept. It has some, if not the most important effect on your own life. This is no exaggeration, rather an understatement.

I had also never really thought much about that concept until an incident happened in my own life. A person came into my life by sheer fate and that person raised my average so much, that it shattered everything I believed up to that point. He challenged me to become more and thereby get more. If I had to draw up a list of people who had some of the most important impacts on my life, he would definitely be on it and today, even though not always agreeing with his ideas and beliefs, I see him as an important mentor of mine. This story will show how important the circle of five people around you is, and by changing even just one person, everything else changes if you allow it. So today I know if I want to move ahead and break new ground, I don't have to change all five people straight away, but get to start with one new person and go from there. This might sound radical and harsh, but believe me - any successful person out there knows this concept and will use it to succeed. While I was travelling to kitesurf I had a silver frequent flyer status with one of the largest airlines in the world. It did not give me too many perks, but it allowed me to carry some extra luggage, which was quite handy with all the sports equipment I had with me during my trips. On top of that it gave me lounge access at most airports in the world. That was quite convenient, because I could relax before a flight, grab something to eat and have free Internet. The other people in those lounges were mostly business travelers and usually quite well dressed. I, on the other hand, had shoulder length blond hair, tanned skin and was wearing flip-flops and board shorts – just as you would picture the typical "surfer-dude" from the beach. You can imagine that most other passengers would frown when seeing me, wondering what a person like me was doing in an airline's lounge. There was no official dress code, but to some degree people expected a suit or at least jeans. Aside of a few bad looks most passengers never spoke up. Before a flight from the US to Germany however, a gentleman approached me and started a chat. His name was Paul and he was well dressed, probably in his late 50s, travelling alone and looked at me quite curiously: "So, seems you have been enjoying your holidays", he smiled. "Actually, I am always on holidays!" I replied with an even bigger smile trying to boast a bit. I was just coming from the world-cup-tour in the Dominican Republic and wanted to show off a bit. "Well, that is wonderful; me too!" Paul threw back. I had not expected such a reply and he definitely did not look as if he was on holidays. Both of us still had some time before our flights and we got into a great chat about travelling and soon went on to talk about kitesurfing, medicine, and me combining both things. He asked most of the questions, and I shared my experiences. I told him I was going back to Austria for an important exam at university, and in three days I would fly to Oman for a Video and Photo shooting session for a kite trip there[8]. My flight started boarding and we shook hands and said good-bye. I had not received much information from Paul, as I had done most of the talking. He definitely seemed like an interesting person and so I asked to stay in touch and gave him my business card. He did not have one but he gave me his email address and we parted ways.

On the flight I wrote him an email to follow up and thanked him for the nice chat in the lounge. Arriving in Europe I also received an email from him, congratulating me on my ventures. He had taken a look on my website[9] and was impressed with everything I had achieved so far. He offered to connect on Skype to stay in touch and let him how my exam went. For a moment I found it a bit weird, that a complete stranger was taking an interest in me. What would you have thought about a man in his 50s wanting to connect? For a brief instant I had the same weird thoughts, but they all turned out to be unfounded. I was studying at the library when I saw him online on Skype. We chatted for quite a while and our conversations ranged from about life in general, my goals and perspectives on all kinds of topics and what I wanted to do with my life. I never had such deep discussions with another person before. On top of that I had just met him quite recently. It felt very natural and easy going, and looking back I know it was because there was a connection on a spiritual level. He was definitely very different from all the other people around me and spending time chatting with him unintentionally started to raise "their average". Paul asked me many questions that challenged my understanding of the world. He wanted to raise the belief-bar in my mind: What will I do after I finish my studies? Where do I see myself when I am 30? When I am 50? What makes me happy? How important is money to me? What would I do with US$50,000

8 You can find this on YouTube if you search for: "Julian Hosp Oman"
9 www.julianhospcoaching.com

a month? What do I want most in life? What excites me most in life? What excited me most right now? Heck, what did I know? I had never thought about these questions. I had just turned 20 and all I cared about was how to pay for my next kitesurfing trip or how to pass the next medical exam, certainly not about such life defining questions. He realized my frustration and he surprised me so much with what he said next and made me completely speechless for what must have felt like an hour: "Take a few hours, and write me the answers to those questions. If you do, I will use my frequent flyer miles to upgrade you to business class on your upcoming flight to Oman." What? Did I just understand him correctly? Did this stranger that I had just met a few hours earlier offer me a free upgrade and expected nothing in return other than me answering him some questions?" He knew I was flying a lot, but that I could only afford economy class. I had told him that in our conversations. Also, he knew that my schedule would be very busy and stressful in the upcoming weeks with my university and kite-schedule. It made no sense, but I was intrigued with his offer. What was there to lose?

I became quite excited, thanked him and promised him to reply the same day. I did have a lot of studying to do, but did not want to pass up on that free business class upgrade. If you have never thought about the questions above, take a quick break and write down your answers into a book, or someplace where you will not lose them. Chances are, it will take you hours to do that. At least, that is what it took me. Almost a whole afternoon went by to answer these simple looking questions, and to be honest it was harder to answer these questions than any of the medical ones I had to study. I pondered back and forth and once I had them, I sent Paul an email. An hour later I received an email that my flights had been upgraded to Business Class. How weird, right? For a moment I had to make sure I was not dreaming. I could not believe the whole story until I was actually sitting on the plane in business class a few days later. On one hand I was confused about what had happened, but on the other hand

I was extremely excited and thankful. It was a night flight, and I could not sleep any of the seven hours to Muscat. I am a WHY person, meaning I ask a lot of WHY rather than HOW or WHAT questions constantly. Why did he ask me those questions? What was so special about them that he would pay to get me to think about them? I did not yet understand during that flight, but I understood it a bit later as you will soon see.

From that trip onwards Paul became one of the five people I spent the most time with. Over the next months we skyped regularly and I even managed to combine my kite trips to Egypt, the Caribbean, South Africa and Asia meeting and travelling together with him a few times. I found out that he owned a very successful business, which he sold a few years before we met, investing his money in real estate. He did not have to work, but was making more money a month than most other people made a year. This allowed him to travel, have fun, and simply enjoy life. One of his passions is to help the people he meets and who he finds fascinating. I was one such person and he appreciated the hard work I was putting in and the attitude I had. He wanted to help me, because he saw all my potential but realized I still had a lid on top of me. Which lid you might be asking? The lid of how people keep themselves down through their own limiting beliefs. For example:

How much money can one person earn?

Is money evil or good?

Do you have goals?

Where do you see yourself in the future?

What do you really want in life?

What is it that you are willing to truly fight for?

Paul wanted to lift my mental barriers and knew he would have to ask the right questions to do so. Upgrading me to business class was pocket change for him, but if that triggered a chain reaction and made me think about the things he tried to teach me. It would make me a whole new person. I understood later that for people at his stage, it was not about getting money in return, it was about passing something on. He took the chance and as you will see it would pay off. Not only did he help me, but also through him I found the motivation to pass on the same spirit to others.

The reason I had never heard these questions before was that I had never been around people who think the way he was thinking. The five people around me that I spent the most time with would be asking themselves different questions, such as:

What shall I wear to work tomorrow?

Will my US$1,500 be enough this month?

How can I sneak out of school or work without my boss noticing?

Why are other people so lucky in life and I am not?

Paul did not think that way, nor did he ask such questions. His mindset was a few levels higher, and by him entering my life he bumped up the average of the people around me. I started to become more, and therefore I would get more. Everything I ever thought would be possible went to new heights by a hundredfold. I believed I could only earn US$5,000 a month – now I knew US$500,000 a month is possible. Whilst I believed that owning one apartment would be great, now I knew that owning as many apartments as I wanted would be possible. Taking one holiday a year was nice – now it would be several trips a year. From him I learned a lot about how to do business, how to talk to people, and how to greet them in the right way. I also learned how to network and value relationships, how to set goals, and how to work towards my future.

I am grateful about many people in my life, but he for sure had one of the biggest impacts on me as an individual person. No one else of the five people around me at that time could have lifted me that much. What is extremely important to add at this point is that the "average" is not related to any specific topic, but as in the earlier examples, to the many important aspects of life, such as lifestyle and career choices, and major personal and family decisions. The reason I am pointing this out is because it is in no way limited to money or wealth but rather open to any measurable concept. After the "five people around you rule" the second thing I learned was what kept people from utilizing these opportunities properly. There is a downside to every upside. I am truly convinced that you will also meet, or have already met a "Paul" in your life in one form or another. The question is, whether you will let them into your life or not. Letting a "Paul" into your life would be the easy part, but by doing so you have to be open to do one of the hardest things possible: to let one of your five people go, someone you used to spend a lot of time with and with whom you may be extremely close. You see, it is impossible to add one person to your group. There is not enough "mental" space to just expand the group, if that is the right way to describe this concept. So, you have to choose someone that will be replaced by "Paul".

Look at the five people again that you jotted down on a piece of paper at the very beginning. If you are now thinking: "I would never want to spend less time with any of my friends or family or anyone else on that list. I want to keep them all and still have more!" then let me tell you this: this is exactly why the vast majority of people will never manage to raise their "lid", because that way they never allow a "Paul" to enter their life. In order for you to get more, you first have to become more. And you can only become more by changing one or more of your closest five people around you. Saying, "Good-Bye" and adapting to change is one of the toughest things emotionally for humans. In order to become better doctors and to understand our patients better, we were taught the five stages that people pass through when being confronted with change or the loss of a loved one. Dr. Elisabeth Kübler-Ross developed this theory in "On Death and Dying". In the case of you having to replace a person in your inner circle it is of course not as dramatic, but maybe these five steps will help you:

1. Denial

2. Aggression

3. Bargaining

4. Depression

5. Acceptance

You will undergo these five steps when having to replace one person of your inner circle. Some of you will get stuck longer at one stage, while others rush through all five quickly. First you reject the information that I am sharing with you in this chapter. It sounds too crazy and so you just ignore it. Next, your inner conscience is telling you there might be some truth to it, and you start hating me for it. I am telling you to move a close person away from you. You feel that it would have been nicer if I had never told you. But then you start bargaining. Maybe it is not so bad, and maybe you can still spend time with your friends or people close by. Maybe you can make it work. But then you realize that you will only be the average of the five people, not six and you start to realize that for you to get more, you have to be more. You become depressed because you know it is true. The last stage is that you accept and adopt the lessons learned. You are now ready and willing to grow by taking action. Of course, not everyone will be able to pass through all the stages and many people prefer to stay in the "comfort zone" of where they are, and unknowingly accept that by doing so, they can never have more.

There is one catch to the concept, and that is the third thing I learned: Other successful people understand the concept as well. Think about the dilemma: If you want to have more, you need to be more, and in order to be more one of the things you have to do is to change the five people around you. This works only as long as you find people who either do not understand this concept or do not care about it. Why? Because the "higher average" people do not want you to decrease their average and will therefore not really like you being around them in the first place. Since most successful people know about this concept, it will be difficult to find someone with a higher average that lets you into their circle. There are only two ways to bypass that: The first way was the one I got by coincidence. Paul wanted to help me and understood I was open to it. A few really successful people out there have such a "giving-back" mindset and they will help you as long as you are willing to grow. They do not want anything in return directly because their return is their personal satisfaction in seeing you grow as a person. The other way is one I will describe in great detail in a later chapter, because I used it over and over again from the time I met Paul. Instead of leaping too far upwards with your average, look for people who are just slightly above you and then try to fit in with them. As an example from previous stories it would have been impossible for me to join an NBA basketball team. They were totally out of my league. But I could join a team of players that were just slightly above my level. Yes, I might have been the weak link, but since I was willing to grow I caught up to them quickly and fit in. Thereby I became a better player way faster than if I had not joined them. You can use the same technique in real life. If you want to grow in a field, look for people that are just slightly above were you want to be, join them, be willing to grow, and you will reach your goal.

I owe Paul more than I could ever repay him in monetary terms. This chapter is dedicated to him to give back to all the people who read this book so that I also have the opportunity to pass this knowledge on to you. I was fortunate to have someone like him enter my life. When he upgraded me into business class it was just a door opener for understanding what was possible, and through his friendship and mentoring I expanded my mental horizons ten-fold. Ask yourself who are the five people around you that you spend the most time with? Are these five people pulling you down or lifting you up? Do you want to stay where you are, or want to move up? Whatever answers you are giving yourself, you now know what you need to do. I had to replace four of the five people (my best friend Daniel stayed) around me, which was one of the toughest things a 20 year old could do. But it is always about what YOU WANT MOST. And I wanted to be more and to give back more, so I had to become more. Be open to let a "Paul" into your life. It will not be easy, because you will feel uncomfortable and unwilling to make space. I know that – been there, done that. Also, a "Paul" will not stay with you if they think that you are not willing to work hard and are not open to grow; you just "kind of" want it. Why should they waste their valuable time on someone who does not try to improve? They would not, unless they see the benefit of helping you to become more. Now that you know this concept, it's time to start thinking about how to apply it in your life. True magic will happen when you take action based upon what you just learned.

SPACE FOR MY TAKE AWAYS

12.

THE FREQUENT-FLYER STORY - THE SKY IS THE LIMIT

"If you can dream it, you can do it!" – Walt Disney

Paul had opened my mind to bigger dreams and goals than I could have ever imagined. But I didn't just want to be a dreamer – I wanted to be someone who goes out and works hard to actually achieve them. I don't know if you have ever made a dream collage? Don't know what that is? Welcome to my club at the age of 20. A dream collage is a board hanging on your wall that you can see every day. On there you put pictures and images of your dreams and goals. They should be big and bold ones – an easy way to test whether they are big and bold is that if you show them to the average "nay-sayer-person", he or she laughs and says that you are nuts. That is a good sign – you want these dreams to big enough so the average person cannot imagine them. You dream of a house at the beach? Well, double the size of the imaginary house at the beach, then go on Google and print out the boldest and biggest house at the beach you can find and that you want to have. Put this picture on your Dream Collage Wall. Repeat this with as many things as possible. For example one of the things I have on there is a flight around the moon. I read about it in a science magazine and it said it would be available for 180 million USD in 2030. I have no idea how to do that, but it is a dream of mine. This sounds crazy, but studies have proven that dream collages work by focusing your mind and programming it to work towards your goal.

I have been using this technique since I met Paul and I created the habit of putting any goal on there. Aside of flying around the moon there are many other things on my collage, ranging from relationships, to business, to the spiritual, money, and health. This story is about one of the dreams I had when I was just 20 years old. I had briefly mentioned in previous stories that while I was kitesurfing and studying medicine I did a crazy amount of flying all over the world. Other kitesurfers could go from place to place directly, but since I had to fly back to university on a regular basis, I had to take three to four times more flights than them. Most airlines run frequent flyer incentive programs for their loyal customers, offering free flights and other perks. Depending on how much you fly with any specific airline or alliance you move up in the ranks called silver, gold, and platinum. As I already mentioned in the previous chapter that I was a silver status member, which was possible for many customers in the program as long as they flew a couple of flights per year. Gold was a lot harder to achieve, yet still reachable, but Platinum was almost impossible for the majority of people including myself. Being from Austria, I would naturally use a lot of the European Airlines from Austria, Germany, and Switzerland. I do not want you to believe that this chapter is any kind of endorsement for any airline, but rather an inevitable need of convenience. I am sure, had I grown up in Japan, I would have chosen a Japanese airline. The German Lufthansa AG group consists of several airlines from the three above-mentioned countries (and some others as well that I did not use much), namely Swiss Airlines, Austrian Airlines and Lufthansa Airlines. To build their flyers' loyalty the group uses a common Frequent Flyer Program called "Miles and More". The concept is very simple: For every flight you take with the participating airlines you get a predefined amount of miles, depending on the length of the flight and the booking class you are in: Economy, Business or First. These miles serve like an internal currency: You can spend them to pay for example for flights and at the same time they represent a measurement for your frequent flyer status. For more details you can go on to their website[10] – and again, this is not advertising of any sort, it just serves to tell my story. As a disclaimer I want to state that while writing this book I am still holding the highest status level in the "Miles and More" program and I am therefore slightly prejudiced towards the benefits of this particular program.

What is so fascinating about such a program is the fact that it brings out the greed for status within humans. I do not believe that people want to earn money just to own it, but because it puts people in to a higher status than others. Simply put: I think it is no fun at all having lots of money if no one else knows about it and you have to live alone on an island. It's a similar situation in frequent flying: I believe the main interest people have in collecting millions of frequent flyer miles is not for the free flights, but rather to use their gold or platinum frequent flyer cards that give them a higher status than other passengers. This might sound silly, but in my life I have taken several private jet flights in a highly luxurious environment (where I was pretty much alone) that were not nearly as much fun as First Class Flights where other passengers could not believe that a 21 year old surfer child would be in the front cabin. Humans are social and they want to rank themselves in society. What would all the millions of dollars mean to the famous and rich if they couldn't show it off to others – it is similar in the world of the frequent flyer.

"Miles and More" has taken a very smart path by establishing a super VIP status called "HON Circle". A lot of rumors fly around this "club" as only a selected few people worldwide achieve it. How hard is it? Well, you need to fly 600,000 miles within two consecutive years. To put that in perspective, that would be around 40 return trips in business class from Europe to the US and back. Flying in First Class means you need to take fewer flights but at the same time cranks up the price significantly. These requirements result

10 www.miles-and-more.com

in the typical HON Circle member being 40-60 years old, male, with a high-level executive job and having close to no life outside of their job, since they are spending pretty much all of their life on an airplane or in airports. Of course there are exceptions, but they are quite rare. Well, at the age of 21, I wanted to be that exception, and I wanted to be the youngest one in the program. Why? First of all I am very competitive and if there is something to achieve, I love to achieve it. Second, I could be the youngest person in the club, which would truly boost my ego. And third, the perks attached to HON Circle are incredible, including First Class treatment at all times, personal assistants all over world, priority over other passengers, seating upgrades, and additional luggage allowance which I especially needed for my kitesurf gear. Looking at the past years of flying, it is amazing how it makes you feel when you get the special treatment.

When I decided I wanted to become a HON Circle member, I had maybe flown 200,000 miles. So to qualify I needed to fly 600,000 miles within just two years. Wow! You might say this is impossible for someone at the age of 21. I probably thought the same but I had the dream and vision to do it. I searched for pictures about HON Circle on the Internet and put it on my vision board. I even photo-shopped a picture with my own card, to visualize what it looked like. My parents saw it and just laughed. They did not understand why I would want to spend so much money and time on something so silly. Money? It would surely cost around EUR 100,000 for all the flights. Second, I was not doing enough flying to get to 300,000 miles within one year – and by far not 600,000 in two years. It was not about understanding the "how" rather than putting it into my mind and being convinced that I could do it. So many times I hear about people who do crazy things like high-speed mountain climbing, or playing chess for four days straight, and while these things sound crazy to most of us, it is perfectly normal for them in their own world. I was committed to achieve the HON Circle status, no matter what other people thought of it. The only person who supported me in my decision was the only person who could relate to it: Paul. That is why the average of the five people is so important.

Most people never put their dreams into action, but if you have a good dream, collage and you see it over and over again you will make your dreams happen, as it will also help you to "familiarize" you with them. Ask yourself WHY you wanted to achieve it and then figure out the HOW later. I described my why above and it was basically status, perks, and the feeling of doing something that most others might not achieve. Now it was about finding the how. I knew there was a way; I just had to find it. Whereas during my early days I had to go to the library to read books about how to play basketball or how to study for the SAT, I could now simply go to Google and type: "How to collect miles quickly?" And guess what? Google knows! Today's technology makes it so easy to figure out the "how", but most people still don't use it. I always wonder how difficult this would have been B.G. (Before Google). Google guided me to a frequent flyer forum, where there were a few other crazy people like myself, who loved to share tips and tricks about flying the globe in a cheap and super efficient way. I spent days reading through the threads, learning the lingo, terminologies and airport codes. I learned how to spell out names in pilot's alphabets, how to talk to airlines' agents on the phone to get the best results and how to maximize the perks and benefits of my silver status. I was studying all that without knowing yet how to apply it in real life. Strangely I noticed so many people were on there, having all this knowledge but never took action to actually make something out of it. I soon would find out why.

What happened next, some people might call luck, but I consider it the point where preparation and hard work pay off. I had a strong desire and I was getting prepared. There was a point where I could call myself an expert on frequent flying. I knew all the airfares, the best deals and top-secret tricks in the airline market. I had learned all the airport codes in the world. I was as prepared as I could have been, and I had a strong desire to make something out of this. And that was when three unexpected events happened at the same time that proved once again that if you want something enough, you have your mind set on it and be willing to do all it takes; the universe will show you a way. First, the kite brand that I was working with wanted me to help them expand globally, especially into regions that they were not that strong yet. Additionally, I received a few requests to offer kite camps at these places to improve people's kitesurfing skills. And lastly, several kitesurf magazines covering the most remote places in the world to kite asked me whether I could write some travel articles for them. Was it luck? Maybe. But I would call it being prepared, with a strong desire to make it happen. I wanted to get great results in kitesurfing, and I was always pushing my own limits in the sport. I had been building great relationships with brands, magazines, and customers. It was a process that had been going on for years. Up to that point I had never been too focused on the travelling side, but rather on competitions. And now that I was building my knowledge about frequent flyer reward programs and all the opportunities to travel the world, I received several offers that allowed me to leverage both my kitesurfing and my frequent flyer goals.

There was no better timing for it and so I think luck had nothing to do with it, but rather I was prepared, so when an opportunity surfaced I was able to grab it. Doing all the travelling and flying meant a lot of organization and logistics, and I am not sure whether I could have done it without all my knowledge. I probably would have needed another person doing all the bookings and arrangements, or would have used a less dense schedule. Both things I could not afford and did not want. There was pretty much no limit to how much travelling I could do. As long as my sales numbers were good, publishers accepted the travel stories, and customers enjoyed my camps, my travel expenses were reimbursed. All of that laid the groundwork for my goal to produce some outstanding results in kitesurfing but at the same time reach the HON circle status as one of the youngest members ever. Groundwork is basically a solid base from which to build. But to actually achieve what I wanted to achieve, I had to do several other, completely crazy things that I will share with you now.

Most people do not know that it is usually cheaper to take a connecting flight instead of a direct one. An airline's flight-fare system price calculations are based on various factors. Through research, I started to understand that when an airline puts a fare for a city pair into its system (for example Frankfurt to New York and return) it assigns each fare with a letter, for example V. Attached to that fare are certain rules. For example whether you are allowed to cancel or change the flight and how much this costs you. If you are interested in studying this yourself go on any flight booking website, do a trial flight booking, and before confirming and paying, read through the so-called "Fare Rules". There are around 25 rules to produce an automated pricing when you go online to book a flight.

I will go into more detail on the routing and stop-over rules, as this is what I leveraged on a lot to get more flying done while paying a cheaper price. As I am sure that many of you love to travel, maybe these tips help you as well. The computer uses the routing and stopover rule to determine which route you are allowed to take between any given city pair, for example a flight from Frankfurt to New York. You might be allowed to take a detour via Munich or via Washington for the same price, as long as the right booking class (in our example V) is available on these connecting flights. You might be wondering: "Why would I ever want to fly more and why would the price not go up if I use a service longer? If I hop into a cab it gets more expensive the further I drive." I have to admit that is somewhat weird, but let me tackle the pricing-part first and get to the longer routing afterwards. To understand airline pricing, forget how you would calculate any transportation normally. An airlines' ticketing systems works by saying: "Ok, we have 250 seats on this airplane, and we open up X amount of seats for this booking class and Y amount of seats for another one." Since the airplane is flying anyway, and they charge you a fuel surcharge for every segment you actually take, it does not matter to an airline whether you fly direct or transfer via other airports, as long as the specified booking class is available. I hope I haven't lost you up to this point. It took me weeks to understand all these rules and fare classifications. But once I did, booking flights was never same.

So how is it possible, that a detour might be cheaper than the direct route if there is a surcharge for every segment you actually take? There are several possibilities and the most obvious one is that on the direct route your booking class is not available so you have to pay more for a higher one. By detouring through other airports you can pick flights where your cheaper booking class is still available. This might allow you to save more altogether, even though you would be paying extra surcharges. However, there are many more extreme examples and this is where all my studying and knowledge came into play: Large airlines such as Lufthansa and many others literally connect the entire world through their hubs, which are their main airplane and operating stations. In the example of Lufthansa, these were Munich and Frankfurt. Most flights went from any outside airport to one of these two hubs and passengers would exit or connect onwards to another flight to reach their final destination. So let's assume you wanted to fly from Cairo or Addis-Ababa or Athens to somewhere in North America or Asia. I am picking these airports as real examples, as these were the airports I used for years. Of course you could choose an airline that has a direct route from Addis Ababa to Singapore for example, but since airlines such as Lufthansa or Swiss also wanted a piece of that market share they offered a fare from Addis Ababa to Singapore. Since neither of them flew that route directly, the fare rules stated clearly how these flights could be routed via their hubs in Europe and also whether you could stop their and continue later or not.

An airline that had passengers transiting somewhere has to offer a better price over an airline with a direct flight, otherwise no one takes the transit route, but rather flies direct – wouldn't you do that too? So, why am I telling you all this? Let me give you my real life examples here. A direct flight in first Class from Addis Ababa to Singapore was around EUR 3,000. So Lufthansa had to offer that flight cheaper, even though the connections went through Munich or Frankfurt. And that is what they did. In order to use that offer I could not hop on in Munich or Frankfurt, I actually had to start in Addis Ababa. Then I flew to Europe, continued to Asia and did the same in reverse for the return journey - Had I started my travel in Europe I would have paid close to EUR 20,000 for the same flights. Someone who is only flying one or two times per year does not really benefit from such insane routings, but because I was on the road constantly, I was able to leverage this often. So the trick is, to not start your trip where you are actually based, but to search for routings that transit through where you are living, thereby cutting the cost by a lot. I know that doing this sounds crazy, and it is, but it is even crazier if you know about these things and do not use them. And "using them" I did. I managed to arrange these combo flights for my destinations all over the world. When I held camps in South America I combined a routing through Europe all the way to Manila, where I held another camp. Flights for filming and photo shooting in New Caledonia did not start in Europe but in Johannesburg, where I did demo work for my kitesurf company. I travelled in Business or First Class most of the time, but paid almost the same price as for an Economy Class ticket starting in Europe. One other useful benefit of these trips was that I was able to network with the world's business high-fliers and some of the world's social elites. These people also have to travel and most of them travel in First or Business Class. Since I stood out with my very casual dress code, long blond hair and tanned skin, they loved chatting with me. One time I was sitting next to Hilary Swank on a flight from Africa to Europe and walked her through Frankfurt airport so she would not miss her connection. Another time I had the chief of the World Bank next to me on a 12-hour First Class flight to Bangkok. And of course, while doing all these crazy flights to kitesurfing destinations over the globe I was collecting five to six times more miles than if I had flown Economy Class for almost the same price. Just a few months earlier I was only reading the theory behind all that and now here I was, getting closer to my HON Circle status collecting hundreds of thousands of miles to redeem.

An important bonus that played into my hands was that I could use all this time on airplanes and in airports to study medicine. Do not forget, I had to study around 10,000 pages per year of medicine and related texts, and while I did get a lot of studying done being at the beach, it was during all those flights that I would do ten-hour non-stop learning sessions. Imagine sitting in First Class next to Hillary Swank without anyone else (no joke) and you having three medical books on the table and her watching in disbelief. Some of the flight attendants even started to know me simply by word spreading that a crazy surfer-child in his early 20s is flying Business or First Class almost every week, studying on the airplane. I booked all my flights to my kitesurfing destinations, and while I did a lot of detours on my flying to collect more miles it was mainly to reduce the prices by 80% or so. If you think that is crazy, wait and see what comes next.

Once I was chatting with a passionate frequent flyer friend of mine in Los Angeles, when he told me about a fare where I could fly from Europe through the US and then back, where I would not only collect a lot of miles for my status, but on top of that the value of the miles collected was higher than the actual ticket price paid. Reading this, you might be asking yourself, "What kind of flights are these, and how can the original ticket price cover free flights afterwards?" Mostly, these flights are called "Error Fares", where an airline's agent either makes a mistake by typing in a wrong price (by missing a 0 for example), or loads the wrong fare rules into the system.

This was the case for this flight: There was no mistake in the price but the fare rules for routing were messed up. According to the rules I was allowed to book a flight to the US and fly around as much as I wanted, as long as I did not stop at an airport longer than 24 hours. Also, I was not allowed to go to any airport more than two times. So this meant I had to pay US$3,000 for this error flight ticket, which was comprised of completely pointless flights that I was just using to build my status and at the same time to collect around 100,000 Miles. I could then use these 100,000 Miles for a flight later on that was worth US$3,000 or more and that I actually needed. So the error flight was actually for "free" but gave me an extra status boost. Such error flights are very rare because airlines notice their mistakes quickly and correct them right away. After talking to him about the details I knew I had to move fast. I calculated the most efficient route, which would take me 2.5 weeks through some cities in Europe and mainly the US, without actually leaving an airport. Fortunately it was June, and my medical exams were coming up in July. I had no kitesurfing trips booked so I could focus on studying during that time. I decided I could study during the trip and so I left for the airport three hours after I had booked the ticket. I only carried hand luggage as checking any baggage would make no sense, plus I had to be careful with the weight and size so I could bring my three medical books, some study card boxes (which triggered a security alert at every airport check) and since I would get pajamas, amenities and slippers in First Class anyway, I did not take much clothing or a toothbrush. It was a crazy schedule of around 28 flights over the next 17 days.

I am not sure if I had ever done anything crazier than just flying around in circles all through the US, going from New York to Tampa to Philadelphia to San Francisco to Portland and on and on. I slept and ate either on airplanes or in airport lounges, and since there was nothing else for me to do it became a highly intense and productive study time. I am sure I hit an average of 16 hours per day, which was more than I could have done back in the library. I have to admit that at the end of my journey I felt a little like an outcast. I had not had any proper social interaction with anyone for over two weeks and my hygiene and living standards were more than questionable. Whoever talked to me on the trip and listened to my story thought I was totally nuts flying around for no reason. Well, I was a nut who totally aced the medical exam and had a great story to tell. Would I do it again? Maybe not a second time, but for sure again as a first time! Eventually I did become one of the youngest HON Circle Members later that year, after having flowing over 600,000 miles quite easily. I received a personal note from the CEO of the Lufthansa Group AG welcoming me into the circle. Today I not only enjoy all the perks, but moreover I reached one of my biggest dreams. Often when I step out of a limousine that picks me up from the airplane, the driver wants to see an ID because he does not believe that he is picking someone up wearing Flip-Flops. This always leads to a good laugh afterwards. I brought tons of revenue to the kitesurf company I was working with and the magazines loved my stories from all over the world. I held several dozen kite camps with hundreds of kitesurfers and helped to improve their levels. These things put a smile on my face, because they remind me every single time how important it is to believe in your dreams, getting ready for them and taking the craziest action possible to make them happen. If you do so, the right opportunities come into your life.

I already described most of the three lessons I took away throughout the story but I want to point them out once again. First of all, you need have big dreams if you want to achieve big things. My dream of becoming a HON Circle member might not have anything to do with what you want to achieve, but that is not the point. The concept stays the same: put your dreams on a dream collage. If you don't know how to make one, look it up on YouTube. I have my dream collage in my living room where I see it every day. Put your dreams and goals on there that may seem insane to others, but are important to you. The second important take away is that when you choose your seemingly unachievable things, you will not know how to get them yet, and that is ok. If you remind yourself WHY you want these things, and that you are willing to hustle to get them, opportunity will strike. Suddenly things start to become clearer and the better prepared you are, the easier it will be to achieve your dreams. The third lesson is that for you to achieve incredible results, you need to take incredible action. I had learned how to work the system, but I was willing to do things that most other people were not. This allowed me to achieve something that those others never could. It is the same with whatever you have on your dream collage. My story might absolutely not apply to you at all and you might think what a waste of time or money – however, that is not the point. Again, it is the concepts behind the story that are important: Dream big, prepare, and be ready to do crazy things to make it happen. Many people stay dreamers, because they never take action to work towards their dream. Yes, at the beginning it seems as if there is no way to get there, but it is the same as going for a long drive: when you leave the house, you have no idea what the next 400 miles will look like. With every mile you travel, more clarity comes into the whole trip. It will be the same thing with your dreams. If you have dreams and goals that others do not laugh at, they are probably too small. Better to increase them and make them crazy.

So, let me ask you this: "Which big dreams have you always had? What do you need to learn to achieve them? Which crazy actions will you take, and are you actually ready to go all the way when opportunity strikes?" Make your dream collage now and take your first step towards achieving your dreams.

SPACE FOR MY TAKE AWAYS

13.

THE REFEREEING STORY - DIFFERENT PERSPECTIVES

"Everything we hear is an opinion, not a fact
and everything we see is a perspective, not the truth"
– Marcus Aurelius

I told you about finishing medicine in the last story, but during those six years, many other stories worth telling happened. The story I am about to relate now happened very early on in my studies, when I was about 22 years old, and is about my transition during my time as an active athlete, from solely pursuing the sport, to becoming active in other related areas. In basketball I had started playing in my first year of Junior High School, when I was eleven years old. Aside from playing in the US when I was sixteen, I also had the chance to play in the "Bundesliga", which is the highest league in Austria. I already considered myself quite good before I moved to the US, but it was the training and mindset there that really got me up to speed. It had been my main reason for moving to the US in the first place and it paid off completely. When I came back to Austria and decided to focus on kitesurfing, I still wanted to stay close to basketball and so I decided to start being a referee. Initially it seemed like a great idea, as I had expected to only referee a few hours a week. I soon realized that refereeing was totally different to competing. Normally I was the person executing the sport, not the person watching or in this case, judging it - which turned out to be completely different to what I had envisioned.

As an active player I had always tried to use the rules of a game to my best advantage but as a referee I needed to know them by heart from a neutral perspective. I had to make instant, educated decisions without guessing what was right or wrong. To give you a quick overview: In a typical basketball game there are three referees, of whom one is the head referee. It is not like in soccer where one referee runs the pitch, with two assistant referees (and in professional games, even a "Fourth Official") who watch the sidelines. In basketball, each of the three referees has an equal responsibility for his or her area of the court. This keeps conflicting calls from different referees to a minimum. The head referee can in theory overrule another referee, but this happens very rarely. Before my first game as a referee, I had to take referee training, which bored me to tears. We had to study the rulebook, watch examples of decisions on video, as well as referee trial games. Only after passing a theoretical and practical exam, were we approved to do a real game. I started refereeing younger children first and over time was upgraded to referee more difficult games with adult players. I progressed quite fast and soon I was refereeing in the "Bundesliga", where I had played as a professional, just a few months earlier. Since most of the games were broadcasted on live television I could listen to the reporters talking trash about me in the replay. I am sure you can imagine how that felt

After a couple of weeks into the refereeing job, I noticed that something unexpected had happened to my basketball skills when I played with some friends for fun. I had become a better player, even though I trained less. I moved better on the court, anticipated plays a lot better and eventually scored more points than before. "How strange", I thought. Did being a referee help me to become a better player? I was skeptical, because those two skills were, in my opinion at the time, not related at all. I knew enough referees that were far from being good players at all and most players never manage to become good referees either. Yet, this was the only explanation that I could come up with and the more I reflected, the more I believed my hypothesis was correct. Usually I had always picked sides, so I favored one team over the other, but as a referee I needed to be completely neutral. Therefore I learned to judge the situation as it was, not as I wanted it to be. I now knew the rules 100% and while in the past I just guessed what was right or wrong, I now knew firmly what actually was right or wrong and what might fall into a grey area. The better I knew the rules, the bigger the grey area became. Believe it or not, even in a century old game such as basketball, there are still some grey areas that one can use: for example, when and how to call timeouts (breaks) or when to switch players. Once I had studied the rules, I learned to understand the game even better myself. I also learned many things from watching other players for two hours a game. I had watched a lot of basketball on television before, but being a referee brought the intensity to a different level. I started to understand which offensive plays were most likely to happen, how the defensive player would react, and what the most likely outcome of a play would be.

You might not be playing basketball or any other sport yourself, but these things that I learned while being a referee apply to many every day things. A fellow Austrian named Arnold Schwarzenegger once said in a famous YouTube Video about his six rules for success[11]: "Break the rules - not the law - but the rules!" In order to do that, you first have to know the rules. In medicine this understanding helped me to know what were my rights and obligations as a student about how much time I had to actually spend in the classroom. In flight travel, I learned to be very exact with the fare rules, so I could take full advantage of them. Later in business, I used my knowledge of the system to get the maximum returns on my revenue or save on tax benefits. So, in whatever field you are, learn the rules, so you can use them as much as legally possible to your advantage. If you are reading this and you are

---

11 http://www.bodybuilding.com/fun/arnold-schwarzeneggers-6-rules-for-success.html

thinking this might be unethical, then be sure a person you are competing or dealing with will know the rules, and he or she will bend them for their benefit. This does not mean that you have to act in an immoral way, nor does your knowledge-based use of the rules for your own benefit necessarily mean that others will be put at a disadvantage. It means that by becoming an expert in your "playing field" you can leverage on that knowledge. Was learning the rules the only reason I had become a better player? Probably not, because especially after another experience from kitesurfing later on I can very confidently say that there is also another important factor that I am going to share with you now.

As I shared with you before, I was kitesurfing on a professional level for almost ten years from the age of 18. Three of these ten years I was also competing on the world tour, being ranked among the top riders in the world. Similar to basketball a few years earlier, also in kitesurfing I started doing more and more travel stories and kite camps, which meant that I did not have as much time to actually train for competitions anymore. Remember, kitesurfing for fun is very different to kitesurfing for pictures or videos and a whole lot different from kitesurfing to train professionally. Same as in basketball I wanted to stay close to my fellow competitors and so I joined the judging panel as one of the main judges for over three years. Again, to my surprise, the same pattern than previously in basketball repeated: my level of skill increased when I became a judge, just this time it could not have anything to do with studying the rules, as it did in basketball. There were simply not that many rules in kitesurfing to study. So, what was it? As a referee in basketball I had to learn to watch the defensive and offensive players carefully. It was really important to define neutrally who was moving into whom in case contact happened. Up until that point I had never watched that many plays so closely. I had to judge over 200 plays a game. Multiply that by around 200 games that I had refereed, and you end up with around 40,000 plays total. This was nothing compared to the amount of television or

YouTube clips I had watched of players shooting, dribbling and scoring, but the intensity was entirely different. As a judge in kitesurfing the same was true, just now I had to closely watch the tricks riders were performing. I had to judge them based on their takeoff speed, the height of their jumps and of course, the difficulty of various tricks. When watching them in movies, I mostly focus on the "Wow-factor", but being a judge I had to observe the small details in order to make a professional decision.

This additional knowledge in both sports made me a better athlete, even though I trained less. I started to become more creative in both sports, learned to improvise and to anticipate what was coming up next, just because I had so much more experience. Even though I have never been a great chess player, I know the same concept applies there. The reason why great chess players can calculate dozens of moves ahead in their heads is not because they calculate every possibility. That would be mathematically impossible. They watch and read thousands of past games and through that experience they can anticipate what is about to happen. It applies to every other sport or activity where you want to perform at a high level. No matter which one it is for you, you need to train a lot, but moreover you need to have great understanding about the sport itself and experience in order to reach the very top. I was refereeing and judging for only a few years, and it helped my actual skill level considerably.

Aside of the above I also managed to build a great reputation being an excellent basketball referee or kitesurfing judge. If you think of either this might sound highly contradictory, as the losing team or athlete will most likely not appreciate the decisions that were made. This was quite different in my case, simply because I understood the main concept: "Care about your reputation, but not about what other people think!" What this means is that your reputation is what you build up over years of putting in hard and dedicated work. What people think about you can change quite rapidly, depending on a single incident. As a referee or judge especially, you will have people complaining or speaking badly about you every time you make a ruling that they don't like. For example, think of watching your favorite team play a soccer, basketball, or rugby game. Chances are, if they win, you won't say anything bad about the referee. But, if they lose however, you will probably complain about bad calls and blame the referee for your team's loss. Am I right? Of course, this was no different in my situation. When refereeing a basketball game or a kitesurfing event I would always try my best to be as correct and precise as humanly possible and I judged any play or a trick following these principles. Most of the participants knew that about me. And still, when people lost, they would have loved to "shoot" me. If they won, however, they said how great I was. But here was one major difference: These were emotions during or right after the heat of the game. After some time had passed however, and the emotions had calmed down, participants would usually admit that I had lived up to my reputation and made a good call. Of course, not everyone was able to "man up" and admit that, but most of them did. This only worked because people knew how accurate and straightforward I always was and still am.

So, how do reputation and other people's opinions come together? I could not change people's opinion right after their kitesurf heat. Many times the loser would have a poor opinion of the judges. My reputation is and always has been that I am hard working, reliable, dedicated, focused, and honest when it comes to giving my opinion. So how does this affect you? Well, first, let me ask you what are you known for? What is your reputation? Are you lazy or hard working? Honest or dishonest? Are you generally late or always on time; reliable and accountable; quiet and reserved, or loud and forthcoming? Whatever it is, it is your reputation. Be sure, you work and protect a great reputation - you only have one. You should however, never care what people think of you because of one individual incident, as long as you stayed true to your reputation. Of course, I could have cheated a bit and make one rider win to get good feedback from him. But this is not I, and people know that. They have to accept me the way I am, and those that do, appreciate me for my strengths and of course also my weaknesses. It is important for you to understand this concept and how important it is for you to clearly understand what you "represent". What are your values and virtues? If you stand behind them, people will not only accept you, but appreciate you. Nurture your good reputation, because it takes a lifetime to build, but can be lost in just an instant. And trust me, every lie, attempt to cheat or manipulate will come back to haunt you big time later on.

The next and totally unexpected thing I learned was to put myself in other people's shoes. Before becoming a referee or judge I was only thinking as an athlete. I never put myself into another person's position. I never thought about what the brands I was working with were thinking. I did not think of event organizers or other judges. I was too ego-focused. But as a judge I moved onto another side of the sport. I started paying attention to all kinds of things that I had never noticed before. I started to notice the challenges that brands were having as I listened to conversations in the judge's tower. I became aware of what media companies really needed, because this was what journalists spoke about in the press tent. I could give you a couple of more examples but the message was always the same. The problem that I was not aware of up until this point was: nobody cared about what I needed, and most people just cared about what they needed. As soon as I learned that I understood that for me to get what I wanted, I needed to combine my needs with the other people's desires. One of the reasons I became so successful in kitesurfing with magazine publishing and brand associations was that I knew what I had to offer them. It was what they wanted. What did they want? They wanted awareness, sales, revenue, and profit. So I had to find a way to get these for them, while getting what I desired, which was publicity in magazines, money from brand partners and the opportunity to kitesurf all over the world. It sounds so simple, but most people actually never ask themselves what does the other person really want? Once I had figured it out, it was easy to convince magazines to print my stories, because they realized that these exact stories got them thousands of readers. I earned more money from brand partners than many other riders just because I tied my income to the revenue I was bringing them. Had I never understood that simple lesson, I am not sure if I would have been able to become as successful in sports. Think of it as the "Win-Win-Win" that I described when opening my sandwich business.

So how does this apply to you if you are not coincidentally looking for a Kitesurf sponsor at this very moment? Well, most likely you are dealing with other people on a daily basis. In your business life, no matter whether it is your boss or your employees, your distributors, customers or business partners. In your personal life, it may be your partner, spouse, children, or parents. Have you ever tried to put yourself into the other person's shoes before dealing with them? Have you ever truly asked yourself what the other person actually wants or needs? Did you ask them? There is a famous saying that goes something like this: "Learn to show people how you can give them what they really want and you will rule the world." You will never learn to know what they want, unless you actually put yourself into the other person's position and start caring. Try it out, before you are about to meet with someone. Take 30 seconds to think about it and tell yourself: "I want to put myself into the other person's shoes, find out what this person really wants and then show him or her how I can help them achieve it!" Do this a couple of times and you will be amazed how much better you are at truly mastering the game. You will understand why your boss is yelling and you will find a way to surprise him or her by solving a problem or delivering outstanding results. Or, the boss might just be crazy. In your personal relationships this is even more important, as many breakups or divorces could be avoided if more people applied this knowledge.

Refereeing and judging taught me these valuable lessons. I learned to have a clear and good reputation and to not care what other people thought just because of an individual incident. I also learned to study the rules and gain experience to increase my game and skills. Thirdly and very important, I learned to put myself into other people's shoes to understand what they actually wanted. My challenge and call for action to you is to identify an area where you are lacking some experience that would push your skills forward. Then write down the names of people around you and figure out what they truly want. Find a way to give it to them and by doing so you will get what you truly want. Last but not least, stop caring about other peoples' opinions – people will have one about you no matter what. So just focus on getting things done with integrity and a good reputation. NOW.

SPACE FOR MY TAKE AWAYS

14.

THE DRUGS STORY - PARTIES, SEX, AND ROCK N' ROLL

"I used to think a drug addict was someone who lived on the far edges of society. Wild-eyed, shaved-headed, and living in a filthy squat. That was until I became one." – Cathryn Kemp

In the past 13 stories you had the chance to see me growing up, from age five all the way to 22 years. Most of the stories I have shared with you had a positive outcome, and the lessons I learned were mostly based on good actions and deeds. As in anyone's life, I was given many lemons and always tried to make lemonade out of them. I managed to do so a lot, but this story will be about some very different back-to-back decisions that I made in a pretty short period of time. I do not want to say I made bad decisions, because in my opinion there are no bad or good decisions. The two types of decisions there are those that you make and those that you don't make. Eventually it will depend on what you make out of the decision you took. It is easy to judge a decision looking backwards, but the important message I would love to bring to you is that you can use any decision for your advantage, even though it might not appear that way initially. That's what you will see in this and the next story.

Around the age of 22 I was, for the first time in my life, earning some serious money from my kitesurfing activities. I had signed great contracts with several brands, was travelling in Business or First Class, and enjoyed being sponsored to go to places where other people had to pay to go on vacation.

To say I had a life that most 22 year olds dreamed of was an understatement. I especially enjoyed spending my time in Brazil, which is an amazing travel destination for wind- and kitesurfing. From September to January there is steady sunshine, a perfect 30°C (86° F) temperature, and constant 25-30 knots of winds[12]. This is pure paradise for a watersport professional like myself. It provided low living costs combined with the possibilities of shooting high-quality kitesurf videos, taking pictures, and meeting other kitesurfers who were also enjoying Brazil's advantages. Countries like Brazil also have other things to offer, like late-night parties, criminals, and drugs. Put any 22 year old into an environment like that, add some spare money and free time, and you can easily imagine what could happen. I was exactly such a 22-year-old. While generally being not much of a party animal, that particular year was quite different. Believe it or not, I had never even taken a sip of alcohol until I was around 21 years old. I just never cared and since my parents had been quite open about it there had never been any real temptation. I had always been involved in sports, a healthy community, and non-drug-friends, so it simply did not fit into my life. But that year I started to hang out with other kitesurfers who were into drinking, staying out late, and even doing drugs. Just as the law of "the average of five" dictates, I started doing the same. Some people might say these were mistakes but let's come back to that question at the end of this chapter, and see which lessons I was able to take away from it, despite my decisions not being the smartest at that time.

So aside of a lot of kitesurfing we did some hefty partying. Many times we were out all night and came home at six in the morning, when the sun was just about to rise, and the wind was already blowing. I can't remember anything serious ever happening during our kite sessions that followed, but it got close a couple of times. One time after an intense party

12 Approximately 50-60 km/h, which is perfect for windsurfing or kitesurfing

I felt like I was in "the zone" and wanted to go for an early morning session. I probably had a pretty high blood alcohol count, so my senses were not the clearest. I pumped up my kite and went onto the water. After riding back and forth a couple of times without any serious difficulties, I decided to show off a trick to some girls who were doing early morning yoga at the beach. I wanted to "nail it" quite close to them, to be sure I would make an impression. Just when I was about to go for it, I suddenly felt an extreme rip, got thrown off the board and up into the air. I think I must have thrown one or two flips, just before crashing hard on to the beach. I had completely misjudged the distance where I actually was and had run straight into the sand for an abrupt and painful landing. Luckily, that happened when I had just launched into the trick, because had I taken off earlier I am not sure how I would have ended up coming down from a 5-meter high jump. I had made an impression on the girls however; it was just not the one I had intended. They were totally shocked, as my crash must have looked quite serious. They came running towards me to help. I was lying still, trying to feel if I had broken anything. Thanks to the soft sand, I just had a few scratches, but was okay overall. After that I decided it would make sense to take down my kite and sleep off the alcohol, not before exchanging name and details with one of the girls, however: there was another party that evening and for sure I did not want to go home alone.

We did live up to the reputation of professional surfers that year and picked up girls faster than "changing our underwear". At the clubs we automatically went into the VIP areas since the club owners were also surfers and enjoyed professionals hanging around. The process that followed was always the same: Enter VIP area; make an impression on sexy girls in the regular area; invite one of the sexy girls into the VIP area and make her feel special; tell sexy girl you are a pro kitesurfer, which got her totally fired up: ply sexy girl with alcohol; take sexy girl home and have fun together. Be a good surfer-buddy and pass her from surfer to surfer, so others could have fun too. Next night: Repeat. Looking back, it was very degrading for any woman, and I do not feel proud of it, but this is how it happened. It was completely nuts and besides the sex, marijuana and cocaine were quite common, in addition to drinking excessive amounts of alcohol. Since the people I was with at that time were taking drugs, I was inclined to also try. One day after coming home from a kite session, my kitesurf buddies had baked hash cookies. They smelled yummy and I was very hungry, as I had not eaten anything the entire afternoon. I was extremely tempted to try and so my friends motivated me to have a couple, but also warned me, not to eat more than one or two on my empty stomach. So after two cookies, which seemed like the best cookies of my life, I just lay back on a sofa and waited for the effects to kick in. Since it was my first time, I had no idea what to expect. I still did not feel anything after what felt like half an hour. "Maybe my receptors for cannabinoids were not yet developed in my body", I was thinking. I was clearly under the influence of the drug already; I just did not realize it. "Ok, I will probably need to double the dose!" I figured. My friends yelled: "Stop eating the cookies, you will completely pass out otherwise!" "Dude, who is studying medicine here?" I replied without making any sense and chucked down two more cookies.

To cut a long story short, my first experience on marijuana worked out somewhat like this: besides feeling like I was in another universe for the entire night, I saw more colors flashing around than probably exist. I firmly believed other kite sponsors were trying to spy on my friends and me by placing little transponder chips into the cereal boxes. I know, that makes no sense, but what does when being on drugs? I have no other explanation to what happened afterwards, other than that I was higher than high, absolutely out of my mind and completely out of control. In order to prove my point I took all the cereal we had and emptied it all over the floor, but I still could not find the "transponder". My friends tried to calm me down, but I was just getting started. While they tried to get some sense into me my mood switched from being paranoid to being scared. I locked myself into the bathroom to prevent them from stopping me from looking further for the transponder. They tried to come in, as they were worried that I would get hurt. That just scared me even more, and I fought a fierce battle to keep them out. At some point, I was so exhausted that I collapsed and passed out straight on the bathroom floor. When I woke up the next morning, I found myself wrapped in towels, lying on the couch in the living room. My friends told me that after they entered the bathroom, I woke up again and started to kick and bite. I have absolutely no recollection of anything and I cannot believe I would ever bite, but they insisted that this is what happened. In order to calm me down and keep me from either hurting them or myself, they had to wrap me into blankets and towels and that was how I woke up the next day. There must be some truth to that as there were still colorful cereal pieces all over the floor. It was a crazy sight and we were fortunate that no one got hurt.

Since marijuana had such a crazy effect on me, the next day my friends suggested that I try a drug that would sharpen my mind, make me laser focused and was said to make the impossible possible. They were talking about cocaine, which was very easy to obtain there. Many dealers on the street were offering the white powder for US$5 for around one gram. It felt like in the movies. We negotiated a little bit, and then bought a few grams each. Back home, we put some of the powder on a table and just like gangsters in the movies we used my platinum credit card to shape it into a nice line, rolled up a US$100 bill, formed it into a straw and snorted the powder. I inhaled forcefully and immediately had one of the worst coughing and sneezing attacks. White powder started flying around in our room. If anyone had walked in that very moment they would have thought we were the biggest druggies ever. Marijuana had made me hallucinate and become drowsy, so I was quite excited to see the effects cocaine would have. Within 15 minutes they set in. Suddenly I felt more awake than ever before. I had the feeling of my senses being ten times sharper than usual. My reactions felt faster, my understanding clearer and I felt as if I was unbeatable. Wow, the drug was really living up to its reputation. We decided to go to a party, and since we wanted to arrive in "good shape" we decided to do another line. This time I was neither sneezing nor coughing. Probably because cocaine is a strong anesthetic substance and my nose was numb. Boom, 15 minutes later I got another even stronger "high". It was wonderful. We arrived at the club and it felt like I was having the best party of my life. The music was better than ever before and the energy was pumping. It was as if my blood was boiling and I had control over every cell in my body.

As soon as I got into the VIP area I was even more on fire: high-fives here, handshakes there. While many other people struggled with self-confidence or sociability I had been quite outspoken my entire life and had hardly ever struggled to speak up in public or be open with other people. What I experienced at the party however was nothing like ever before. Approaching any girl and chatting with her openly was like the most natural thing ever. Gone was any slightest fear of rejection or insecurity. It felt as if I was in control of the entire room and everyone wanted to talk to me as long as I said they were allowed to. Of course that was not the case, but cocaine let me believe so. I wanted the evening to go on forever. Two hours later, my friends pulled me aside and said: "It's starting to wear off, let's get another line!" "Let's do it!" I thought: "Sure, what the hell!" We went into a back room and had more cocaine. Boom, even more speed, more clarity, more fun, more of everything. At 7:00am in the morning, while the sun was rising, we were still out partying and dancing full speed. Wow, it was unbelievable; I wanted this feeling to never go away. We went to bed that day at 10am with more girls than ever before. Neither of us could sleep until the early afternoon, but with all these girls that was not the plan anyway.

I have no idea when and how we actually fell asleep, but when we woke up, my mouth was extremely dry and I had a wicked headache! I had totally forgotten to drink water regularly during the party, and since the air conditioning was off in our room I had been sweating like crazy. I felt as if I could not move a single muscle in my body and it was worse than having the flu. I had been partying the entire night, but I had done that before and it had never felt that bad the next day. The girls were gone and I was lying naked on my bed. I did not even know what day it was or how long I had been sleeping. The sunlight hurt my eyes as if little knives were poking into them. I was now feeling as terrible as I had felt wonderful the night (or two nights?) before. All I wanted was to get back to the state I had been in. My friends were also starting to get up and one of my friend's first questions was: "Wow, how awesome was that?! Ok, so how can we get some more coke to get rid of this hangover!?" My initial reaction was to reply "Heck yeah", but then I hesitated. "What was I doing? How the hell did I end up where I was?"

That was the moment I realized how dangerous it had all become. Yes, it had been a lot of fun, maybe even the best party of my life, but taking the drug again would get me into a death spiral. I would feel worse tomorrow and I would need cocaine again and I would start a viscous circle. At that moment it started to dawn on me how quickly I had come so close to the edge. Here I was, a successful athlete, made good money, having lots of fun already, and pretty much enjoying what most other people dreamed of, but I found myself on the edge of drug dependency. It started with alcohol, went on to marijuana and then cocaine. What would be next? I had always believed only bad people with bad backgrounds would get into drugs; not people like me. I then realized that it could happen to anyone in the blink of an eye. At that moment I decided it had to end. It was the first and last time that I ever took cocaine. It was also time to change my friends and focus on medicine and kitesurfing: without drugs. I am thankful for this experience however, as it let me take away a lot from that trip. Now, I want to answer my question from the very beginning of the chapter about whether the decisions I had made there were good or bad. There are no bad decisions, as long as you make the best out of it. And that is for sure what I did. I learned about the dangers of drugs and saw in real life how powerful their effects were. The experience allowed me to say NO a lot easier during the many other times when I was offered a cigarette, alcohol, or anything else.

Have you ever done drugs? Are you doing them at the moment? Do you drink too much alcohol, smoke or take marijuana or cocaine? Anything else? Up to today I have never touched a cigarette. Looking at the risk-rewards ratio, smoking is as stupid as it gets. That is right. If you are reading this and you are a smoker, get help, NOW! There is absolutely no benefit of smoking that you could not get from something else, but there are dozens of related diseases and health risks. If you are not convinced, Google, "effects of smoking on the human body" and you will get thousands of examples[13] Enough with the lecture, it is your choice to stop, but looking at one single corpse and comparing it to someone who didn't smoke is all it takes. Why should you stop now? Well, our human body is so amazing that after 15 years of no smoking, it can pretty much restore itself and all the tissue affected is repaired. Sounds like a second chance, right? It is, and you should take it! So smoking had always been out of the question for me and I have never been much of an alcohol drinker. Now that I have tried marijuana and cocaine I have had my fair share of drugs and feel no fear of missing out on something.

As I pointed out already, my second take away was that you will never know how close either you or anyone around is to get involved with drugs. What I mean is that even though you might think you are as far away from them

---

13 http://www.dailymail.co.uk/health/article-2531279/A-cocktail-cyanide-arsenic-New-graphic-images-damage-caused-smoking.html

as possible, it sometimes might just be one wrong person offering you something. I personally feel my parents had prepared me well when growing up. They never made a big fuss about alcohol or cigarettes, and so it was never a big deal for me either. When there was something to celebrate, they had a glass of wine or my dad drank a good, cold beer after a hot summer day. There was never any excessive drinking, but also no hiding, which would have made me suspicious and maybe would have made me want to try it even more. If alcohol or cigarettes are already a part of your family life you should try to quit as soon as possible. As for drugs, the best thing to do is to be informed about the kind of damage drugs can do. Studying medicine gave me a huge advantage when it came to that. I knew the harmful short and long-term effects. Even if you don't dig into the nitty-gritty details, there are some impressive pictures and short reports out there that show the harmful effects of cigarettes, cocaine, alcohol, or any other drug. It is important to understand that even though everything seems to be "safe", it does not take much for someone to drift into addiction.

So how did I almost shift to "the dark side"? The answer is very simple: I had too many people around me doing drugs and so it started to feel normal. This is the 3rd take away – your circle of friends matters a great deal. You will do what your friends are doing because you want to fit in. This fits with the law of the average of the five people with whom you spend the most time. If you want to stay healthy- be around other healthy people. Are you a parent wanting to protect your children from harmful things and people? Children choose their own friends and trying to prevent a child from seeing a friend just makes them more determined. The key is to treat your children with respect and to acknowledge them when they take a stand for what is right. If you tell them not to do something… chances are they will do it even more. So the key is that they enjoy hanging around other people that don't get them into trouble. For example when I was around 13 or 14 years old and just hitting puberty I asked my dad whether

I could have an air rifle. He told me I could, but he wanted to take me to a model plane store first, saying that he wanted to buy a model airplane for himself. We went to the store and of course now I wanted a model airplane as well. He told me I could either have the model airplane or a shotgun. Well, guess what I chose? Of course, it was the model airplane. I never brought up the gun again because now I preferred flying my plane. Why am I telling you this story in that context? You are a child's first role model when growing up. One thing I learned is that most people do not what you tell them to do… rather, what they see you do. So since you will be one of the primary people in your children's lives, you will be a primary role model and an important influencer. Walk the walk and not only tell them what to do, but rather show them. My dad did not want me to get into guns, so instead of just telling me not to do so, he swung me over to model airplanes by actually taking me by the hand and "walking the talk" - I am very thankful for that. When I got older, it was up to me to choose my friends wisely. Most often I did. Like I said… most often does not mean always.

So, understand the consequences of what you are doing, and be aware that it can happen as quickly as one, two, three that you slide off from a successful path. Pick the people around you wisely, and if you are using drugs, binge-drinking alcohol, or smoking – get professional help. It is 100% worth it; not only for your own health, but also for that of the people around you. You have only one life, so don't mess it up by doing drugs. Be in control and do it now.

SPACE FOR MY TAKE AWAYS

15.

THE BRAZIL STORY – THE EIGHT
WEEK, EUR 90,000 COURSE

"If a man with money meets a man with experience, the man with money will have the experience and the man with experience will have the money." – Anonymous

It is surprising how many great memories I have from Brazil, despite everything that happened there. In the previous story I told you about my party excesses there and now I want to tell you about my money experiences. Before we dig into that let me ask you this: How long does it take you to earn EUR 100,000? If you are among the average income earners in any developed country it is around five years. And how long does it take you to save EUR 100,000? Probably a lot longer, and many people may never achieve this during their entire lifetime. When I was 23 years, old I was making more than really good money through all my kitesurfing contracts and publishing deals and coming out of an average background, it was more than I could have ever imagined. I had always been doing my own accounting and was very accurate with my finances, and therefore I managed to get my total savings up to EUR 80,000 by that age. A lot of that money came from profits I gained from stocks, which were soaring high in the years prior to 2008, right after the "dot-com bubble".

Part of getting into the wrong circle of people in Brazil was not only my involvement in taking drugs but also doing the wrong things with my money there. Some of the people I met were actually quite decent whereas others were convicted criminals who looked for refuge in Brazil, a country with a pretty corrupt legal system. Of course, if you are inexperienced, you do not see that straight away. They pursued their hobby of kitesurfing while making money through all various questionable and / or illegal schemes, such as online trading, online gambling, suspicious real estate projects, or other scams. Up to that point, I did not have much contact with any of those activities, so I did not realize the upcoming danger. The bit of knowledge I had learned about investing my money mainly came from YouTube. It was very straightforward to learn and all the knowledge was free as long as you searched for it. It was 2007/2008, and the whole housing and stock markets were heating up. If you are not familiar with the economy during that time, you can simply google the "Housing Bubble of 2008" or the "Fall of Lehmann Brothers" to give you a better idea. That year stocks plummeted by double digits and housing loans became unaffordable for many borrowers. Millions of people lost their fortunes and many ended up in near bankruptcy. It also started to affect me, since most of my money was tied up in the stock market. There were some warning signs prior to the collapse that was about to come, but since I had been on a roll I wanted to continue the ride. I was making money in sports, in the stock market and I was more successful than ever before. Why would I ever listen to other people if I knew it best myself – right? Sure… I had absolutely no idea about the actual business world and my investment strategy was less like an actual strategy and more like gambling. Remember the lessons about making money on the buy and only investing into things you understand? Well, I did not follow either of these rules here.

While hanging out with other kitesurfers at the beach or bars, it was natural that aside from discussions about kitesurfing, we talked about other topics such as money. I had never bragged about my income status or equity stakes, but I am pretty sure an experienced person realized that I had liquid capital and that I had no idea how to use it in a smart way. That made me a perfect and easy target for any experienced con artist who wanted to take advantage of me by getting me into a shady business deal. I met another Austrian there, who had been living in Brazil for quite some time. His name was Jose Ralf da Silva, and he was such a con artist, who used Brazil's extradition laws to hide from charges he would be facing in other countries. He spent a lot of time at the water lagoon where I trained and shot videos, and personally I found him quite friendly. Yes, there was something weird about him, just like his questionable hygiene or his many tattoos all over his body, which at the time I tended to associate with criminals and gangs. But that could have applied to other people as well. People had warned me that he was not to be trusted, but I kept telling myself: "What do they know?" One day he told me about a real estate project that he wanted to set up along the coast a bit further north from where I was staying. He told me he had acquired the seafront land and he would love to set up a kitesurf resort there. He was looking not only for investors, but also connections to people in the kitesurf industry who would work with him on the deal. He got me excited immediately and since I was extremely well connected I told him I could help him out. He offered to pay me a commission on any investor I could land a deal with, and on top I would get a special price on one of the lots of the land in case I wanted to invest myself. I was totally stoked – I had never been involved in real estate before, and now I had an opportunity to get a special deal on a land right next to the water, which could be worth tenfold in the future. It sounded like a dream come true.

What can I say? Looking back, I should have realized that the reason he had to come to me to ask for help was because no one else wanted to work him. If something sounds too good to be true – it most probably is. Writing these lines makes my blood boil, because I still feel the pain of the mistakes I made back then. I think you can already see where this is going. I was the wildebeest grazing contentedly on the savannah, and Ralf was the lion hiding in the bush, ready to pounce. We had no luck finding any investors, so the project stalled. He told me that if I invested EUR 50,000 now, we would become equal partners, and with that money he could start the project straight away. It would buy us time and we could continue to look for investors. It did feel weird that all the other people looking into the deal were backing out. That should have been my first of many warning signs. What did I know about real estate in general? Nothing! What did I know about real estate in Brazil? Even less. Regardless of all these facts, the outlook of an estate right next to the beach in a prime location for EUR 50,000 that could be potentially worth EUR 500,000 was extremely tempting: and once greed sets in, your brain shuts down. Remember the rules of investing? I was not applying them by far.

In any person's buying decision the initial response is rather an emotional than rational one. Otherwise hardly anyone would buy a pair of shoes for EUR 2,000 or a watch for EUR 50,000. Afterwards the logical side of the brain looks for reasons why the purchase made total sense to justify the initial, illogical decision. In my case, greed was the emotional driver and not the rational rules that I should have applied. I saw myself being worth half a million Euros. My gut told me there was something fishy about the deal, but my vision stayed blurred. I justified my decision afterwards by saying that the stock market was indeed heating up too much, and it would make sense to liquidate some profits that I could put into this project. The deal in Brazil sounded too good and I did not want to miss out. I sold the stocks, withdrew the EUR 50,000 in cash, and brought it to Brazil. This was the next awkward sign that should have been another huge red light: Ralf needed the money in cash. He made the excuse that banks charged too much money on international transfers. Since I was not experienced and he claimed he was, I believed him. I did not use my own lawyer for the contracts either… why would I, right? It all felt like a family anyways, and everybody had the same goals, so Ralf suggested using his lawyer to save on the legal costs. "Makes sense", I thought. "What a nice guy trying to help me out!" We signed the documents and it was just before the kitesurfing season was ending. Everything had been taking too long already and I had to leave to go to Bonaire for a video- and photo-shoot of the new kitesurfing gear. Ralf promised to keep me in the loop and to finish the project while I was gone. The plan was that six months later when I would be back, everything would be set up and running and we could have the first guests at our kitesurfers resort. I left Brazil full of excitement. It had been a crazy trip, with lots of kiting, but too many parties, drugs and weird people. I was glad it now seemed to all work out and was looking forward to being a business partner of this resort.

I tried to stay in touch with Ralf while I was on Bonaire. I kept asking for updates but reaching him became harder and harder. At some point his phone number stopped working and his email address started bouncing back. I have not heard from him since. It took me quite some time to understand what had happened. I had just lost EUR 50,000 to a fraudster and all the hard work over the last few years was for nothing. My nest egg had shrunk to around EUR 30,000. I had made so much money during the prior years and now it just disappeared into thin air. I found out later that he actually did not even own the land and neither of his other claims was even close to being true. It was time to consult my real friends and they all advised me to get a lawyer, to at least try to recover some of the money that I had given him. I found a very competent lawyer in Munich, who looked through the contract that I had signed. She said my chances of ever seeing even one Euro were very slim, but she would try her best. At the time of writing this book, the case is still ongoing and my lawyer is doing a heck of a job trying to chase this fraudster down. So, if you are reading this on a Brazilian beach and you meet a smooth-talker by the name of Jose Ralf da Silva by any coincidence, please report him to the police in Brazil – I would gladly appreciate your help.

My next thought after the legal consultation was that I had to earn back what I had lost. But I was on a kite trip in

Bonaire and I had no idea how. I remembered that during my time in Brazil I had made some other "friends" who had been in stock trading and seemed to be very successful. They claimed they had found a way to make money through a "foolproof" system. Back then I was not that interested but now the situation had changed. I needed to cover my losses and I wanted to do it fast. What I had heard from them seemed like my best option. I tracked one of them down on Facebook and told him I was interested to talk about his system. I told him the story about Ralf, who he had also met in Brazil and about losing the EUR 50,000. I told him that I had come to him for advice on how to make the money back. He seemed very compassionate and tried to cheer me up by telling me that his system could definitely do that. However he was not sure whether I was able to use his system, as it was designed to only be used by a few people. He had to check back with his partner whether there was an open slot from someone dropping out. I was devastated when I heard that. He had been my last hope of a bulletproof system and my plan seemed not to be working out anymore. "I will explain you the basics, so just in case there is a slot, you are ready to roll!" he then added. I was relieved. So there was a light at the end of the tunnel: or so I thought!

I did not see that that light because this tunnel I was running into was his perfectly set-up sales funnel. He had spotted my need, had given me a little bit of hope just before taking it all away to increase my interest. Now he had me dangling on a short string, waiting for him to throw me the big rope. It was a perfect sales script. He explained that for me in order to use his system, in case there was a free slot, I had to pay EUR 2,000 for the license. I gulped when I heard the number and he noticed my hesitation on Skype. "Listen Julian, this system will bring you tens of thousands of dollars. If you are not willing to invest EUR 2,000 for that, you better tell me straight away to save each other's time." Boom, I had not expected such an answer, but now he had put me on the spot. "No, I am interested. The EUR 2,000 makes sense." I heard myself saying. I was getting pushed further down the sales funnel. He was doing everything right and I was doing everything wrong. "Ok, let me explain how the system works", he continued, once I had confirmed that I would pay the EUR 2,000 in case there was an opening.

He sent me their website and explained some details to me. It looked great and it showed their performance over the last couple of years. They had made over 100% every year according to their numbers. I was stunned and desperately wanted to have the same. On top of that, he had some sort of certification on their website and so I was sure their system was legit. The way it worked was by analyzing thousands of graphs and data of stock transactions and then giving clear instructions to the members. It would tell me what to buy, when to buy and when to sell so-called stocks options. It seemed foolproof. Anyone could make money, and once I heard all that, it made sense to me that only a limited amount of people could use it. As the system was into options trading, it meant I could use my money to leverage and make more money with this leverage in shorter periods of time. That also meant that because of this high leverage I could lose my money faster, but of course he did not tell me that. Up to that point I had only invested into blue chip stocks[1], which are pretty much the largest companies in the U.S. So, if those were performing well, I was making good money and since the stock market had appreciated a lot over the years from 2003 to 2007, it was easy - even for a clueless investor like me to make good returns. I firmly believed that I was a skilled investor, and the reason I had been making so much during those years was because of my knowledge in picking the right stocks. As I realized later one of the worst situations one could possibly be in was to be incompetent as well as ignorant of that incompetence at the same time. Anyone could have made good money in the stock market during that time because of its overall performance – not just me.

To give you a general idea: When buying a stock, one basically owns a piece of that company. If the price moves up by 10%, one earns 10% of the original investment. If the price on the other hand moves down by 10%, one loses the equivalent 10% of the original investment. That is easy to understand, and that is why I had chosen stocks before. The downside of doing so is that stocks don't usually move 10% up or down, but maybe two or 3% per year on an average. So making money can sometime take quite a while there. And that was what I did not want at that moment. I wanted quick and easy money. I hoped the stock options would make this happen. Stock options can make quick money, but also lose money a lot faster than regular stocks. They are quite complex, and for the sake of keeping it short I will cut out a lot of information and simplify the explanation. For those who are interested, more detailed information on stock options is available on Investopedia.com. You can almost compare stock options to doing a bet on a stock price. The person buying the option is betting for the stock price to go one way (up or down) and the party selling it (mostly a bank or broker) wants it to go the other way. The difference versus a bet is that an option is not an all or nothing outcome. This means, that if you "bet" on the stock price to go up, and it does, you can make a lot more money if the price goes up even further. However the same is also true the opposite way. So if you are "betting" on the price to go up, but the stock plummets, you will lose more money the further the price goes down. Additionally, one of the many advantages of options is the possibility for "leveraging". What that means is that there is a multiplier in the conversion from the stock to its option. So if we use the example from before and the stock goes up 10% with an option leverage of 5, we would be either losing or winning 50% depending on what we were "betting" on. This means that with the same amount of money one can now earn but also lose five times more compared to buying the actual stock. That was the reason why my friend on Skype suggested using options, where I could leverage my money to make my EUR 50,000 back a lot faster. I hope this is somewhat clear and I tried to keep the math to an absolute minimum.

When he was almost finished with his explanation on Skype however he had only been covering the upsides, and not the downsides. Suddenly his phone rang and he told me he had to take it, as it was his business partner. They chatted back and forth briefly, before I heard that out of total "coincidence" one of the slots had become free. If I was fast, I could take it right away and get started on earning my money back. I was not prepared and felt quite pressured. But what were my options? This was a once in a lifetime opportunity and I felt so lucky that that slot had just opened up. I gave him my credit card number and we processed my data for the newsletter information system that would give me all the information from now on. Later I realized that he did not care at all about me actually making money on the stock market. All he cared about was selling these licenses for the newsletter system. All I could see was the upside, but I definitely did not understand the potential downside. I was sure the system would take away any risk and so to me it was a given that I would be making money. I had been doing so already during the past years trading stocks and now with the stock options, which sounded even more promising it was going to be five times faster. At least, so I thought. The first newsletter-update came in and I started with EUR 1,000 to get a feeling how this leveraged trading would turn out. Within 20 minutes my options had such a tremendous change in pricing that I literally had made 28x more. I could not believe it. Earning EUR 28,000 would take an average person over a year to do, but I had just done it in less than half an hour. The system was working and I was rocking it. This was the point that I should have realized that I just had been lucky. I should have realized that while such trading systems might work sometimes, there is no such thing as a magic pill in the stock market. I should have realized that I had just gone into the world's largest casino, had bet on any random number because a system had told me to do so, and had actually won due to an incredible amount of luck. But I was now only EUR 22,000 short of getting back my EUR 50,000 and any rational reasoning had stopped. I thought I was the one ruling the game, when I should have known that the house never loses. After winning EUR 28,000 within 30 minutes I was more euphoric than ever to get the next newsletter update. The next day the system's indicators were showing a high possibility for the markets to recover after the last days' drop (where I had made my EUR 28,000) and so I should buy options to "bet" on the markets going up. I planned on doing another EUR 1,000 and I was sure I could pull off another great trade just like yesterday and maybe even break-even. And hey, in case I lost my EUR 1,000 I was still EUR 27,000 net positive. Right?

I entered the trade and since it seemed to be a slow day, I decided to go for a kite session in the beautiful Bonaire Lagoons while getting rich through my bulletproof system. Unfortunately the markets during the upcoming few hours not only dipped, they literally dropped in a free-fall after news broke out that the Lehmann Brothers Holdings Inc., a global financial service firm and back then one of the biggest investment banks in the US was insolvent. When I came back, I could not enter any order. Stock market trading was suspended as people all over the world, including myself, had started to panic. Initially I thought I had only lost EUR 1,000, but soon I realized what was happening. My "bet" had gone so wrong, that the same leverage I was benefitting from the day before when I was making EUR 28,000 profits was now seriously harming me. I could not yet estimate the exact damage, as I had to wait for the markets to open again. During the night, the markets fell even more and I knew it would get horrible. I was worried I would lose my entire EUR 27,000 profits I had made. It turned out to be one of the largest drops on the US stock exchange in a single day since the 1930s. The system could not have foreseen that incident, but I should have understood the actual risks of what I was doing. While I did not know them beforehand, I was soon going to find out: The next morning I received a "margin call" from my bank as soon as trading was open. All my money was eaten up by the losses and the bank wanted an additional EUR 40,000 from me. I did not understand! How is it possible that I could lose more money than I actually had? It took me some time to gather my senses when I realized that the options I had bought had gone the wrong way by 6,900 %, or 69 times of my initial investment of EUR 1,000. I hope you are as confused as I was back then, because I had assumed I could never lose more than 100%, which would have been the EUR 1,000. Well, with leveraged option trading you can; and I had found that out in a very painful way.

I knew the bank always covers their risks and they would come after me for everything that I have, if I did not add the EUR 40,000 as soon as possible to my account. My problem was that of the EUR 80,000 I had eight weeks ago before I paid Ralf, there were only EUR 30,000 left. And now I owed EUR 40,000 to the bank. I was left with minus EUR 10,000 and had lost EUR 90,000 in just eight weeks. That day was the only time in my life I had seriously considered killing myself. I was ashamed of my failure. I was disappointed in myself and not only did I feel worthless, but actually I was worthless, in monetary terms. If anyone asks me: "What has been the lowest point in your life?" This was it. How was it possible going from a successful medical student and professional kitesurfer to being completely broke? Was it just bad luck combined with a few bad decisions? Could it have been prevented? Should it have been? I was lying in bed when I started to cry. I had not cried in a very long time. The last time was out of joy when we had won the Basketball Championship. But this time I felt like the biggest disappointment in the world. I had worked so hard for the past several years, and what had been the result? I ended up with less than I had at the start.

In medicine I learned the different stages a person would undergo when committing suicide. It was one thing for a person to consider killing him or herself, but it was another to actually make the preparations to do so. Even though I

things like that coming up again in the future, so point the figure at yourself, and start to learn your lessons.

There are certain things that are unavoidable, such as natural disasters. But these are rare and eventually it comes down to your own personal mistakes. I could have blamed the stock market, bad people, or the system for stock options. I could have blamed anyone else, but remember: when pointing one finger at something else, three fingers point right back at you! That EUR 90,000 "course" made me make a pledge to myself: No more investments that I did not understand. No more gambling with money. No more trusting other people blindly. In all my years since then, I only broke that rule one time. I trusted a girl called Laura with a model agency in Hong Kong, without properly understanding the investment, and boom! I lost another EUR 30,000. The big difference there however was that my net worth was already much higher compared to back then and so it did not wipe me out completely. I hope that you have learned from my story and that you will not have to pay for the same "course" – if you understand what I mean.

The first and most important lesson whenever you put money into something is to understand what is happening with your money. What is your potential risk? What is your potential upside? I am still amazed that so many people love giving money to the bank: Potential Risk: Losing it all. Potential profit in 2015: zero %. Disagree? Well, then you better study the terms of your savings account. Oh, you didn't read them when signing up? Welcome to the club! Normally putting your money into a savings account in a bank with a good reputation is quite safe – I agree. But what about the mutual funds your banker might have recommended? Always understand what happens to your money. Had I followed that rule, I would have still lost EUR 50,000 in Brazil, but at least I would not have lost EUR 40,000 trading options on the stock market. If you do lose money, understand why it happened, and learn from your mistakes. Do not be scared to invest again. Otherwise you will have your money under your mattress and get nothing out of it at all.

The next lesson is to only listen to people's advice if you are sure it is in your best interest. Do you really believe a banker cares whether you make money in the mutual fund he or she is suggesting? Probably not, and definitely not as much as you care, because all he or she is interested in are the commissions they earn when you buy the fund. Today I only listen to people about financial advice if I want to follow in their shoes and want what they have. If you want to be like the banker, then listen to his or her advice about investing. Otherwise, look for investment advice from someone that you want to emulate. That would have kept me from investing with Ralf, because I would have never wanted to be like him. But I would have been tricked into using the trading system. Again, it was my own fault that I used it, and I don't blame the sales person. It was in no way was his fault that the stock market dropped so dramatically. I should have known better. I could have avoided that by listening to my gut feelings, instead of being driven by greed. Ralf's deal was completely out of this world and, as the saying goes, if something smells fishy, it's probably a fish. You should walk away, no matter how tempting it sounds. The trading system also sounded too good to be true, and I should have realized that the sales person only cared about his commission, not about whether I would make money with his system.

I invested with the wrong people for the wrong reasons. Over time, I have learned to quickly notice if something or someone is not right and I walk away. On top of that, I also learned to use professional people to check my contracts and legal documents, since I have no experience in that field. So, does this mean that you should not trust your banker? Absolutely not! Actually, you should be building a strong and trustful relationship with him or her. Why? If you are smart, you will use both the upsides and the downsides of working with a bank. Getting a loan for your real estate investment?

I love working with banks on that. Getting advice on what investments to pick? I never listen to my banker about that, simply because the bank's suggestions are only in the bank's own interest. Banks are corporations, so their job is to make money for their sales, not to make money for you. Believe me on that. However, going to them to borrow money for true investments is a win-win for both of you. Why? You get a good deal on your loan if you bargain, and for the bank it is a great income. So follow your gut, learn to judge wisely and listen to the right people.

The 3rd lesson of this story is my advice to you about what you should invest in: YOURSELF! By reading this book you are doing this already, which is a great start. Any time you are not sure where to put your money, invest in the one thing that will give you the highest return on investment. An investment in yourself is not only 100% foolproof but it is guaranteed to give you amazing returns. As a side note, that is also the reason why it is close to impossible to bankrupt on your student loan.[2] Since it is an investment in yourself, the ruling is that this will benefit you for your entire life and therefore, it is hard to imagine it will bankrupt you. So, what does this tell you? Even the highest institutions in the world advise you to invest in yourself first; otherwise there would not be such a ruling! So, whenever you have a few dollars left over that you want to invest in something, invest in a good course about the topic first, no matter whether this is real estate, the stock market, a language or anything else with value. I believe that you will have a 10-fold return or more on this investment, guaranteed, if you take action based on what you learn. But you should know that from following my advice at the end of each of these stories.

Looking back at when I was 23 years old, it was the most painful but also the most important time in my life so far. I shared with you in the past two stories about how I did drugs, lost all my money, and trusted the wrong people. These were all decisions that nearly wiped me out. Some might say they were all stupid and I should have avoided them. These people might be right, but had I not experienced them at that age, I would have experienced them later for sure, at higher stakes. I am 29 at the time of writing this book, so I still have a lot of life ahead of me and a lot to learn. Maybe someday I will write a story where I took a EUR 500 million course for a one-day seminar. I hope not, but if so, I would take away the lessons and go from there to become a better me. My call for action to you is to not be scared of investing your money wisely. If you don't know what to invest in, do a course about investing. So, look one up now, and take action.

SPACE FOR MY TAKE AWAYS

16.

THE MARATHON STORY - 24 HOURS ON A BIKE

"The bicycle is a curious vehicle. Its passenger is its engine." – John Howard

I am always true to my word, no matter whether in business or personal life. So when I told the banker I would pay back the money within a year, I was committed to do so. This meant I had to work even harder, make even more money and cut down on my expenses. Since most of my expenses came from travelling, I decided to cut down on my freelance travel when I was not flying somewhere for a magazine, event, or other paid trip. Also, I started flying more on mileage-paid trips, since it was very easy to keep my frequent flyer status with the many hundreds of thousands of miles I had already collected. I had planned on using them in the future and purchasing actual tickets to reduce my taxes through deductible expenses. But since I had lost so much money, taxes were no longer a big issue. All in all, that meant I would spend more time in Innsbruck, but also, that I would be studying more at the university and not on the road. This was not so bad either and it was pretty much the only year that I felt like an actual student. Also I started going to the gym more often, which I had enjoyed doing a lot while playing professional basketball. With all the kiting I was doing I had stopped going there, but I actually missed it a lot. The gym I went to in Innsbruck was open 24 hours a day, which was perfect for me since I would study from seven in the morning until around 10pm (these were the opening hours at the university), and then I could hit the gym either at 5:00am or at 10:00pm. I started to make friends with the gym manager, Stephanie, and one of the trainers, Jochen.

One day Stephanie told me she was organizing a 24-hour cycling-spinning marathon where people could cycle for 24 hours on a stationary bike for a good cause. You didn't have to do the full 24 hours; you could do as much as you wanted. For every hour on the bike, the fitness studio would donate some money to a charity for children with cancer. Being a medical student, I felt a special connection to that, and so I was quite motivated to join at least for a few hours. I had never been much of a cyclist, and so I spoke at length to Jochen who was one of the main trainers in spinning and cycling at the fitness studio. He was convinced that because I was a professional athlete, if I trained hard for a few weeks, I could complete the full 24 hours. Up until then, I think the longest I had ever performed a sporting activity non-stop was kitesurfing for around seven hours when the conditions were good. After that I was completely exhausted and could not move for the rest of the day. How about cycling for 24 hours on a stationary bike, looking at the same spot on the wall, and going a full day and a full night? The idea was unthinkable for me at that moment. Yet, talking to Jochen motivated me. He seemed to know what he was talking about, and since the event would take place in seven weeks, I had some time to get ready. Together with Jochen I worked out a fitness plan to train towards the 24-hour marathon.

I'm not sure if you have any clue about what spinning is: It is basically a group of fitness enthusiasts in a room on stationary bikes, who cycle according to the rhythm of the music that the trainer is putting on at the front. A good trainer will try to imitate an actual cycling course with difficult uphill as well as fun downhill parts – all combined with slow or fast music. Jochen was such a trainer, and so I especially enjoyed his sessions. My first spinning class with him was a total disaster. Since I had never been on a bike very much, I was totally saddle-sore after just one hour, and my cycling shoes were rubbing blisters on to my toes. I felt miserable. How could only one hour destroy my body that much? The suffering continued during the entire first week. My quads and calves were sore all the time. Even though I was supplementing with magnesium I got muscle cramps during the night and fatigue muscle twitches during the day while studying. As my butt was so sore from the bicycle, I had to bring a donut-pillow to the university, since normal sitting on a chair was unthinkable. At first, I tried to explain myself to fellow students, but after nobody believed that a stationary bike could do so much damage, I just let them believe I had undergone surgery.

I had never eaten so much in my life either. I needed five or six proper meals a day, and was still losing weight. Even though I was eating kilos of pasta and rice, and downing high-energy drinks, I lost three kg in just two weeks. And I was already under ten percent body fat. It was insane. However, coming back after a short break in the second week, I had more energy than before. I still had five weeks of training left and so the plan was to increase not only the training frequency, but also the riding time as my training progressed. Jochen told me that it did not make any sense to train longer than four to five hours a day, as I would just be depleting my body's glycogen stores, which would inhibit me from proper training the days after. Most spinning classes went for 90 minutes, so I always arrived two hours before, cycled at around 60-70% of my maximum heart rate and stayed through the course. I brought my study cards with me, which I would be writing during the day at university, so I could rehearse on the bike. It helped to pass the time while still being productive. During the 90-minute spinning class I went full power and then I added another 60 minutes cool-off ride at 40-50% heart rate to get the lactic acid out of my muscles.

After two weeks on this regimen I took a few days off, and then I repeated the same training cycle again. Jochen told me that he was 100% sure my body would be ready for the endurance race, but 99% of the people who attempt to do it would have that as well – yet, they still don't finish. "The 1% who finish, have a stronger mind", Jochen informed me. "The body is not meant for such endurance riding and sends out signals to the brain to stop the torture. Most brains respond and most riders therefore give up. But with proper training of both, mind and body, a strong rider can push through and make it happen." He gave me a book to read during the last two weeks before the 24-hour non-stop spinning session. The professional cyclist Wolfgang Fasching, who wrote the book, described his long endurance races in the Race across America and what tips he would give to anyone attempting something similar. It was unbelievable to read about the pain he endured and how he trained his mind to keep pushing to finish the race. Jochen was right: It was important for me to read it, as it was essential to prepare me mentally for my exhausting 24 hours plan.

The 24-hour spinning marathon started at 5:00pm. That way, the first 12 hours up to 5:00am would lead to a Cortisol[14] spurt at half time. I had been "resting" for the three days leading up to the race, only cycling two hours each day at very low intensity. Around 80 other people had registered in total, but only a fraction of them wanted to do the full 24 hours. And of those who planned to do the full time, only a few would actually finish. I had done the math in advance so I knew how much I would need to eat throughout the 24 hours (around 600-700 kcal an hour times 24 hours, which was around 14,000 – 15,000 kcal throughout the entire race). I had read studies that showed that under such extreme circumstances the body could only absorb 75-80% of the nutrition it was given – best in liquid form. That would mean I had to eat around 18,000 kcal, or around 25 McDonald Big Macs over the next 24 hours, which was impossible. Therefore, I had

14 Cortisol levels increase around 2-3 hours before waking up and this is the most important alert-hormone in the human body

bought specially designed high caloric meal replacements, which were gels full of pure calories. Those, combined with a few proper meals should give me the energy I would need.

The first six hours of the marathon up until 11:00pm went by fine as I was used to doing 4-5 hours of non-stop cycling and was only going at around 50% of the maximum intensity. I could visit the toilet, but I had to keep the time down to just a few minutes every few hours. During the first six hours I only went twice. I had been monitoring my fluid and food intake closely, my heart rate was running at 130 beats per minute, I kept changing my body posture regularly to loosen my muscles, and up to that point everything seemed to be going great. I felt as if the next 18 hours were going to be a piece of cake. But after midnight, with the prospect of a long night ahead, plus my body not being used to the long endurance, I started to feel worse and worse. At 2:00am my butt started to hurt badly, my legs started to burn and I began feeling drowsy. The spinning trainers had been rotating so none of them was doing more than two hours at a time. Jochen returned for the 2:00 – 4:00am session and so I was happy to see him. When he came in, I must have looked horrible, because he came straight to me and checked my pulse. He looked deep into my eyes and cheered me up: "Julian, you can do this! What you are going through is completely normal. It is the point where the body is telling your brain that what you are doing is completely crazy. Your body is trying to trick your brain into quitting. You must not give up now. It is all in your mind. Remember what you read in the two books: Believe you can!" I didn't really understand half of what he was trying to tell me, but it gave me hope that what I was going through was normal under these circumstances. Up to this point, around eight others had been going with me non-stop. I glanced at them and they looked terrible as well. Jochen realized what an important part this 2:00 - 4:00am session was. His two-hour session was just one hour before halftime, and if he was right in saying that the mind is everything, then getting to halftime was a crucial point of having a feeling of success. He adapted his training for the eight of us who were still fighting to go for the full 24 hours. I could not imagine how I was going to make it through the next 14 hours, if I was already so exhausted and drained. Jochen kept telling us stories of his hour-long races, and how he kept himself motivated to keep going. I was listening to him, staring at a point on the wall. I am sure I started to hallucinate a little at some point because I thought that people actually came into our spinning room to cheer for us as we were cycling up and down a mountain. Maybe they did, or maybe it was Jochen's motivating stories that made me believe that, or maybe it was just my brain trying to get my body to stop.

I told my brain to tell my body not to give up. I remembered my basketball coach telling me: "Son, don't you ever tell me that you cannot go anymore. You have to be lying on the floor puking… then I believe you. Up till that point you simply don't want any more!" But I wanted to keep going. My body said no – my mind said yes. My mind was stronger. I ate my gels and drank around 600 ml of fluids every hour and I kept going. I kept pushing the pedals, kept staring at the dot on the wall, kept fighting, and kept going. I don't even remember what else I kept doing, but before I knew it – halftime was here. Probably it was the Cortisol kicking in, combined with my body's endorphins[15] that started to make me feel invincible. My butt had stopped hurting, and the pain in my legs had been so constant that I had just accepted it being there. It was just after 5:00am, and I could see the sun rising through the studio windows. It was one of the most exhausting, but most beautiful moments at the same time. I told myself: "Julian, you made it this far, cycling back is farther than to just keep going!" I believed that if I used a mental trick of simply telling myself that I had been cycling in a circle and now I was half way through, then maybe my mind would be tricked into believing I needed to finish as the way back was longer. It seemed to work. The hours kept

---

15 Hormones that act like the body's own opioids

counting down. Eight hours to go. Six hours. Five hours, it felt like the 24 hours would be over soon. Full of motivation, I reached down to an empty water bottle and that's when I realized I had dropped out of my patterns that were supposed to keep me on the track to success.

I had not been drinking any water for hours and my eating patterns had become irregular. I had taken off my pulse meter because it started to rub against my chest and I was starting to have a skin-rash. Since I could not monitor my pulse I must have cycled too fast and too slow for different periods, killing my body's reserves. Oh no! That could be a fatal mistake and I had only 4.5 hours left to go. The negative thoughts pushed my own exhaustion and suddenly I saw other people quitting. There were only four of us left. One of them collapsed on the bike and the emergency doctor had to assist him. I could not believe it: I had come so far, and now my body was giving up. I had drained it of every last bit of reserve energy. I started to have blurry vision again and my body started to shiver. Clear signs of being close to breaking down – I did not need to be a medical student to understand that much about my own health. There is a powerful saying that goes something like: "As long as the water cannot seep through the wooden hull of a ship, an entire ocean cannot bring a vessel down." My negative thinking was the water creeping into my strong mind, trying to bring it down.

I had only two options: Give in, and always ask myself what if – or push through and run the risk of falling of the bike in a spell of dizziness. I knew what I had to do: I stepped off the bike, and with my head held low I walked towards the men's changing room. I was limping, but it felt so wonderful to get off the bike. I walked to the toilet. I had not taken a pee in hours. While I was standing at the toilet, I had to lean against the wall with one hand to avoid collapsing. I remembered Henry Ford's quote: "Whether you think you can or whether you think you can't – you will be right!" It was unbelievable what I had achieved during the last seven weeks. I had become an excellent endurance cyclist through hard training, dedication, and pure focus. I had to smile… "No, I was not done yet! There were still four hours left to go, and I would, "Never give up, Never give in, Never surrender!"[16]! I was a fighter and if I was leaving the studio it was either in victory or in an ambulance to the hospital!" I pulled my cycling pants back up. Everything was hurting: not only my butt but also my hands, I had blisters on my palms from holding the bike's handles. At that point I had made a decision, and making a decision is one of the most powerful things a human being can do. When I was back on my bike just a couple of minutes later, the trainer who was holding the next two hours saw my dedication and just smiled. I believe he must have felt the aura I had around me – success was my only option, failure was not acceptable. I forgot about my pain, forgot about the time, and forgot about everything around me. I just focused on succeeding. I cannot remember how many other people were around me, how hard I was cycling, how much I was eating or drinking. My body was in auto mode – my mind was in the zone. All I focused on was to succeed and push through the next couple of hours. My mind had triumphed over my body – just as Jochen had promised. My mind pushed my muscles to keep cycling and complete the 24 hours. I only went to the toilet one more time, simply because I did not drink or eat anything anymore. There were three of us who completed the full 24 hours. The press was there to celebrate that surreal moment. It was 5:00pm, and the gym was packed as it always was in the afternoon. Hundreds of people who had been following the last few hours were cheering and congratulating us all. The moment I realized that I had made it, the tension inside myself melted away and I must have collapsed on the bike, because when I woke up I was lying on a couch with the doctor next to me. My mind had won, but once I had finished it gave in to my body's total exhaustion. But it was ok – I made it. Victory was mine.

---

16 Famous quote by Winston Churchill

I stayed on the couch for a few minutes. I had blisters on my hands, on my feet, on my chest, and on my butt. I was a wreck, but even though I was completely depleted and unable to move, I was happy. I opened my last energy gel that I was supposed to eat an hour before the finish and drank another liter of fluid to rehydrate my body as much as possible. I took my phone and called my best friend Daniel to come and pick me up, since I was not able to drive my car back home. He couldn't believe I had made it and was totally stoked and excited when he heard the good news. I asked him to bring a pair of crutches that he had at his house, as I was sure I was not able to even walk to the car. The next day, I read about the event on the front page of the newspaper, where there was a photo of me with the other two cyclists who completed the 24 hours as well as Stephanie, the manager. It was an amazing moment and I knew that if it were not for all the tips and motivation from Jochen, I would not have succeeded. The mind is a hundred times stronger than the body, and reading this should be a great reminder for all of us of what is possible, as long as we make a firm decision.

Even if you are not planning on cycling for 24 hours straight, the lessons you should take away from this story are very important and applicable to everyday life! First and foremost, you need to understand how crucial your mind is. Therefore be careful what you feed it. If you feed it with negativity from the press or from the news, it will be consuming bad and destructive things. Your mind will then not be functioning at a high level. Stay away from these negative things and listen to great audiobooks, watch motivating movies, and read great and inspiring success books from the field in which you want to thrive.

Second, is once again to understand the power and importance of making a firm decision. I have shared this concept a couple of times already, but I had never felt its consequences so immediate than when I was standing in the toilet ready to give up. You need to develop a mindset of "I WILL DO IT NO MATTER WHAT!" When was the last time you said something like that to yourself? "I will make the absolute greatest (fill in the blank with your goal) in the world and no one will stop me!" This is what you should be saying to yourself. One trick and tip I can give you that I learned during this time is to wake up in the morning and speak aloud 15 or more things you will achieve and/ or are grateful for. For example: By the end of the year I will weigh only 79 kg. I am so grateful for my health. I am so grateful for my wonderful friends. My business will make US$1 million revenue next year. The universe will test you as soon as you make a real decision. For me this meant that my body was trying to give up, and my mind had to overcome that pain. If you decide to really do something, be prepared for the people or things around you to suddenly get in your way. Starting a new business? Well, be prepared that just after you start, something will happen to make you want to quit. Going into a new relationship? Some challenges will come up. You will not be able to avoid the universe testing you, you can only arrive prepared. This is what I have been doing, and will continue to do. The 24 hour marathon was a great reminder that keeps coming back to me whenever I am struggling with a new venture and am about to give up because some seemingly insurmountable obstacle is getting in my way.

The third lesson is that you can do anything you set your mind to, even if it is something you have absolutely no experience doing. I did have a good fitness background to do the 24-hour marathon, but so do many other athletes, yet most did not make it through. It is not about what your body can do; it is your mind that dictates your success. The more diverse the challenges you face, by putting your mind into them, the stronger your mind grows. It is just like a muscle that needs constant stimulation. Try out something completely new for once; something you have never tried before; something that sounds absolutely absurd. There is a man from the Netherlands called "The Iceman[17]" who has such a strong mind, that he can control his autonomous nervous system. His real name is Wim Hof and the things he learned are absolutely incredible. He can raise or decrease his body temperature or stop anaphylactic shock without medication. These things are all tested and proven, and he can explain in great detail how he does it, and if you wish, he will even teach you. You do not have to be that extreme, but start with something small such as running a 10K-race, a half-marathon for a good cause or climbing Kilimanjaro, the highest mountain in Africa. Put it on your bucket list and go for it!

So what happened to my loan? I kept my promise to the bank and made enough money to pay back the EUR 10,000 loan even ahead of time. Since I was using my air miles for my flights and kite-camps, very soon I did not need the extra EUR 10,000 line of credit that I had initially requested. My bank was extremely surprised and probably even a bit disappointed, as they had no doubt expected to collect interest on the loan. Well, they lost out on that score but I did borrow from them at a later date when buying some investment apartments. I got back on track, learning from my lessons, and back stronger than ever before! And now it is up to you, to take action based on what you have just learned. Which firm decision will you make right now and let the universe test your strength to resolve? Go and do it – you can! Your mind will be stronger than anything else around you. Believe in yourself, and take action now.

---

17 http://fourhourworkweek.com/2015/09/07/the-iceman-wim-hof/

SPACE FOR MY TAKE AWAYS

17.

THE CASHFLOW STORY –
NOT WORKING AS A DOCTOR

"People never change; they just become more of who they really are." – Dr. House (Hugh Laurie)

The year after the spinning marathon was a very special one. It was 2009/2010 and everything seemed to fall into place again. I had just turned 24 years old and I was back on track. I had learned from my pitfalls and was pushing hard to become a better person. Every evening before going to sleep I made the goal to be just a little bit better than when I had woken up. I am sure you know the concept of improving just one teeny tiny percent a day – it will compound to a huge amount over time, and that was what I wanted. Besides all the kitesurfing and travelling, I was also finishing my medical studies in 2010, expecting to start working as a medical doctor after the summer. My final exams in June were the most nerve-wracking of my life, so far: not because they were so difficult, but rather because after that I had the feeling the studying would be over - which of course would not be the case, as I realized later. Still, it felt that way. Once again I had done an enormous amount of studying and I was confident that I would pass with either an A or B right after I had turned in my final examination papers. I was simply so well prepared that you could ask me the page number in my medical textbook where a disease was described – I would know it. Let me give you an example: In Central Europe, the "Herold company" is responsible for publishing telephone books. Their phone books are printed on extremely thin paper to bulk and reduce weight. We used a medical book with over 1,000 pages with the same kind of paper from an author who was also called Herold. Pretty hilarious coincidence. I had memorized the entire book into hundreds of memory palaces and so you could have opened the book on a random page and I could have told you what was on that page, in full, correct detail.

Aside from the time in Brazil, I had never been much of a drinker or partier, but after my final exam I was sure to get hammered. As soon as I arrived home my best friend Daniel, my friend Thomas from university and my kitesurfing buddy Martin, started opening wine and champagne to celebrate. The result was one of my worst hangovers ever – but it was totally worth it. I was finished with all the medical studies and receiving the official M.D. title would just be a formality that should take place a few weeks later during an official ceremony. I would then start my work in the traumatology station, where I had already done a lot of my practical work during my studies. The plan was to use the summer for my final year in kitesurfing, and then to get started with full time work in the fall. Doesn't that sound familiar to just seven years earlier, when I had come back from the US to "just spend the summer" in Austria to return to the US for college? Not only does it sound similar, it would turn out to be version 2.0. That summer in 2010 was the first time in my life that I did not have to do any studying and I started to feel completely unproductive. Only kitesurfing was just not enough, as I had to challenge myself mentally and I was missing having to go through dozens of medical books. On one of my trips to Denmark a French kitesurf buddy was reading a book called "The Secret" by Rhonda Byrne. Up to that point I had not read many self-development books and I had never heard of that one, even though my friend told me it was extremely popular. He told me most of the concepts in there are quite logical, but most people would not be actively aware of them. I started reading and was so hooked by the ideas that I finished the 200 pages in three hours. My friend was right: most of the concepts were quite logical, but I was not actively applying all of them. One of the most important ones is the idea of our thoughts not only being affected by our surroundings, but vice versa - our thoughts actually affecting our surroundings. I had understood the science of quantum theory since my early medical studies and so I was aware about the concept of the observer being able to affect the outcome of an experiment. In quantum theory, this is called the observer problem[18]. In the social sciences, we have the Hawthorne effect (named after the Hawthorne factory in the USA, where a study on factory workers' productivity in relation to improved lighting conditions also demonstrated that their productivity was affected by the mere fact of them being studied, as this led to unconscious behavioral changes). It had never crossed my mind however that this would be applicable to everyday life. More simply put, "What we think about we bring about". This quote is quite popular, yet few people, including myself up to that point, were acting upon it.

I had always loved freedom and was constantly looking for ways to avoid being tied up in rigid environments. I assume this was the reason why I enjoyed travelling and kitesurfing so much, as these allowed me to be as free as possible. On the other hand I also knew that my professional kitesurfing career would come to a natural end within the next couple of years, due to me not being able to perform at a high enough level for brands to continue working with me. Medicine would become my new source of income soon, but being a medical doctor and having to work for 70 or 80 hours a week in a hospital, which seemed like a prison to me, was exactly the opposite of being free. When I read Rhonda's book I realized I had to change some things if I wanted to stay free. Therefore I decided to go back to my vision board (the one that I had created when I met Paul) and change some things: I removed anything from the board that would connect me to medicine, and started focusing on pictures more related to building a business, as I figured that this would be the

---

18 https://en.wikipedia.org/wiki/Observer_effect_(physics)

only alternative. I added images of expensive cars, real estate, stocks and successful business leaders such as Steve Jobs and Richard Branson. I was hoping that this adapted vision board would help me get on the "right track" - I had no idea that just a year later all of it would start to become reality.

"The Secret" was the first book on what became my personal, lifelong reading list. My first question after finishing it was: "Which book should I read next?" I went onto the Amazon Bestseller List, and spotted an author called Robert Kiyosaki, who had written a book called "Rich Dad, Poor Dad", which had been selling close to 26 million copies worldwide. I had never heard of his book either, but I wanted to read it. I downloaded the book's audio version. One trick that allows me to get through more books faster than usual is to adjust the speed to 50% faster than normal while listening. Try it - other people might think you are crazy, but I guarantee you will get used to the speed soon. If you have never read any self development books other than the one you are currently reading, I would suggest to take the same path that I had taken, starting with, "The Secret" and moving on to "Rich Dad, Poor Dad" as well. Be careful though, not everything in there is to be taken as gospel. Some of the ideas are great concepts, but none of it will work if you are not committed on taking action. Both books will give you a good base however, from where it is easy to move onwards to many other excellent books. In his book "Rich Dad, Poor Dad", Robert Kiyosaki talks about the two different dads he had in his life. One being poor, the other one, you guessed it, rich. They had different philosophies and ideas about literally everything, when it came to education, money, and investing. You should read the book yourself - I simply want to lay out Robert Kiyosaki's most famous concept: The Cashflow Quadrant.

The Cashflow Quadrant is not new, unheard of, or revolutionary. Similar to "The Secret" it is an easy and understandable concept that the average person can easily grasp. Other books might also have covered the same idea, but none of them managed to put it into laypersons' language that well. The concept of the Cashflow Quadrant is simple: Everyone on our planet is making a living through one or more of four different options, which are laid out as four squares. The left upper quadrant is quadrant E for Employee. People in there are employed and therefore working for someone else. This is what almost 80% of the population is doing (including, most likely, you). The profession of a medical doctor is also part of the E-quadrant. The next quadrant is the lower left quadrant, which is quadrant S for Self-Employed. Some employees start their own small businesses, working for themselves to gain some time-freedom and flexibility, but take up significant financial risk at the same time. Around 15% of the population tries to work in this quadrant, but only a few actually manage to stay there; the others in this group drop back into the E-quadrant. Maybe you have also tried to start your own small business, but gave up once you realized all the commitments necessary to maintain it. As a professional kitesurfer, I was already part of this quadrant. I could choose my projects freely and was responsible for my own finances. Both quadrants are called the "left side", but I prefer to call this the "non-scalable income" side, because the income you can get from either quadrant depends 100% on your own work and cannot really be scaled People who work in these quadrants exchange time to earn money. For example, as a medical doctor at the time I was getting paid around EUR 40 an hour. If you work as a construction worker, secretary, lawyer or work in any other employed or self-employed profession, you will be able to break down your income per hour as well the same way. However, since a week has only 168 hours, and you cannot raise your charges per hour ad infinitum, there is a ceiling to your income. That is why I call the left side "non-scalable".

The right side of the quadrant follows different "rules". The upper right side is the B for Big-Business quadrant. People, who earn money from this quadrant, leverage other people's time and use networks to deliver value and earn money in return. Best-selling authors, "Sell-out" performers, or high-ranking business people like Steve Jobs, Bill Gates and others earn their income from this quadrant. The fourth and last quadrant is the right lower quadrant or the I-quadrant for Investors. People who earn money from this quadrant make their income by leveraging their own or other people's money in investments. Both quadrants on the right side are independent of time, because you are leveraging either on people or on money. I call the right side the "scalable income" side, because in theory you can scale the income from there as high as you want. I will talk in more detail about these quadrants in later chapters, because they are very exciting and allow you to become "financially free". I hope the concepts described are easy to grasp. To learn more, either read Robert Kiyosaki's book or google the "Cashflow Quadrant" concept. While reading I was caught in the ideas immediately. Except for one time, when I was 14 years old and wanted to make some money on the side by taking a summer job at a local factory, I had never really been employed. And that experience was not exactly a positive one: I quit after a couple of days because I could not being told when to use the bathroom, when to have lunch, or when being allowed to go home, just to earn eight Euros an hour. Back then, my mom had been really upset because I had quit something, but I think she understood that I was really miserable and felt caged-in. What I had not been aware of until reading the book was that as a medical doctor I would go back to exactly that, just at a different income level. I would start trading my time, not for eight Euros an hour, but for around 40 Euros an hour. It was a lot more money but still the same concept and I would still be in the E quadrant. This revelation was earth shattering to me. At that moment I promised myself that I would find a different way to produce an income: one where I would not feel imprisoned.

It was a crazy thought, considering I had just finished six years of studying and everyone around me was expecting me to start working as a surgeon at the end of the summer. I really liked the idea of trying a different path, but I was not sure at all how I could tell that to the people around me. My parents, friends, and other colleagues would be shocked for sure and would try to "talk some sense" into me. The thought of standing in front of my mom, telling her that her son was not going to work as a doctor, gave me the shivers. She would surely lose any bit of respect for me, never mind what other friends and family might think. I believe that many of us are in such situations almost every day, where we are expected to do certain things, just because it is "common sense" or because this is what one is supposed to do. I am sure you can relate to this yourself. As in the other stories you may have read so far, it is not the situations themselves that are unique, but how we react to them. I knew what I truly wanted for my life, and being "locked up", even as a medical doctor, was not it. In order to keep the people around me from changing my mind I secretly cancelled my official graduation ceremony and delayed it by a year. Without my M.D. license I could not start work as a doctor after the summer. This bought me some time to come up with a better solution. Not only was my mom furious when she found out, but moreover, friends and study-colleagues expressed their clear disagreement. I had a very hard time, not only explaining to them that what I was doing was right for me, but also staying convinced myself. I promised everyone that I would do the official graduation the year afterwards, and if my goal of finding an alternative did not work out, I would start working as a doctor then.

By postponing my actual graduation I had bought myself another year of living the life I wanted, finding solutions to move to the right side of the quadrant. You might ask what is so bad about being employed. There is nothing bad about it, it just depends on if you enjoy what being employed means to you: your days, weeks, months, years; in fact, your entire life, is mostly pretty much mapped out. 48 weeks of "nine to five", for 45 years. You may earn a few promotions and then hope you can enjoy your retirement (if you don't lose your job or, as the cliché goes, get run over by a bus). I knew I did not want that. It does not matter whether you are ten years, twenty years, forty years or sixty years old when you are reading this book. Anyone can, if they want to do so, change their life in small steps. Maybe you are just like me back then, and you really want to quit your day job and move over to the right side of the quadrant, but you have absolutely no clue yet how to do that. Welcome to the club! Step by step during the next stories, you will see the things I went through during those years, and you can learn the lessons that will empower you to become financially free as well, if you want that. Moving from the left to the right side of the quadrant will require a change of mindset, and it will not happen overnight. As you will read in the next stories, it took me around four years from age 24 until 28 until I had completed my transition. You can do it faster or slower, it absolutely does not matter. The important thing is, to get some valuable tips as well as important skills that will allow you to transition as well – and I will teach and give you the most crucial ones. So be prepared for some of the upcoming stories to have some intense content, and you might want to read them two or even three times to absorb that content completely. Just like the tree story, do not become impatient with your own transition – rather - delay gratification. Do not listen to people around you who have no idea what you are going through, but have faith that it will all work out.

2010 was my breakthrough year business wise and it had all started with me deciding not to work as a medical doctor. I did graduate the year after, in 2011 to finish my degree as I had promised, even though I knew that I would never actually be a practicing physician. It was an extremely emotional moment when I walked over the stage during the graduation ceremony with my family and friends attending. I was reminded of all the hours of non-stop studying in the library and about how many other people would love to have the chance to finish medicine, but can't, for whatever reason. Here I was, having put in so much hard work for this dream, just to decide not to actually work as doctor. I took my oath "to do good and not harm", received my medical license, degree, and title and thereby became officially a "God in white", which I think is a ridiculous name by the way. My grandparents, who are over 90 years old, do not know I am not actively pursuing my medical career... and I hope you help me to leave it this way :-) So if you ever meet them surfing or cycling (yes, they are over 90 years old and still kicking hard!) just tell them what a great grandson they have. Many people ask me, why I actually pushed through with all the studies, or whether, looking back, I feel that it was a waste of time. My answer is that first, you should always finish what you start – it shapes your character and builds your reputation. Second, I am able to apply the knowledge in so many things on a daily basis, just like this book for example. And third, who knows? Maybe I will build a business in the future where my medical degree comes in handy. Steve Jobs once said: "You can never connect the dots looking forward, only when looking back!" And that is exactly what I think will happen in my case. So if you are reading this and currently studying for a degree, do not see this as motivation to abort your studies! You want to finish it, and reap the rewards just as I have done, even if that means not using it actively right now.

I learned a lot of very valuable lessons that summer, but probably the most important one was to understand the difference between scalable and non-scalable income. What did that mean for me? I was still totally committed to kitesurfing but also learned about how to move, step-by-step, to the right side of the quadrants. For example, understanding scalable income opened my mind for writing a kitesurf book called Kite-Tricktionary, which is one of the most successful kitesurf books today. I would not have put enough focus on it, had I not realized the kind of income a book could bring. I did not make any money during the year while I was writing it, but since its release at the end of 2011 I continue to receive monthly royalty checks. There is always some work to do for marketing, but it is scalable. That means

I can reach more customers through various techniques and can thereby earn more money in the same amount of time. If I sell my kitesurf book to ten times more people, I will make ten times more money. That is why the right side is more favorable compared to the left side, as it lets me scale my income without necessarily having to spend more time on it. My book was my first true right-sided income endeavor, but many more followed that year, as you will soon read. Once you understand the importance of scalable, right-sided income, it will change your life forever, just as it changed mine. You will want to find ways to move from the left to the right side as quickly as possible as well. If you do not know how to do that yet, do not worry. I will cover a lot of ground during the next stories about exactly that and you will receive some great input, so keep reading with an open mind.

This brings me to the second lesson: If the right side is so great, why isn't everyone doing it? There is a simple, yet disturbing answer to that: "The power of the average of the five people around you". Think about it – which side are your parents in? Your teachers? Your co-workers? Your spouse? Your friends? Over 95% of the population is on the left side because this is what is being taught in schools and universities. So chances are most of the people around you are on the left side, too. As soon as anyone tries to move to the right side, the person's surroundings try to pull him or her back straight away. It was the same for me: When I told my parents that I was not going to become a doctor, imagine the arguments that followed: "You cannot be a kitesurfer forever. Writing a book is not safe. Being a medical doctor is such a respected profession. What will your friends think about you? Business Owner?! You will go broke!" They were all talking from a left-sided view and could only see the benefits of having a monthly, fixed salary. They did not understand the benefits of the right side, with its flexibility and scalability. So your take away should be to speak with people from the right side, if you want to get helpful feedback. People on the left may not understand your decision, just as we do not understand a foreign language until we take the trouble to learn it. Just like a foreign language they could study the right side of the Cashflow quadrant, but sadly few will do so.

The third lesson for you is what made me eventually realize that the right side was the solution. While reading the self-development books I was reminded of the quote about being stupid if you did the same things, but expected different results. I looked at the colleagues who were already working for five years at the same surgery station that I should have been starting at. When I asked them, some of them told me they were not happy, and were only there because they were hoping for things to get better. So I asked colleagues who had been working there for over ten years. Same result: 90 hours of work per week, no family life and some of them said they were not happy either. They too were hoping for things to get better. So I talked to people who had been 20 years in the hospital: Same answer. 30 years in the hospital: Same answer. There were even people I asked that have been a medical doctor there for over 40 years, and even some of them told me the same thing. Finally I am reminded of an article published about the biggest regrets dying people had: they regretted of not taking up opportunities, but living a standard life to fit in with the norm. All that made me realize that there was no way I wanted to follow in their footsteps. Don't get me wrong, I love and respect the profession of a medical doctor; it was just not the path I wanted to walk. So make sure to look at the path you are about to walk, and look at people that are following that path 5, 10, 20, 30 years ahead of you. Do you want to end up where they have ended up? For things to change you have to change - everything else would be a form of defining stupidity!

Step by step I was moving into the world of business and my vision board was shaping into reality. My streams of income had started to change, and it was not coming from the employee quadrant as a medical doctor, but from the scalable income side on the right. I want you to take this as inspiration and challenge yourself to take baby steps towards that one thing you always wanted in life. If you already live that life, then keep living it without changing it. Otherwise, start with taking that first leap of faith and try something new – something exciting. Remember, you only live once and you want to make it a life worth living. So take action now, and check your future that is ahead of you by looking at the people who have been walking the same path. You like it? Stay on there. You don't like it? Change.

SPACE FOR MY TAKE AWAYS

18.

THE DIVING STORY -
CALLING TIME OUT

"A man can be himself only so long as he is alone, and if he does not love solitude, he will not love freedom, for it is only when he is alone that he is really free." – Arthur Schopenhauer

With all these new projects at hand in 2010, I started to become busier and busier. Soon I was surrounded by technology non-stop that I could use to stay in touch with family, friends, and of course business partners. I had always loved technology, and when the first iPhone came out back on June 29th 2007, I wanted to be one of the first to have it and so I purchased it the first day it was available in the U.S. Three years later, I purchased the iPhone4 and the brand new iPad, and I was more reachable than ever before. Initially I thought that was exactly what I wanted, but then I realized I could barely survive without my computer, iPhone, and iPad anymore. First thing in the morning, I checked my messages. During breakfast, I read and replied to emails. At lunch, I updated my Facebook status, and at dinner I made blog posts. Sounds familiar? Well, guess what? I was totally submerged in the technology boom and there was no sign of this obsession getting any better. At that point however, not many people were concerned about the upcoming trends, and where once there was exciting chatter over a topic at the lunch or dinner table, now people were focused on their mobile phones.

That year I had the opportunity to go diving in Cocos with a group of friends. I had taken a Padi Diving course in

Mauritius a few years earlier and had been diving every once in a while when the weather was not good for kiting. Cocos is known not only to be one of the best diving locations in the world, but it is also one of the largest uninhabited islands on our planet. It is one of the few places in the world where you can dive with hammerhead sharks, whale sharks, manta rays and many other fascinating creatures. There are extremely strong currents at these diving spots, combined with great depths and other conditions, which are ideal for the sharks but are challenging to human divers. What scared me aside of that was that there was no access to the "connected world". I would be cut off from any Internet access for ten days straight. No phone, no email, no Facebook, no Whatsapp, no nothing. I also get seasick very easily, which is pretty funny considering how much time I spend kitesurfing on water. I really was not sure if I could handle all that, and how all the business I was doing could survive without me being plugged-in 24/7. Any person running a business is thinking similar things, but as it turns out, a good business can survive even if "the boss" is out of touch for ten days. After some planning, I decided to go anyways and booked a flight to Costa Rica, from where we took a two-day boat ride to Cocos. I had bought some extremely strong anti-seasickness pills that the pharmacist would not have given me had I not convinced him that I was a medical doctor. I knew how sensitive I would be on the open water inside a closed cabin, and the plan was to sleep through the entire two days by knocking myself out completely. I dosed them carefully though, to be sure that all the meds were out of my body before starting to dive.

The thought of not being able to react to any issues from kite camps, respond to sponsor or magazine requests, or to just chat with friends and family was quite scary. It was mind-blowing how fast the world had been moving ahead, considering that just a few years earlier it was almost impossible to communicate seamlessly across the world. Now, with all this technology and wireless global communication, that luxury had become a necessity. I had set auto-responders and replies to advise people that I was out of connection. Looking back it was hilarious what a huge fuss I made out of it, but the hyper-connectivity had made me dependent on technology. After I had shut down my computer, I knew it would be the last time for the next ten days that I would switch it back on. I wanted to use the opportunity to completely relax throughout the trip and I had brought several good books to read and audio books to listen to. I kissed my telephone and Internet connection good-bye and we started the trip.

I cannot remember much from the 2-day boat ride over the choppy waters of the Pacific Ocean. The medicine's dosage was perfect and other than eating and using the toilet I was completely knocked out flat on my bed in the boat, dreaming of still being connected. Once we arrived, the effects from the pills started to wear off just in time, and I went outside to get some fresh air. The boat had anchored right in front of the island, and I saw one of the most magnificent views of my life. If you have ever watched Jurassic Park, you might remember the scene where a helicopter is flying through a valley of a deserted island, where the dinosaurs supposedly live. That movie was filmed on Cocos Island, and the director of the film chose that location because it is completely secluded in the middle of the Pacific Ocean, without any human structure that could distort the pristine, natural view. The island had the "freshest green imaginable" and was covered with forest and foliage. Everything around was water for thousands of miles. We had arrived in the morning and the plan was to have breakfast and then rest for a few hours before going for a first test dive to check our gear. It helped to drag my thoughts away from what might be happening online and what I might be missing. Did I get any emails? Who had posted on my Facebook wall? I had no clue… At that moment some doubts had set in as to whether it had been a wise choice to go on this diving trip or not. Fortunately, we were going for our first dive soon, and that got me thinking about something else. Up to that trip I had always been extremely scared of sharks, even though any surfer knows that the chances of an actual attack are slimmer than being hit by a coconut on the beach. But that fact did not help overcome the fear when being out on the water, not knowing what was beneath. I was hoping to conquer that fear by looking a shark in the eyes. And I meant that literally, as Cocos' clear waters are famous for being shark infested. You are pretty much guaranteed to see a shark if you dive there. It was gut-wrenchingly frightening, but at the same time it was the only way of overcoming my fears.

On my test dive I only went down ten meters and stayed there for around 15 minutes to check the gear, get to know my diving buddy and get used to the water after the long boat ride. All went well and we went back up onto the boat. I wanted to do the same thing that I would do when coming off the water from kitesurfing: Get online. I was amazed at how quickly habits can develop and shape our character. Since I could not get online, what else was there to do? This sounds crazy, but I was pretty clueless. Entertaining myself with other things turned into an interesting challenge. You can try it out for yourself: Don't use the Internet for the next 24 hours. Just 24 hours: I dare you. The significance of habits became very clear to me that day. In one of the books I had read, I learned that you cannot prevent yourself from doing something that you are in the habit of doing. For example you cannot just stop smoking or overeating. You have to actually replace that habit. For me on the boat, that meant that I had to come up with things to replace my urge to use technology. Since after long dives my logical mental functions were not as clear, I had to use the creative side of my brain for such activities. I had never been much of an artist, but with no other alternatives I started to develop the habit of drawing pictures after these dives. Drawing replaced the habit of getting on to a computer, and it has since become so strong that even when I had a computer on later trips, I still drew pictures after being back on land following a diving trip. It is incredible to see how easy it is to train the human mind.

Over the next nine days we would be doing four dives a day, which was going to be an exhausting but wonderful program. The dives in Cocos were the most fascinating ones I have ever done, having the chance to dive with huge whale sharks, carefully touch manta rays, and experience incredible night dives with hundreds of black tip reef sharks. Halfway through the week, we planned on going down to a very special dive site: It was a mountain shaped cone in the middle of the ocean, the top being about 15 meters down, and eventually dropping off to hundreds of meters in depth. As it was a very exposed spot in the middle of the Pacific Ocean the currents were especially strong and we had to go down one after the other, grabbing a rope tied to the mountain that was also moored the boat. Some of the divers (there were around 20 of us) even used special hooks to stay attached. In surfing I had experienced some serious currents, but these were different. They were like a river in the midst of the ocean and they could force your mask of your face if you looked in the wrong direction. With such hefty currents, there were always big fish around, waiting to snatch some prey. We hoped to get the chance to dive with Hammerhead and maybe even Tiger sharks. By then we had been diving with smaller sharks already, but the upcoming dive would become one of the most frightening, but also one of the most memorable experiences. Since we were diving with Nitrox[19] we had to be careful not to dive too deep, as that could cause irreversible damage to our bodies. At the same time, we wanted to dive as deep as we could (close to the 40m if possible), as that is where the big sharks would most likely be hunting for prey. I was quite nervous about not becoming the prey for them.

I did a buddy-check with my dive buddy and then backflip-dropped into the water. We had agreed to glide down next to the rope, and tl.en wait at the top of the "mountain". If everything went smoothly, we would have around 45-50 minutes of diving time considering safety margins and a proper

19 Oxygen enriched nitrogen gas

safety stop every five meters when resurfacing. Ascending too quickly could cause diving sickness, which was close to a death-kiss, being two days away from civilization. Therefore, the safety stop was important to give the body extra time to get rid of the excess nitrogen from the deep dive. After I had dropped into the water, I was already a few meters away from the rope. The current had pushed me away immediately and was so strong that it took me a lot of effort to fight my way back and grab the rope so I could go down to the mountain top. It was important to avoid excessive activity as much as possible, as that meant using up too much oxygen, which in return would mean having to shorten the diving time. I wasn't really off to a good start, already being out of breath after two minutes in the cold 11 degree (C) water, which caused me to consume more oxygen as my body had to work hard to stay warm. Normally we should have arrived at the end of the rope after just a few minutes, but since I had wasted valuable time struggling against the current, and my diving buddy couldn't get his under-water-camera working, it took us at least twice as long. We finally got there, re-organized and did another quick buddy check. Now it was time to go deeper, and that meant our compressed lungs would need more and more oxygen with every breath we took. Also, the deeper we went, the more risk there was of either depth sickness or irreversible damage to our bodies from the excess oxygen. I had never experienced depth sickness before, but I head learned about its symptoms. Divers described it as acting as if drunk or confused because of the increased nitrogen in one's brain. If we wanted to see the big fish, we had to reach the edge of both risks, depth sickness and irreversible oxygen damage.

We climbed further down meter-by-meter, holding tightly on to the rock to avoid being washed away by the strong current. 20 meters, 25 meters, 30 meters. The goal was to reach around 38-39 meters, while trying to stay above 40 to avoid breaking the limits. When we reached around 33 meters, I wasn't sure if I was hallucinating or not, but suddenly I saw one of the largest hammerhead sharks imaginable. Not only one: I suddenly I saw three. Then eight, twelve, and then twenty or more of them! They were everywhere. Had there not been water, I would have screamed 'HOOOLLLYYYY SH$#@$@#$@$T!!!!" I looked at the other divers, and they all were staring in awe at these huge animals that were circling around. I took out my GoPro Camera and started filming the 25 or 30 huge sharks that were moving around elegantly as if there was no current at all. You can see the footage on my YouTube channel, even though the lighting at 35 meters depth is not too good, but it is incredible to see these huge animals just a few meters away. With all the excitement I had forgotten that I was actually just a few meters away from dozens of extremely dangerous sharks that could make a meal of me. I had learned that sharks could smell blood and pheromones just like we can see light, so I realized that me being extremely scared was not sending the right signals to them. Oh no! I was now even more afraid than before. I kept my GoPro camera pointed at the dozens of sharks that were now also swimming above us. The other divers were also filming and taking pictures. I looked at my diving computer to check the statistics. I was at 35 meters and I had around 11 minutes left at that depth without having to go into forced safety stops. I knew as soon as I went further up, that number would increase easily. I turned around to look at my dive buddy, but I could not see him next to me anymore. Where had he gone? Had he been washed away with the current? Or had he started to ascend? I looked up, down and around, I could not see him. All I saw were other divers and sharks; lots and lots of sharks.

More fear was building up inside of me. What should I do? Was I too exposed for the sharks and was that why my diving buddy had moved? My best guess was that he had also become scared and had gone even deeper, as it seemed that there were fewer sharks down there. It seemed reasonable and so I started to descend further, looking for him; 36 meters, 37, 38, 39, 40. I was reaching the limits of what I was allowed to do, and my computer started to beep and warn me that I was getting too deep. However, I was sure that I had to get deeper, to find him and to be safe from the sharks. 41 meters. 42… The visibility was less than a few meters. Suddenly I felt a super strong grip on my left leg. OMG! A shark must have grabbed me. I tried to kick backwards to shake off the shark, but I swiftly realized that it was not a shark, but my incredibly worried dive buddy. He held me with a firm grip, trying to pull me back up. Our computers were sounding off like crazy. Both of us were too deep and were running the risk of not having enough oxygen left.

What had happened? I came to my senses and realized I had gone too deep, so that the nitrogen had blurred my brain. Wow! Divers' depth sickness symptoms had just started to strike me. I started to be aware of my actual surroundings. Many of the other divers were watching us and two of them came swimming towards us to check whether everything was ok. I looked at my diving computer and it said I had only one minute left before having to do forced safety stops, and a total of only eight minutes of oxygen left in my tank. Even though my initial reaction was to panic, I stayed calm. I had to climb up meter by meter, without wasting too much energy and air. The higher up I went the more my allowed time under water would increase, and the relative time of air would go up as well. I looked up towards the pinnacle of the mountain, 25 meters further up from where we were. I could barely see the top, and the surface, which was another 15 meters further, I could not see at all. All I could see where dozens of sharks circling around chasing for smaller fish, and me having to be the first one of the divers to start ascending. Oh my gosh, I felt like I had the choice of either being eaten alive by the sharks, or running out of oxygen if I stayed down. I had no choice. I had to overcome my fear of the sharks and hope that they did not see me as bait on a fishing rod. Time was working against me but I could not ascend too fast, otherwise the increased amount of nitrogen would again let my body run into the risk for divers' sickness. I reached 30 meters, trying to move up slower than the bubbles of air I was exhaling, which was harder than one might imagine with the diving computer beeping to tell you to go up faster. I checked the numbers and they were improving slowly. I still had around eight minutes of air left, but the number of how much longer I was allowed to stay at that depth had "normalized" to four minutes. The further up I would go the better they get, but there were so many sharks and so little space. So much current with so little time left. It all didn't matter; I had to keep going if I did not want to drown.

My mind was clear again and the "fog" of being down too deep had disappeared. I had now reached the top of the underwater mountain. I still had 15 more meters left to go to reach the surface. I looked up and I could see the boat rocking on top of the waves at the end of the rope. I checked my computer once again right before grabbing the rope to drift upwards slowly. I had less than ten minutes of air left and the other number had become irrelevant, as I was now up far enough. Were there any sharks trying to attack me? I understood that my fears were completely unreasonable and none of the sharks even cared about me while they were chasing after the small fish. I was relieved. When I reached seven meters I checked my computer. I had around eight more minutes of air left and I would normally do a safety stop of only a couple of minutes. Since I had been down very deep I did not want to run any risk and decided to stay as long as possible at that level to wash out as much nitrogen from my blood as possible. One by one the other divers came up. Their tanks also nearing empty and they did their safety stops next to me. They all seemed quite worried and checked whether I was ok. I was, and also the current didn't seem to be as strong, or I had become accustomed to it – probably the latter.

After around ten minutes waiting there, my computer started to beep. It was the signal that I only had three minutes of air left. A few other divers were still coming up and I decided to ascend together with them. Slowly I reached five meters, then three meters and then popped up on the surface. Total

dive time: 51 minutes. Maximum depth: 43 meters. Yikes, I
had come so close to getting injured on this dive, but getting
so close to the sharks and experiencing the depth sickness
made it quite an incredible experience. I pulled my mask off,
and took a deep breath of fresh air. My dive buddy was already
on the boat, looking out to help me up. It had been a truly
memorable dive. The rest of the week was just as amazing,
but less nerve wracking. I had the opportunity to dive with
some of the greatest people and see some of the most unique
creatures of the ocean. I connected with the water and nature
like never before and I learned to switch off completely from
the busy world that normally surrounded me. Getting back
on land after being cut off from society for ten days was a very
special and actually overwhelming experience. Having over
a thousand unread emails, Whatsapp messages and missed
calls was a challenge in itself, not only because of the amount
of messages, but because I had developed the habit of not
needing to be connected to technology so much. It is amazing
what ten days of total disconnection can do to one's habits. I
would have never given up Internet for ten days, had I not
been forced to do it. The entire experience empowered me
more than anything else that year, as I learned that the earth
keeps spinning with or without me being online 24/7. Some
problems actually solved themselves without me intervening
and once I was back on, people were happier than ever before
to hear from me. I did not think this trip would ever teach me
valuable lessons for my life, but it did. I would like to share
the three most important ones with you:

The first lesson is to understand the power of habits.
They can be either good or bad, and in the case of my near-
addiction to the Internet, it was difficult to deny that this was
a bad habit. If you are also annoyed with a habit you have,
and you want to get rid of it – you have to REPLACE it with
something else. Simply giving it up will not be enough; you
will go back to it. Want to quit smoking, snacking or lying
on the couch? Find something to replace the bad habit, and
after around 2-3 weeks, the new habit will start setting in.

The first week is the hardest, just as it was on the boat for me when there was no Facebook or Email. But I managed to replace it with reading a book, writing in my journal and drawing. Replace smoking or snacking on chocolate, for example, with attractive, healthier alternatives that suit you. Later in the book you will see how efficient your day can be if you have certain rituals set up, especially in the morning and evening, and you will learn that, believe it or not, it is all programming in your mind.

The second lesson was to see the power of overcoming my fear of sharks by submerging myself with them face to face. The fear of sharks is to some extent driven by the media, but that knowledge did not help me when I was surfing in the water. Neither did the fact that I was more likely to be killed by a coconut or a car accident. You might not be scared of sharks, but I am sure you have fears too. It is extremely empowering to work on overcoming them, either through therapy or like I did, by going "all in". Please note that this advice is in no way meant to substitute that of a trained mental health professional. If you suffer addictions or phobias that are affecting your life, you should seek professional help. The most common fear is public speaking, which would actually be one of the best skills to develop, as you will see in a future chapter. Or, if you are afraid of flying on an airplane, heights, snakes, the dark, or anything else, your fear will be very limiting to whatever you want to do in life. Once you get over your fears, you will be a different person. For me diving with all these hammerhead sharks freed me mentally to enjoy every second of kitesurfing, without worrying unduly about a shark attack. Many fears are irrational, but that does not mean that they are not any less difficult to handle. Such fears exist, so it makes sense to tackle them, one step at a time. Just imagine being able to give a speech in front of a group of people, or to step on to that airplane without many worries. For some of you this might mean you need professional help, while for others, you could do what I did - overcome it by yourself confronting it face to face. Remember that the definition of courage is not having any fear, but rather, acknowledging that fear and dealing with it. So, have the courage to overcome your fears and live a free life.

Last but not least, the ten days of being completely disconnected from the online world showed me the power of taking time off. When I came back from the break I was so energized, more than I had been in a very long time. The human body and mind need to recharge every once in a while, but I did not believe that before I left. I thought I was still running at full speed. When I returned however, I knew what full speed actually meant. Suddenly I could work 18 hours a day again, seven days a week. From that year on, I have taken breaks of seven to ten days at least once or twice per year. It is important to shake things up completely during this off time. This means no computer, no phone, no Internet. Nothing that reminds you of your regular day that you would have throughout the rest of the year. I love going on a cruise, simply because it is as different as it gets, compared to my everyday life. I also know people who love to lie on a beach all day with a book in their hand. That would not be for me at all. A good friend of mine goes on a nine-day trekking trip two times per year to completely disconnect. Every person is different in regards to the type of timeout that is best for him or her, and there is no right or wrong way to do it. Time wise, I have come to find that nine to ten days is the perfect time span for me. Shorter than that and I do not relax fully. Longer than that and I become bored during the last days. Your needs might be different, and you might have to try different lengths to find what works best. Understand that while you might think you are losing time while you are gone, you will actually make up for it threefold when you are back with all your energy. On top of that, it will allow for some things to resolve on their own, even without you being around. That should be a great feeling as well. If you fail to re-energize, your ability to work at full capacity will be affected, or in a worst-case scenario, you may even suffer from "burn-out". This may take months to redress. So, remember: Be in work mode 100% when it is time to do so, but also be 100% in play mode when it is time for that. Taking some time off is wonderful, and you should make every effort to build this into your life. Your body and your mind will thank you for it.

What I want you to do right now is to write down one habit that you want to replace at this very moment, and most important – with what? You will be amazed how powerful this will be, and your personal growth will be stunning doing just this one thing. Take action NOW.

SPACE FOR MY TAKE AWAYS

19.

THE CRAZY STORY -
LIES DON'T TRAVEL FAR

"True forgiveness is when you can say, "Thank you for that experience." – Oprah Winfrey

So far I have shared only a little of my personal life, and most of it was about my childhood or later on partying. Interestingly, totally contrary to my wild time stories that I shared before, I had always been more of a relationship person. However, I firmly believe in "playing the field" when not with a partner, but keeping it together and being loyal when being in a committed relationship. My mom mistakenly told some of my stories of my in-between-relationship-times to my girlfriends, which resulted in quite some follow-up discussions, as you can imagine. Yep, my mom loves me, but sometimes she doesn't know when to keep quiet. Anyways, my first two serious relationships were during the times while I was studying medicine, kitesurfing, and playing basketball. You might be wondering how I managed to fit in a relationship, or maybe why? Why bring sand to the beach… Literally speaking. While you might be right wondering why I would not be non-stop partying and sleeping around during all the kitesurfing trips (which I did during the times I was not in a committed relationship), I want to reiterate how important efficiency and consistency had always been in my life. This might sound weird, but it was really great knowing there was someone you could always go back to. Plus, I have always had quite forgiving girlfriends, when it came to not having much time left to spend with them

– which was one of the reasons my relationships actually lasted considerably long.

In Brazil in 2008, I was "sleeping-off" my 2nd relationship there, but afterwards I wanted to bring more stability back into my life again. Before I shared this more from a financial and business perspective so far, but his story will be about my personal life during the years 2008 to 2010, when I was dating my 3rd girlfriend. It won't be until 2011 until I get to meet the wonderful person I am together with now, but more about that in the next story. After my trip to Cocos I returned to my regular life, which meant kitesurfing and developing my first business. I then went to Canada for a tour-stop of the kitesurfing world cup and that was where I met my now ex-girlfriend, who was one of the staff at the event. I would post her name here, but I do not know her real name after being together with her for almost three years. Yes, you read correctly. This may sound crazy, and it is - as Bette Davis's character said in the film, *All About Eve*, "Fasten your seatbelts; it's going to be a bumpy night". Have you ever heard stories about people talking in interviews about others they thought they had known, but when a completely unexpected turn of events happened they could only say: "Wow, I would have never seen that coming; he/she always seemed so nice!" I am sure you have, and after reading this upcoming story you probably also would say: "Oh gee, come on Julian, you must have noticed something odd about the woman you were sleeping with for three years!" Well trust me, even though I was together with that girl for so long, neither me, nor anyone around me knew who she really was. I learned, after the fact, hat she was a mother of three, an ex-convict, and, if not a diagnosed psychopath, someone whose behavior was very typical of one. Claiming to be different persons in several separate lives, committing serious crimes through credit card fraud, smuggling, and identity theft. Neither my parents, my best friends, nor my kitesurfing buddies; none of us, although we spent a serious amount of time with her, noticed what was really going on or saw her true character – until afterwards.

So how did it all happen? Boy meets girl. Girl says she is working as a pilot for Air Canada but is tired of her job and wants to start travelling. Boy says: "How awesome, I am a pro kitesurfer, let's travel the world together!" Girl says: "How fun, but before that, let me take you on a plane ride so you see that I am telling the truth". No, she did not say that, but before we left Canada she offered to hop on a small private plane and show me the local kitespots from the air. The crazy thing about this part was that she did not even have a pilot's license: a fact that I figured out later. I don't know how she managed to get us onto that little turbo-prop-plane, but I assume it was through her professional identity theft skills. Have you ever met a stranger, and just because of one small detail you start to trust that person? Her telling me that she was a pilot reminds me of the movie, "Catch me if you can", where Leonardo DiCaprio's character assumes the identity of a pilot and uses this to build trust, and this also worked on me. Looking back I should have never gotten on that plane with her. Surprisingly even though she had no license, she actually knew how to fly. I have to admit it was one of the most incredible experiences, flying in that little plane. I was even allowed to fly it myself for a while. We did some other crazy stuff in the air that I cannot put into print otherwise the book may get an XXX rating, so I leave that to your imagination.

Getting to see all the kitespots from mid-air was incredibly impressive and I have never experienced anything like that again since. Aside of her claiming to be a pilot, everything else of what she told me also fit together: She was driving a fairly expensive car and living in a very comfortable Villa – of course, since she said that she was a pilot it made sense that she could afford all that. There was one odd thing right at the beginning though, when we left for the airport. She just left. What I mean is there was a strange feeling of finality and no mention of when she would return; she just packed two bags and left everything else behind. Just like that. On top of that we left in quite a hurry, which surprised me because I had assumed she would want to say good-bye to family and friends, whom I did not even meet. She was quite good at telling the fanciest stories about all kinds of things. When we arrived at the airport she stopped her car right in front of the check-in area and told me that as an Air Canada pilot she would have valet parking. Golly… I was so naïve! Later I realized that she had left so quickly because her creditors were catching up to her, and so she had to leave as quickly as possible.

While travelling in Europe she always had a mess with her different passports. I asked her about why she had so many different ones and she responded that this was because of the English-French duality in Canada and her having Indian roots. I cannot really recall the actual reasoning but it made sense back then and she seemed to be the friendliest and most caring person, so why doubt her? All my friends and family liked her and thought she was a "nice girl", well at least most of the time. Sometimes she had these weird freak-outs, which seemed to come out of nowhere. Looking back, they happened mostly when plans changed unexpectedly. For example, one time we were supposed to meet up after I had finished going to the gym. I decided to surprise her by showing up a bit earlier and bringing take-out Italian food. She had a major tantrum! Looking back I am certain she had to cover up some fishy business that she was organizing and I almost caught her in the act. Another time, things could not be arranged as she wanted them, so she suddenly developed extremely strong headaches, which today I am also very sure were just faked. My poor sister had to take her to the hospital several times (sorry about that sis…) for check-ups. She did not want to be hospitalized but as soon as my family and I made the arrangements that she wanted in the first place, her headaches stopped. What a miraculous cure, but none of us suspected anything. Many people mock me about all these months and years, claiming they would have noticed straight away – trust me, other than one incident, she never really harmed my family or me directly, and I think that was why she managed to pull it off. She never showed any bad feeling towards us, or we likely would actually have sensed it. One time however, she could have destroyed my life.

We were on our way back from Australia. While I was stopping over to visit some friends in Singapore, she claimed that she wanted to meet a pilot-friend in Indonesia. Whether she actually went there or whom she actually met, I have absolutely no idea. We met up again in Singapore a few days later. In the cab to Changi Airport she asked me: "Honey, can you take one of my two bags? I am only allowed to take one as hand luggage and you can take four bags." Sure I would, what a question. She was my girlfriend, right? I was flying in First Class and had my HON Circle status, which gave me almost unlimited baggage allowance. She was using her "cheaper Pilot tickets", where she was mostly booked on standby and was not sure to get on the actual flight. So she was mostly only carrying one piece of hand luggage. It was a no-brainer for me to take her other bag, as I am sure you would agree. Only later did I find out she had made up the "Pilot tickets" story and was actually using stolen credit cards to pay for the tickets. The reason she was flying different routes was probably to avoid suspicions or to get her "business" done at these locations. At the airport I took her brown bag and went to the check-in together with three bags of my own. I had 150 kilos of luggage since I had three surfboards, eight kites and clothes with me. For some reason my ex seemed worried. Maybe she thought I would be charged extra, but the check-in agent did not flinch, and tagged all four bags on my name without hesitation. We waited for the bags to disappear on the luggage belt and her mood lifted again. Maybe I was just imagining all of it, I thought.

While she was flying via Bangkok, I enjoyed the First Class flight on the A380 directly to Munich. Since I arrived a few hours before her I went to wait for her at the First Class Lounge, where I could do some work and freshen up. When she arrived, she was quite surprised to meet me at the gate, and not at the baggage claim area or outside of the security part of the airport. She was worried that someone had taken my luggage in all these hours and she started getting nervous again. I told her that one of the lounge agents had called the luggage handler after I had arrived to inform them that I was not coming out until a few hours later. It did not calm her down, which surprised me. She knew from past experiences that they would store the luggage safely until I was able to pick it up. We went to the luggage storage together, and I asked to pick up the four pieces. It took a few minutes for them to bring them to me. When I turned around, my ex-girlfriend was not there anymore. Where the heck had she gone? That very moment I received a text message from her, telling me she had already left the security-area and was waiting at the taxi transfer. What? Why would she not help me with the luggage? It was not the first time that I had taken one of her bags, but she had been acting extremely weird this time. Maybe she was still tired from the flight?

I walked towards the exit channel. One was red where you had to go to claim something, the other one was green, which was the one I took. Since I always had a lot of luggage it was normal that a police inspector or security personal stopped me and inquired where I was coming from and why I had so much luggage. I always had my Austrian passport ready to show them I was just "coming home". While walking through the green channel, I did get stopped. "Sir, may I ask whether you are carrying taxable items with you?" the agent asked. A few years later when reflecting on the entire incident I learned that high-tech security cameras were picking up every reaction I was making during this questioning. A team of highly trained analysts would then see if I showed any signs of lying, abnormal level of insecurity or nervousness. Of course it is normal for anyone to feel uncomfortable during such a confrontation, but any innocent citizen will behave quite rationally. The security cameras with a team of body language experts were scanning me without me knowing it, while I gave him my passport and replied: "I am just coming back from Australia and I am a professional surfer. I live in

Austria and I have nothing to claim as everything belonged to me already when I was leaving to Australia." Aside of my ex-girlfriend's bag that was 100% the truth and I was not thinking of her bag at all. The officer looked at my four bags and the large surfboards on the luggage trolley. They looked a bit dirty and sandy. I was wearing flip-flops, shorts, was tanned and the salty water had bleached my long blond hair. I fit the story. "So how were the waves?" he inquired. I would learn later that officers were trained to ask such random questions out of the blue, to check how my reaction would be. In order to save time and not having to pull out everyone, they would rather ask such a "surprise-question" and have their team in the back analyze a person's response. "Oh man, they were freaking awesome, some of the best surf in my life", I responded and my face lit up. It was the truth. The four weeks in Western Australia and The Gold Coast had been a blast and I had enjoyed some of the best surf and wind of the year. "Welcome home", the officer replied, handed me back my passport and waved the next passenger over. His team must have informed him via headset that I was telling the truth.

I was telling the truth, but at the same time I might have been lying, since I had absolutely no idea what was in my ex-girlfriend's bag. As soon as I was through the security channel, she came towards me, and took her luggage off the cart. "Great, now that I am already at the taxi, she was willing to help", I was thinking, but didn't take further notice. On the drive home she had the bag right next to her in the passenger compartment. There was enough space in the back of the shuttle, so I assumed she had it there because she wanted to change her clothes or whatever. Arriving in Innsbruck, I expected the two of us to relax for a few days after all the travel during the last months. Surprisingly, she told me that an old friend of hers was in Italy and she would leave straight away for a few days to meet with her. I was surprised to find out about that on such short notice, but since I would then meet with friends myself, it didn't bother me very much. After her trip to Italy I never saw the brown bag again. Although I never found out what was in the bag, her behavior was very strange, and I suspect that I may have I dodged a bullet there, especially after getting her "full background" afterwards. I am pretty sure she tricked me into smuggling something for her from Asia to Europe. She must have known that someone could only pass through so easily when travelling on a local passport and the security cameras were not picking up any suspicious activity. She had absolutely no risk since she sneaked through with just one piece of hand luggage. If it existed, I was the one carrying the actual "problem-bag" and if anything had happened at the checkpoint, she would no doubt have disappeared into thin air, since she had already walked through ahead of me. So what do I think was in her bag? I am not really sure, but I doubt it was drugs. They pop up too easily with all the screenings and sniffer dogs. Maybe it was a bunch of stolen credit cards, passports or actual cash – or all of the above. Something that does not show up in a bag screen, but would raise some serious concerns if the bag were opened for inspection. The above items would fit, as she was and probably still is involved in these crimes today. In Europe she may have been passing the money on to other parties or selling the credit cards and identifications to other criminals. But again, this is all supposition, albeit based on some strong behavioral evidence. I just know that I am more than happy that nothing bad happened that time. The next time you carry a bag for someone else, think back to my story here. Believe me, I do every time, even though, I would still take a bag from my girlfriend any time she asks me.

So what happened to the both of us? The relationship was destined to fail. It would just be a matter of time before I found out about her criminal activities, when her web of lies began to unravel. Had I actually paid more attention during the first two years of our relationship, I would have noticed it a lot earlier. Sometimes me confronting her with some of the inconsistencies she was trying to tell me, ended in her slapping or hitting me. One time in Egypt it was so bad that the hotel management had to call security. She was yelling and going off in front of the bathroom door, shouting and screaming at me. Imagine the scene, when a quite pretty and naked girl is hammering at the bathroom door trying to get to you, and all you hope is that the door is strong enough for her not to get in. When staff arrived they were amazed to find me, and not her, locked up in the bathroom. In one of her freak-outs she had bruised and scratched me so much that this was my only place of refuge. I am pretty sure that the staff had assumed that it was happening the opposite way when other hotel guests had called them to come and check, as they had heard screaming and yelling in our room. I tried to break up with her over and over again but to extend our relationship she was using crazier and crazier tactics: One time I was in Mauritius for a video shoot when my parents surprised me with a call and told me that my ex was with them. I had told them not to let her into the house and to change the passcode for the front door. She said that her father and brother had died in a boating accident. Even though I had never met them, I felt sorry and worried. And not only myself; everyone that I knew who heard the news started to support her – of course, this makes sense – but only if it had actually happened. We found out later that she just made up that lie to buy herself some time. It worked for her, and instead of breaking up in the fall of 2010, her ruse kept me in tow for a little longer. The break-up eventually happened a few months later in early 2011. Social Media helped me notice what was really going on, when suddenly her location on her Facebook status did not match the story she was telling me. She had told me she would be in London visiting a friend, but her Facebook just said that she had just eaten in a restaurant in France. When I asked her about these inconsistencies she had another tantrum. My family and friends called me insensitive but I kept telling them that I had reached the end of my rope and she had to go. Eventually I forced her to pack all her stuff, used my miles to book her a one-way flight back to Canada and had a good friend take her to the airport. Finally she was gone.

It was a big relief at first, but then something strange happened. First, the airline refunded the miles back on to my account, telling me the flight had not been taken. What? Then her email account started bouncing, her Facebook profile was gone and her Whatsapp never showed that she had read any of my further messages. I understand some people needing distance from the other person after a break up, but even common friends all over the world started to write to me to ask about her whereabouts. A few days later, some light was shed upon the mystery – and it was not pleasant. I received a call from a friend in Australia who told me that her credit card had just been misused for over US$25,000 for rental cars, flight bookings, hotels and expensive clothes. A few hours later, another friend in Germany told me that her credit card company had blocked her card after bookings were made for expensive goods in Florida. Another US$10,000 gone. I received two more emails from people who had all lost tens of thousands of dollars to her in credit card fraud. All of these statements and receipts showed my ex-girlfriend's name. I was in shock. I immediately blocked all my credit cards, changed my passwords and told my close friends and family members to do the same. Police reports were filed, interviews were taken and the picture became sickeningly clear. Still, it was not even close to what I would find out next, after receiving an unexpected phone call from someone very close to her.

As mentioned earlier, I had never met neither her friends, nor family in person. This had been her method of preventing me from finding out about her true nature. So you can understand my surprise when I suddenly received a phone call asking me: "Hi, am I speaking to Julian?"

"Yes", I answered.

"This is your ex-girlfriend's mom. I tried to reach out to you earlier, but never managed to. I have a lot of things to tell you!"

She certainly did. We were on the phone for over two hours. Afterwards I felt like I needed therapy to help me overcome what I had just found out. My ex-girlfriend had always been a troublemaker, repeatedly getting into trouble with the law. As mentioned above, she was the mother of three children, but she was not allowed to see them due to her criminal acts and her dangerous influence on them. The police had been trying to find her for years, but she managed to change names, switch identities and pull off the same frauds over and over again. Nothing about what I thought I knew about her was true: neither her age, her name, her profession, nor any of her other stories. It was unbelievable back then and still is today, knowing I had been quite close to this person for almost three years and I did not know her one little bit. It took me quite some time to get over that. Not to get over her – that didn't take me much longer than an instant, but getting over having been deceived and lied to in such a brutal and manipulative way. How could I ever trust anyone else again? I thought that it would take me a while to do that. But a few months later, in mid-2011, I met someone who showed me that you CAN trust other people; my partner, Bettina. And I have been with her ever since. I have never heard back from my ex-girlfriend and it is probably for the best. I just know that she will continue to steal from and dupe people until she is stopped. They even have a website now to warn others about her, but I know she is still doing her thing. What can I say? Lies don't travel far - they have short legs!

I hope this story is not one to which you can relate directly, but that it will teach you some valuable life lessons if you read in between the lines. The most important take away should be that you have to learn to accept the past being the past. This may seem like a horror story or a fiction, but actually living it is 100 times harder than just reading it here in this book. So of course, I could tell myself to never trust someone else, or decide that I will never fall in love because I will get hurt, or I will never take my girlfriend's bag. But that would mean remaining in the past and therefore not progressing forward. Of course I started to become more careful in certain things, but it has not inhibited my lifestyle. I meet so many people who get hurt once, and then never ever try something new, in fear they get hurt again. No matter whether it is losing money on a business deal, getting one's heart broken in a relationship or getting disappointed by a "friend". Although these things are horrible, you have to accept that you cannot change them. They are your past. Be thankful for the experience and the lessons you take away so you can become a better person. If I was able to forgive my ex-girlfriend for all the trouble and stress she had caused me, then you can do the same for whatever you are upset about from your past. Accept the things you cannot change, learn from them, and focus on having a better outcome the next time. Not for their best, but for your own.

Second, I learned to never judge a person or situation if you are not in it yourself. This story taught me that it was nearly impossible to ever say "This would never happen to me" or "Oh my gosh, why did you not realize that". It is easy to judge and connect the dots in retrospect, but it is a totally different story when you are actually part of the action. Many people read or hear stories about others reacting seemingly irrationally towards certain happenings, but let me tell you this: There is a reason why the U.S. army has the rule of never judging a battle situation that they have not been in themselves. It is simply very hard to do, even though it might look easy and straightforward for an outsider. So the next time you feel tempted to judge someone else's situation, pause for a moment, and consider whether you as an outsider have the right or the knowledge to make such a judgment.

The third lesson is also a famous quote from Mark Twain's notebook (1894): "If you tell the truth you don't have to remember anything". A web of lies will inevitably collapse sooner or later, and if you don't want the people around you to leave you and call you untrustworthy, it is best to stick to the truth – even though it might hurt sometimes. Many times people say that I am too upfront and that I should sometimes be more soft spoken in conversations or answering questions. They might be right, but I believe people should know what they are getting into with me – what they see is what they get. No hidden agendas. Especially in one of the upcoming stories about my travel to Asia, you will learn how awkward it is when you talk to people and they lie to your face, just to avoid hurting you with the truth. I understand, different cultures, different rules. However one thing that I found also in the Asian culture, where "face" is extremely important, is that successful business people here will always be very straight and upfront. Take this to heart: If you want to be successful in the long term, you must understand that nothing builds better than the truth. Lies will not get you very far.

In my life I have met thousands of people, and only a very small percentage of them have been really bad. The world is good and wants to be good. If you look for the bad, you will find the bad – If you look for the good however, you will find the good. So it came as no surprise that the girl I met a couple of months later would become the girl of my dreams! Had I dwelled on the past, not forgiving my ex-girlfriend, or myself, I would have been stuck and not been open for this new relationship. In order to move to the next chapter of your life, you have to leave the previous one. If you are struggling to do so, use this inspiration to truly forgive someone, and let the past be the past. Take action now and be open for exciting things to enter your life

SPACE FOR MY TAKE AWAYS

20.

THE RELATIONSHIP STORY - FINDING TRUE LOVE

"Cause all of me, Loves all of you,
Love your curves and all your edges
All your perfect imperfections
Give your all to me, I'll give my all to you
You're my end and my beginning
Even when I lose I'm winning
'Cause I give you all of me
And you give me all of you!" – John Legend

Cleaning up the mess my ex-girlfriend had left took some time in early 2011 and some people probably would have never managed to forget. I am happy to say that I was able to put it behind me after several months, as otherwise I could not have experienced that year as the wonderful as it turned out to be. In my life so far, I have had a couple of "leapfrog years". These are years where I experienced, compared to the other years, a huge leap forward. The leapfrog years did not just happen; they were the result of all the groundwork I had put in leading up to those years. 1999/2000 was my first leapfrog year, at age 13, when I had the most progress in basketball. 2003/2004 had been my intellectual break-through year. I had excellent SAT scores and I was sailing smoothly through my medical studies. 2007/2008 was my break-through year in kiteboarding. Doing the math, it seems that I was having "leapfrog years" every four years or so. All my basketball training, studying, or kitesurfing efforts were finally paying off during those times. I previously mentioned that I finished my medical studies in 2010 and started to get ready for other fields, especially business. The last six stories in the book will focus on these years from 2011 culminating in 2015, the year I wrote this book. As you might imagine, 2011 was one of those leapfrog years... and 2015 seems to be another (more about that in my final story).

2011 was my apex in kiteboarding and I managed to gradually shift my life more into business. I was finishing my "Kiteboarding Tricktionary" book and I re-negotiated better kitesurfing contracts with my partner companies. I had started to apply the business lessons I had learned into my life, which resulted in my highest income in one year up to that point. For my 24th birthday, I received a wonderfully designed wine-cuvee set as a "Thank-You" gift from Lufthansa Airlines for extending my HON Circle VIP membership. Everything was going great that year and so at the end of May, being back from lots of travelling, I decided to call up some friends and celebrate. I had been enjoying the single life for the last couple of months, and I was doing my fair share of partying. We had great fun that evening, first at my place in Mils in Austria, and then when hitting the city center of Innsbruck. After a few glasses of wine, I was quite buzzed. The others always made fun of me, since I was such a sissy drinker – but so what? At least I never had to spend much money on alcohol to get hammered. Haha!

While dancing with a light buzz in one of the most popular clubs in Innsbruck, I noticed a girl with very dark hair and a huge tattoo on her back. Normally I did not like tattoos, but hers seemed really interesting, almost as if telling a story (which it actually does). I was slightly under the influence and so it came easy to walk over to her and say 'Hi'. We chatted briefly and then I remembered one of the key sales lessons I had learned in business: always make the customer feel as if it is not a 100% certainty that they can have the desired "product" – it will only make them want it more. My girlfriend firmly insists that this is not how it actually happened, but this is the way I remember it, and this book is about being as truthful as my memory permits. At some point, my girlfriend may decide to publish her side of the tale. What I did next was what I call the ideal go-getter technique: "The-Take-Away-Pick-Up". Sounds like a line from Barney Stinson's (*How I Met Your Mother*) playbook, but it is an original "Julian". I said, to her: "I would be looking for a place to stay over for the night - what a pity that I have a girlfriend, so it won't happen!"

So, that girl I was hitting on back then is now my girlfriend, and her name is Bettina. Up until today she claims that it totally turned her off, but if so, why did we end up getting together? I am sure part of it was my take-away tactic in the pick-up line but also, because she is a smart woman, she could probably see that there was more to me than just that. After talking a bit more we exchanged Facebook details and had some more fun dancing together. We did not sleep together that night; I suspect that she knew my strategy, and played "hard to catch". We stayed in touch and met again a few days later. What can I say? Boy meets girl. Boy clicks with girl and girl clicks with boy. Similar interests and focus. We fell in love – wonderful. That is the short version of the beginning of a now over four-year, ongoing, and fantastic relationship. I was still travelling a lot for kitesurfing so I was not in Austria much, but when I was, we spent a lot of time together having fun as a couple doing sports and other activities. The hilarious thing is that while we met each other partying, we haven't partied in that way since. Neither one of us actually likes the wild nightlife. I feel it is really important to make it clear in a relationship from the start what you really want, and that was one of the major points. Do not fake being someone else. It will only work for the short term. So, even though we met through partying, we both made it clear that this is not what either one of us really enjoyed.

A few months after we started dating I was supposed to fly to Oman to hold a kitesurfing camp there together with a group of kitesurfers. Martin, my friend and photographer had joined me many times in the past on these kite camps, but due to some work engagements he couldn't come that time. I needed someone to take photos and since Bettina is a quick learner, I asked her whether she wanted to fly with me on a paid vacation to Oman. The only catch: She had to learn how to take photos and film videos within the next couple of weeks. She was open to it and so we flew to Oman and Dubai for two weeks. It was her first time flying First Class and she could not believe that I slept through the entire flight and did not take advantage of the service. It probably was my 100th flight or so in the upper deck, and it had lost some of its special touch to me. What a sad thing to think, looking back. We had a blast and the photos turned out to be quite good too. Most important to me however was the fact that Bettina and I got along, even when together 24/7. Many couples are fine being together for a few hours, but putting them into a room for days together and throwing in long-haul flights is a pretty good test of a relationship.

She was really special to me and so I wanted to make sure things were working out between the two of us in all kinds of environments. Being apart for weeks while travelling? It worked. Being together for weeks, backpacking and moving in and out of hotel rooms every day? It worked. Similar interests? Yes. Sporty? Yes. So, I was quite confident that even after the 3-month "honeymoon" phase, the time of the initial love-crush, we would be a great fit. I am by no means a relationship expert, but if I can give anyone only one relationship tip, then it would be that the base of your relationship has to be solid and working well. If the base is not good, just like anything else, a relationship will inevitably fall apart. However, never forget that a good relationship is hard work, almost like a good business. If you do not put energy into it, it will never work out, no matter how good the base is. Many people tend to forget these two requirements, and either they invest time and energy into a relationship without a proper base, or they fail to continuously work on their relationship, even though there is a good base. A lot of Bettina's and my friends call our relationship "perfect". Actually it isn't, we each have our rough edges. We did make sure however the base was good and we never stop working on our relationship. So despite not considering myself as an expert, I want to share with you what I found are the things that make our relationship great.

First, I want to give you some tips about having the right base. Keep in mind that every couple is different, so some might work well for you, and others won't at all. I feel that in a long-term relationship, not only the couple should get along, but also the bigger family. With that I mean getting along with each other's parents and brothers or sisters. My former girlfriends had always found my parents very easy to get along with, sometimes too easy as you may have noticed in the previous chapter, and aside from my mom's loose tongue about stories from my past, she has always treated any of my ex girlfriends as part of the family. At the beginning of our relationship, Bettina had told me that her dad had "put down" a few of her ex's, so I was a bit fearful the first time I was invited over to their house for a BBQ. Picture the scene, me coming up their driveway, imaging that this afternoon would turn out like a clip from the movie "Meet the Fockers". I would be put down and ridiculed. Well, none of that happened. I got along really well, not only with her parents, but also with her brother. Also, when the two sets of parents met, it was equally great, like one big, happy family. I had ex-girlfriends where that was not the case, which had always created a sense of unease. I don't know how your family situations are with regards to your personal relationship, or whether the idea of your families getting along with each other is actually important to you, but for us that was a big green light when we decided to take this relationship to the next level.

Another important factor to me is having common interests. These can be sports, music, art, games, computers or anything you enjoy doing. I am not a big fan of doing everything together, but I do believe that having certain common hobbies will help couples bond and avoid living separate lives. One very nice thing Bettina and I do regularly is going for a morning run, a beautiful mountain hike or a stroll by the sea, now that we are currently living in Hong Kong. We don't do that every day, but knowing that there are activities that we can enjoy together, helps us bond even more. If you are extremely athletic and energetic, but your partner prefers to stay at home, watch movies or play computer, I personally think each one of you would rather spend time with other people, than with each other. To a certain degree that might be ok, but I think it is important for a healthy relationship to have a common denominator with your partner. I do spend a fair amount of time travelling, and when I am at home, I also want to spend time with friends and business associates. One of the top factors that kill a relationship (aside of cheating of course, which is absolutely unacceptable!) is jealousy. If Bettina were to constantly check up on me, read my Whatsapp messages or check my phone calls, I would not be able to be together. And she feels the same. Trust is a two-way street and needs to be built mutually over time. Jealousy pops up if one partner stops fully trusting the other. If you are ok with that, or that is even what you like, then that is fine of course. For example I have this good buddy who is married to a South American girl, and she flies into a rage if he is just 30 minutes late, or does not pick up her phone call instantly. It would totally freak me out, but he loves her overly "caring" character, which I would rather sense as "possessive". Again, there is no right and wrong, it is just that you need to be aware of what you want, and make sure that this is what you actually have.

Bettina and I do a fair amount of activities and travelling together, and while sometimes it is just the two of us, many times it is together with other friends or business associates. In past relations I did not get along with my ex-girlfriends' friends, which was quite awkward when going out for lunch or a drink. I am not a very social guy in the first place, but then spending time with people that have totally different interests than me, is a total relationship killer. You do not have to become best friends with your partner's friends or vice versa, but it helps if you can also have a great laugh together every once a while. Yes, there will always be some friends (Bettina's, or mine) whose company one of us can do without, but in general it works out well. One of my best friends used to have a girlfriend that over the course of three years I have only seen once or twice in total. This was because she didn't like being around us, who she called, "those kind of people", whatever that meant.

Another important base to cover at the beginning is for each of you to share your focus and general plans in life. Do you want to get married, and if yes, when? Children? How many and when? Here is a tip if you are reading this and you are younger than 25: Live your life! Do not get attached too early, as you risk later on feeling like you are missing out. A common reason for people having the so-called mid-life crises is because they feel their time is limited on this planet and they are scared of having missed out on experiences. If you ever get the chance to talk to my mom over coffee, she (to my embarrassment) will gladly share the stories when I was lining up girls in front of the house, living room, garden and my own room, so I could juggle back and forth with five or six girls on the same day. I have to admit, having had these crazy experiences while travelling but also at home gives me peace of mind that I have had great life experiences. If you are reading this at the age of 17, and you are in love for the first or second time, and you feel it will last forever, believe me, with my first girlfriend I thought the same, but trust me, live your life, follow your heart and only commit when YOU feel ready, not when others, including partner, say so. Your older self will thank you for it.

If you are slightly older, just like me right now at the age of 29, and you are looking for, or are already in a serious and committed relationship, you should get together with your partner and talk about what you both want: your plans and your focus, as discussed above. I still remember how Bettina asked me quite early in our relationship whether I wanted to have children, and by what age. It was an uncomfortable question back then, but a smart one. So what are our plans on this? Over the next couple of years we want to grow our businesses, and then start a family preferably before the age of 35. Then we plan to take some time off from work (not fully, just to focus on the children more) for the next 5-10 years, and then return to work full on.

Do you have a ten- or even twenty-year plan for yourself or your family? You will read in one of the next chapters how important this is. If you don't have a clear goal and plan in mind, you run the risk of simply drifting and missing important opportunities in your life. This brings me to an important point. Do you and your partner agree on your focus and plan? I have a good friend in London who told me his experience with a girl he would have loved to date for a longer period of time. He is extremely focused on business and being productive, while she was taking a year off from university and not doing much, other than partying and hanging out with friends. This worked only for a couple of weeks, which was not what he wanted. He would have preferred a long-term solution. If one of you is totally into personal development, just like Bettina and I both are, but the other is not, it is a given that after a few months you will no longer be a good match. If one wants children, and the other doesn't, one will be unhappy. Goals and plans can differ for brief periods in time, but the long-term visions about work, family, and life-style for both of you should be similar.

I know that I have mentioned it already, but I feel that sex is an important part of a relationship. It is a topic that is often brushed under the carpet in conversations between couples. If there are issues in this area, and these are not discussed, this inevitably leads to problems within the whole relationship and the possibility of partners cheating. Although you may not feel comfortable discussing sex, you need to discuss issues like the level of intimacy you share, the type of sex you both prefer, and the frequency. You might be surprised how many sexual fantasies are out there that do not get fulfilled. Do you know your partner's fantasies? But often times, these are not shared, due to fear of rejection. A good friend of mine in Asia has a girlfriend, that I am 99% sure he will break up with, just because they are not a sexual fit. She likes it soft, while he is more interested in bondage games. So what happens? He cheats on her to fulfill his sexual fantasies, and I personally think the only solution in the long run is to end such a relationship. Bettina and I are very open about sex. In our monthly relationship meetings (yes, we have that), we always reflect on this topic, as well as many others of course.

Last but not least on the list of things I love to cover as a good base for a relationship, are your methods of communication and the fire in your character. Bettina and I literally never argue. There might be a small disagreement once a month or so, but never a big fight or argument. Both of us have relatively calm characters and want to make it work. A good friend of mine in Hong Kong genuinely fights with his girlfriend once a day. He says he needs it. If she doesn't scream at him or he doesn't get to scream back, he doesn't get to have make-up sex, and this is what he wants. Their relationship seems to be going extremely well, but just because their way of arguing and communication fits. I couldn't handle that, and neither could Bettina. So if you prefer a peaceful and harmonious partnership, then make that clear to your partner, if you prefer it to be wild and fiery, do that as well. No matter how good your base, your relationship will never work out in the long run if you don't put effort into it. Bettina and I have been together now for over four years and the most important difference compared to my past relationships is that both of us are putting in a lot of work. Yes, the base is good, but if we only relied on that I am sure we would not have made it more than a year. I understood that I had to treat my relationship as seriously as I was treating a business. A business, no matter how good its foundation, will fail if you don't continuously work at it. How do we do it? I feel it is really simple, and I am sure most of you actually know these things, but knowing is of no use without execution and action.

Throughout the day we do little things for each other. These little things make a big difference. For example since I normally get up a bit before her I use that time to spoil her with a freshly made cappuccino. We also write each other little love messages on Whatsapp throughout the day. Remember, what you think about, you bring about. So, if you think about your partner, and write to him or her, it will inevitably bring you closer together. Every once in a while I leave little notes on the table or I send her an email with a funny picture. Think about it. These are gestures that take you just two or three minutes, and if you set yourself regular reminders on your smartphone or computer it will be an easy and automated process that brings great value to your relationship but only take very little effort. It is important that you and your partner are on the same page with this, because a friend of mine in the U.S. sometimes doesn't talk to his girlfriend for a week when he is travelling. Both of them are cool with that, so it works. I had similar experiences with ex-girlfriends too, but sending a few love-messages a day, has cemented my relationship with Bettina a lot.

A healthy relationship is always a mixture of give and take. While you should give without expecting something in return, the relationship will not work in the long run if only one of you is stepping up "to the plate". So, yes, I do give to Bettina without expecting anything in return, yet she gives back equally. I feel this is important and I probably could not be in a relationship where that is not the case, even though we do not keep count. Whenever we part, we kiss each other as if we might not see each other again. It is something that has been imprinted in me when realizing how quickly life can be over. I believe it is crucial not to part in anger but always in love. I cannot remember one time that I had ever parted with someone in anger, and didn't regret it just soon after. If you truly love your partner, sort things out always before leaving. If you are travelling as much as I do, it helps if you bring back little gifts from your travels. It does not have to be anything big. For example from one of my trips I brought Bettina a Hard-Rock-Café-Stuffed-Animal. It was a silly little gift, but she loves it and always has it right beside the bed when I am gone.

One thing that has brought great value to our relationship is a weekly relationship lunch. How does that work? Once a week we have a romantic lunch together. Just the two of us. If you don't have the luxury like we do to being able to schedule your day as you want, then maybe do it on the weekend. If you have children, make sure you carve out some time for the two of you at least once or twice a month: just the two of you, so you get to talk about things you could not talk about with children around. And if you do get to spend this rare time together, make it count. We have a rule of not using the phone or computer during that time. It is just the two of us. We pick lunch because we hardly ever eat dinner to avoid big evening meals. We choose a different place every time and have lots of fun doing so. If you are on a tight budget and you can't afford to eat out often, do another regular activity together – just the two of you. This could be sports, or cooking at home, or art, or a hike, or whatever takes your fancy. Spend a few hours of quality time together every week. Use this time to reflect on what has been going on. Listen to the other person and make sure that your partner understands that you care. If you can, dress up nicely for each other. At work or with friends you would always dress your best, so do the same for your partner!

We also do monthly and annual things on a regular basis. As mentioned briefly earlier, once a month Bettina, who is the self-appointed and undeniable relationship-appointee (whatever that means), calls for a relationship meeting. I always have to come prepared, like I would for a business presentation. We would go through a couple of points about things that we should improve and make plans for the next few months. We talk about what is on our bucket-list and if we are missing big things from the other person. No phones or computers are allowed during these events – it is not so much about quantity rather than quality. All in all, it is basically time we spend for ourselves, and personally I feel it is one of the key factors why our relationship has been going so well. Think of a well-run company – you would do the same thing there too. Daily updates, weekly meetings, monthly scheduling. And if you see your relationship as an actual partnership it only makes sense to have these too. Remember, a good relationship, no matter how great its base, will always require work to make it stay awesome.

You can follow these tips whether you have a lot of money, or no money; whether you see each other a lot or are in a long distance relationship, and whether you have children or not. The principles and ground rules always stay the same. Since Bettina and I both have packed work schedules, we make it our business to have some fixed relationship dates in our diaries. Just as a company has an inauguration date, fixed holidays and some other special dates, for us, both of our birthdays, our anniversary, as well as Christmas and New Year are the five fixed relationship dates in our calendar that we commit to spend together. So far we always managed to do it, even though a few times it has been close. If you put enough value on something, you will always find a way. For example on our first Christmas together I was supposed to fly to the Philippines for a photo-shoot. I told my partner company that I would only be going if my girlfriend could join me. They agreed. As you see, relationships are work, but if you put in the work, you will enjoy the benefits, that good relationships have to offer. Together with Bettina I have started several extremely successful businesses and we share the most amazing, mind-blowing and funny experiences together. For example, we once decided to do a liver cleanse together, and after consuming dozens of grams of Epsom salts both of us were either lying in bed in pain or puking in the toilet and emptying our bowels. It will be these special and many times awkward moments and experiences that will bond you forever. No one remembers the nights when you were sleeping, but rather the crazy ones when you are up non-stop partying or having the best time of your life. That is also why we went on a several-week road-trip through the U.S. when we were in Las Vegas for business, or did city tours in Paris and London while touring Europe. We have travelled around Asia together, spending time in Chiang Mai with tigers, getting massages in China, and surfing in Bali. Make every day with your loved ones count, just as if it was your last day with them.

All of the lessons I am taking away from this story have been described in great length above, but I want to summarize the three lessons that I consider to be the most important. The first lesson is to see a relationship as similar to a business. It needs a good foundation. If you and your partner share different values, goals and ideas, it will be very difficult for you to get along over time. The second lesson is also connected to the first: any relationship, no matter how good its foundation, requires work. If you don't give, you will not get, and eventually you will start to live apart and the relationship will break down. Small things count; the more regular you make your efforts, the easier but also the better they will become. The third lesson is to create strong memories with each other. It will help you bond and get you through the rough times that you will inevitably face. I have found that these powerful memories can remind you of how wonderful the other person actually is, even though in that very moment you cannot stand him or her being around when you are in disagreement. I am not a big fan of dwelling in the past, but if you think of past experiences, you will always remember only some special moments, never the entire story. Build many of these memories with your loved ones. No one is perfect, including you. Accept the other person's weaknesses and enjoy his or her strengths. If you are "there" for the other person, you will get through the hard patches in life together. I hope you agree with me that nothing is better than sharing the joy of life together with a special someone!

Our relationship is not perfect, but we are working hard at it. We want to make it happen aside of all the craziness around us on a daily basis. I hope this chapter gives you some tips on what you could be working on with your partner, so that your personal and family life becomes more fulfilling. What you should do now is follow the lessons above. If you are in a relationship already, work out a plan on how to make it special and give value to each other. Build up memories together and make them count. If you are looking for a partner, define what a good partner is for you. You need to know what kind of person you want; otherwise you will never find him or her. Remember, knowing is worth nothing without execution and action. That is the key. So go out there, and take action with your loved one.

SPACE FOR MY TAKE AWAYS

21.

THE NAMELIST STORY -
SIX DEGREES OF SEPARATION

"Finding good partners is the key to success in anything: in business, in marriage and, especially, in investing."
– Robert Kiyosaki

"What would you do with US$10,000 a month?" And by that I mean, what would you be doing if this amount of money were coming in constantly, as if you had for example won the lottery and you had a guaranteed monthly income for life? The average income in the U.S. is around US$1,700 per month, so for most people, including myself, it was quite a challenge to answer that question during a seminar on investments in 2011. Up to that point, the maximum I had ever made a month was half that amount, and so imagining how to double that was quite hard. Eventually I wrote three things down on a piece of paper: First, save some money for later, second, buy an apartment, and third, buy a nice car. What would be your three? Take a minute and write them down.

The seminar host gave us a couple of minutes and then announced: "Most people will write down: first, pay off debt, second, save money for later, and third, buy an apartment!" Strike! I had nailed it! Or so I thought. But then he continued (to the best of my memory): "If you wrote down these three goals, it makes absolutely zero sense. Why save money for later if you were guaranteed to make US$10K a month? Why invest in an apartment? Why not buy a proper house? Why not use the money to actually have fun living? "Wow, he is right", I thought. I was so consumed in looking at what I did not want, that I completely forgot to actually define clear goals for what I wanted that year. The speaker finished with "If you don't tell the universe your goals and dreams for how you would use US$10,000 a month, you will never have US$10,000 a month!"

Wow, what a bold statement. However, I had read similar points in "The Secret" and in "Think and Grow Rich" and I knew: "What you think about, you bring about!" When I got home I thought about the "smart things" to do with US$10,000 a month. If you have written down similar things to those I wrote down, try to come up with three new things as well. My biggest challenge was that I was not thinking big enough. My thinking was stuck at buying a car for US$100,000, which I would have paid off after around a year. I had to dream larger. By a lot. I started working on my vision board – again. But this time, I was completely dedicated to pushing my own limits. I once learned that if you truly want to achieve things in life, you have to 10x your goals. It really stated it like that: 10x. What does that mean? If you want to make US$10,000 a month, you have to think as if you want to make US$100,000 a month. "If you shoot for the stars, you might miss but reach the moon!" meaning that if you set an incredibly high goal of earning US$100,000 a month, you might not make it, but maybe you might end up making "only" US$10,000 month – which is probably more than you were making when you started. What if you are already making US$10,000 a month? Set a goal of making US$1,000,000 a month – you might fall short and end up with 100K. Very nice!

The 10x principle can be applied to any other concept as well of course. So what goals did I come up with? First, I kept the goal of a new car, as I was driving an old EUR 1,500 Golf Volkswagen back then. I already had an Audi A7 on my vision board. Second, I wanted a house right next to the beach so that I could go surfing. I also had that on my vision board. Third, I wanted to start my own business to give value to people without having to draw an income out of that same business. That was also already on my vision board. Looking at that, you might be as confused as I was back then. If all these things were on my vision board already, why didn't I think of them in the seminar? Then I realized my mistake: I had not put a price tag on them. I had made the simple mistake of having a vision board with great dreams on it, but I never took the steps of actually turning my dreams to into clearly defined goals. I had not asked myself how much money I would need to get what I had on there. And since I did not know what I actually wanted, how could I ever achieve it? Did you follow the steps from chapter eleven with Paul and make your own vision board? If yes, did you add price tags? No worries, I made the choice not to tell you then, so that you would have a bigger revelation on the power of having concrete goals in this story now. Were your three things you just wrote down on what you would do with US$10K a month already part of your vision board? If yes, awesome, and "Welcome to the club!" That day I put a price tag on my year (2011), and since I had consistently been making around US$10-15,000 income a year, I had to 10x it this time. So I promised myself to have my first ever 6-figure annual income, meaning that I would be making US$100,000 or more in a single year. Considering that an average household in a developed country makes only about US$20,000 per year, I was not sure whether I could achieve that, or better it, and especially how?

So I went on to Google and looked for "How to make a 6 figure income a year". Hundreds of websites with shady schemes started popping up. Tons of systems were advertised and I was sure that these were not the solution. So I searched for "What do 6 figure earners have in common". The answers were not much better either. Hmmm, maybe I had to 10x my thinking. Let's see and so I typed, "what millionaires have in common" into the search bar and the search produced a flood of extremely well researched articles on what millionaires in the U.S. had in common. You can try it for yourself on Google and you will find all the articles. I browsed through the various suggestions and started making notes on what these articles were saying: hard work, frugal spending, business owners, investors, team builders, smart, good education, etc. The problem I had with all of these statements was that while they were true for many, they were not true for all millionaires. The articles seemed to state facts while contradicting themselves, often within the same paragraph! For example: millionaires are hard working. I knew a few millionaires in person, and some of them were absolutely not hard working. They were also not the frugal spenders the article had suggested. One of them for example had inherited the money and another had bought three real estate properties over his lifetime during good market conditions that had appreciated to over US$1,000,000 by now. I had met doctors who were millionaires and I knew millionaire athletes who did not have degrees. How did that all fit together? What did the professional soccer player have to do with the person winning the lottery? I could not believe that these millionaires had no actual common quality. I kept browsing when suddenly my inner light bulb switched on.

"Of course, millionaires hang around millionaires!" This was the only true commonality that all the millionaires shared. The professional athlete was in the same millionaire income bracket as the medical doctor. All the millionaires I knew in person were around other people who were millionaires as well. I found this particular revelation quite interesting, since this also relates back again to the concept of "being the average of the five people around you", that I have discussed in previous chapters of this book. This seemed to be pushing it to the next level, because the next question I asked myself was, "Can just the fact of being around millionaires, make me a millionaire?" I typed the question into Google but did not get a proper search result. "Fascinating", I thought. I will go and find out for myself then. I took my vision board and pinned a piece of paper on there. With a blue marker I wrote: "Meet new millionaires!" Great, the only question now was: "How to start?" Anyone who has great dreams has to start with an exact goal pinned down. But most of the time one has absolutely zero idea where to start. So as I sat there thinking, I looked at the notepad from the seminar, where I had taken pages of notes. One of them jumped right at me: "It is not about knowing the answer. It is about knowing the question!" "Such a powerful statement", I thought. If I wanted to know how to get where I wanted to go I needed to start asking the right questions first. I opened Google again and typed: "How to connect with anyone in the world". I pressed enter, and a Wikipedia entry came up as the first result, that was initially hard to believe.

It read: "The entire world is connected via six links[20]". I was skeptical and so I crosschecked the references in the article. They seemed correct. I continued reading. The article stated that every person in the world could in theory connect to any other person by just using six other people as referral links. So for example if you wanted to reach the famous soccer player Leo Messi, you could in theory talk to your soccer playing friend (1st link), whose coach (2nd link) might know someone playing soccer in Barcelona (3rd link), who might know someone in the Football Club Barcelona (4th link) who might know a trainer of FC Barcelona (5th link), who then might know Leo Messi (6th [and final] link) in person. That was mind-blowing, as it meant that I could in theory reach Michael Jordan, Bill Gates, Warren Buffet, or even the President of the United States of America through the same principle. Of course it had to be the right people, or otherwise you would not be successful. The concept of the "average of the five people around you" did not really apply in this case, because it did not necessarily mean that the people you needed to connect with to reach others were part of your inner circle. More of a networking system was needed that could leverage the power of the six links. I kept searching for famous people who had been great in networking and Google gave me the former U. S. President Bill Clinton. It is stated that

20 https://en.wikipedia.org/wiki/Six_degrees_of_separation

he was able to remember the name of every person he had ever asked for his or her name. I don't know if it is true, but I am sure there is at least some truth in it. I decided to give this idea a shot and started my own project "Name List for Life". Since I was not sure whether I could remember everyone's name, I wanted to write down the names of everyone that I knew on paper, and could thereby follow up with him or her on a regular basis. This would allow me to keep track of my existing network and help me find more "millionaires" and "billionaires" at the same time.

Initially I planned on using an Excel spreadsheet, but then I found some online applications that could do exactly what I needed. They were called CRM tools, which is short for Customer Relationship Management. These are basically online versions of the good old paper phone book. A few of them were free to use but there were also some for several hundred US$ a month. I don't want to advertise for them, so I won't give any names. You can do the research yourself online, and if you search for my name and include CRM you will find a couple of online podcasts where these programs had interviewed me about why I was using them to become successful. I started with a free CRM tool and upgraded to more expensive ones over time. Today I pay around US$200 a month for it, which is a rather expensive, high-end service. My assumptions were 100% correct and the only common denominator successful people had, was their excellent networks to other successful people. Using these CRM tools has been one of my key factors to success and so I believe that I am getting real value for money in paying such a fee. You will realize that your name list has immense value and millionaires or billionaires are where they are because of the huge connections they have built up over decades.

The first thing I did was to "import" all the people I already knew from my phone and email lists into the CRM tool. I ended up with around 500 people. I had a lot more people on Facebook, but as I did not know most of them personally

I did not add them. You can copy what I was doing, and you will see amazing results. Looking at Twitter statistics, there is somewhat of a trend that people with a lot of twitter followers also tend to have a high net worth. Now don't get me wrong, I understand that there are thousands of examples, where people with billions of dollars have no twitter followers and they might not even own a twitter account. I have however never seen a person with one million Twitter followers who is not worth at least one million dollars. Please let me know if you find otherwise. Based on that observation, I drew the conclusion that if I could increase the number of people in my CRM tool, I might also be able to make more money. My hypothesis turned out to be correct and the more people I managed to get into my network, the more value I started to create, and the more money I was making. What is important to note here is that it is not enough to just add people into your CRM tool. It is really about actually conversing with them. You need to create value around your name list. Soon, I was facing a new challenge: My CRM tool was great for letting me have an overview, but the more people I was adding, the more I lost control of how and with whom to stay in touch.

The best solution for the "who" part of the equation was to find a way to rank these people to figure out who were the "right" ones. Focusing my time on them would increase my chance of building a network with value, without spending too much time with the wrong people. Easier said than done. After some contemplating I came up with a five-star system that I teach everyone today during my seminars or coaching sessions. It has helped me so much myself to get to the next level. So how does this five-star system work? Most people love spending time with people they "like" or "get along with well". So when they choose to spend time with someone over dinner, lunch or coffee, they pick exactly these people. There is nothing wrong with that, but it is not very likely to help you in terms of your goals. For my five-star-system to work well it had to be based on something other than personal relationship preferences, so I came up with a value-based system. The idea is simple: Whenever people interact, value is exchanged - value does not have to be measured in money; rather it is a subjective measurement, for example one person helping the other person with a tip, psychological or emotional support, or guidance. Eventually, you rank the people around you within five categories. These are not absolute however, but relatively ranked to you. You always start by giving yourself three stars. Even Leo Messi would give himself three stars. So, any other person around you that exchanges the same basic value with you also goes into that category. Again, this can be but is not necessarily measured in money. As a side note: I personally believe it is wonderful if your life partner is also a three. That will make sure that similar value is exchanged, and in the long run no one feels that they are falling short. If he or she is a two or four it is also fine. So in relation to your own value, whose value would be a two? This would be someone to whom you are giving slightly more value than you are receiving. With three as your pre-set value, a "four' would be someone who is giving you slightly more value than they are receiving from you. Values one and five are the extremes, where the values exchanged between the two of you are seriously unbalanced, such that one person in your relationship is totally out of the other one's league.

I want to point out once again that this has nothing to do with downgrading or upgrading people. It is a relative value - measurement for you so that you don't do lose track of the right people to include in your network. Initially, it might be a bit tough to rank all of the people in your network, but over time you will get the hang of it. You will find that there are people who have a lot of money, but simply bring you no value. They would be a one or two. The opposite is also true, and you will meet people with little money who but who rank highly in other values. They would be a three, four, or five depending on how much value you can return. Time could also be a value factor: Who is always there to help you? Who disappears into thin air if you need them? I hope you get the idea. Keep in mind that since it is a relative system the stars will change over time. A two can become a four or vice versa. And a three for one person could be a one or five for someone else. Everyone gets different value from different people and that is the great feature of this system: it will give you a clear idea of who to focus on around you and who to network with. It will be quite hard to spend a lot of time with fives, simply because you are probably a one to them, if they are following the same principal, so try to spend time with threes and fours. Reach out and connect with them; meet them for coffee or talk with them on the phone. Learn to give value to anyone with whom you converse. Always! The more often you manage to give value, the higher you will rise in another person's ranking, even if he or she is not doing it consciously. Over time you manage to catch up to your fives, as they have now become fours or maybe even threes. Once you make yourself so precious to other people that they never want to lose connection with you, you have mastered this system. A great example would be Mark Zuckerberg. He is bringing so much value to over a billion people through Facebook that no one ever wants to give it up. That is the reason why he is worth US$ 40 billion and seen as one of the most powerful people on our planet.

So, now that we talked about who to talk to, let's move on to the how to do it. Update your name list daily. Aside of the five star ratings, I include a few other things in the CRM tool that help me organize the thousands of people. For example I always make notes about how and where I met them the first time, or what stood out about them. I include the home location and where they are living right now. Why? In case I fly into Los Angeles, I always have someone to meet up. Need someone in Europe? South America? South Africa? South Korea? This allows me to build a worldwide network. Another thing I mark down is their personality type, which I categorize into four different ones: Red: the action takers. Blue: the strategists and thinkers. Green: the social and harmonious group. And Yellow: the attention seekers and entertainers. There is some generalization to it, but it is an efficient way for me to remember how I think people tick and what drives them, in readiness for when I meet them again. There are many courses about color personalities on the Internet, and you can make a very detailed categorization, I tend to keep it short and simple. Using these 3 factors of stars, locations and colors, I have an efficient and fast way to have an overview of tens of thousands of people in my name list of life today. Of course I add important background features every once in a while, but the more time you spend on updating your system, the less time you actually have to use your name list. You need to find a good balance.

That brings me to my last important point on what to do with your contacts to network effectively: A year only has 365 days. The reason I say "only" is because let's say you can meet or call only one of your super important people a day. That would mean that you would connect with only 365 people from your list in one year. Maybe even fewer than that. So remember, you want to focus your attention and time on the key people. Sometimes you might manage to meet with a five-star, but during these meetings it will be quite obvious that he or she is just doing you a favor. The four stars and sometimes also the three stars will help you to grow the most without giving you the feeling of there being a gap in between the two of you. Meet these people in person or if you are on a tight budget or your job does not allow for that, have a phone call with them. Build meaningful relationships with them and show them that they are important to you. When spending individual time with someone it has to be to network "upwards". This is a key concept in the law of building a powerful network. If you meet with four or five star people, ask them if you can join them for an event that they attend. I was invited to a Harvard Alumni event that way once. Just imagine how many four and five star people where there! Hundreds! This is the power of focusing your time on the right people and giving value to them, as they will always give back. That is the nature of a three, four or five-star. Once you work your way up the networking ladder you will have more and more one star and two star people relative to you. The best way to stay in touch with them without losing sight of your key three, four and five stars is to send a monthly newsletter email. Give people a quick update about what is happening and make everyone feel you are in touch. This doesn't have to be a long text, even a great quote you read, or quick, valuable tip you came across can be very effective. Tell them that you are extremely busy to avoid hurt feelings if you don't reply to everyone's call. Focus on spending individual time with the higher stars, and use mass communication with the lower stars. Again, this is not discrimination or devaluation; it is how the world works. Try to contact Mark Zuckerberg. If you are not one of his close advisors you definitely will not get an hour of individual time with him. So what does he do? He uses mass media such as Facebook or Newsletters to give you a peak at his life and work. Absolute five-stars use the same system, so believe me you should do too. It will change your life in ways you cannot imagine.

I have shared with you step by step how I was doing it, so you can just copy my system. Focus on the lessons and you will be successful. The three most important ones are: First: Start your name list as early as possible and build it over life. As time is an important factor when building trust and relationships a young age to start is definitely a plus. Update it regularly to avoid forgetting someone. Second: Rank people using the five-star system, based on reciprocal value, as I have described above. Additionally, add people's locations and color personalities so that you don't forget how they tick. Third: Focus on spending quality time with three and four star people and network your way up to the five stars. The further up you go, the more need you will have for a mass update system for all your one and two stars, to keep them in the loop. It is as simple as that, but many times it is the small and simple things we do that have the biggest impacts on our lives!

The day I realized that building a name list for life would help me get connected to hundreds of thousands of other people through the law of six degrees of separation, is the day I had a true mental breakthrough on my way to a six-figure annual income. Suddenly I was reaching out to more and more powerful people, who connected me to even more powerful people. I did buy my Audi A7 that year and what a wonderful feeling it was, knowing that I had achieved it through clear goal setting, planning, and taking massive action. I found great new ideas and lifted my "lid" even higher, to finally "become more", and thereby "get more". I wish someone had told me all that when I was 16 years old! Well, it is better that I started when I was 25 than never. No matter how old you are when applying this concept, you will benefit from it massively. The earlier you can do this of course, the better. This is your call to action. Start your name list for life NOW. Rank the people in your five-star system and get started. Yes, it might take you a full Sunday to do so, but it will be worth it a million times over.

SPACE FOR MY TAKE AWAYS

22.

THE ROUTINE STORY -
THE 100 HOUR CHILL WEEK

*"The secret of your future is hidden in your daily
routine." – Mike Murdock*

Through my name list for life I managed to connect with
many different people from all walks of life, which helped me
grow as a person. People that go to renowned universities get
a head start in life because of the combination of excellent
educational programs and the relationships and connections
they build during their time at university. Think about it: If
you go to school with the son of a high-ranking corporate
individual, it will help you succeed as well if you can reach out
to that person in the future. I never went to an elite university,
and even though many of the people I met in med-school
are wonderful, most of my relationship building that I use
today happened after my graduation. In one example, my
networking brought me to a Spanish business owner who
clearly was either a four- or even a five-star.

He also kitesurfed, so we could both give value to each
other. He gave to me through business, while I gave him
tips on kitesurfing. He was living in Barcelona where we
met a couple of times for lunch. During one lunch we were
at a typical Spanish tapas bar. We ordered delicious local
snacks and talked about the differences in work hours
between Austria and Spain, and the resulting productivity
and time management. As you might imagine, it was a
fierce discussion, and I told him how I had been especially

productive and working at full power mode since I had been back from Cocos earlier that year. When I told him that he looked up: "That's interesting, what changed after Cocos?" I was not sure if he actually was interested in the answer or whether he was just trying to inspire me to keep digging for our ongoing discussion about productivity. I replied by quoting Steve Jobs to him: "Every time in the morning when I look into the mirror I ask myself whether I enjoy what I am about to do. And if the answer is 'No' for too many times in a row, I know I have to change it." I added: "I really enjoy what I do." He smiled at me quietly, waiting for me to continue. I had probably been correct; he just wanted to inspire me! That's what I love about high-star people. They always give value, either directly by giving you great tips, or indirectly by making you think of things yourself. I knew I had not answered his question, so while picking up another piece of sausage my brain was sorting my thoughts. "What has been different since then? I have definitely been creating massive value for the entire year; that's why it is the best year of my life so far. Also I have never been working in an actual job and have never experienced actual employment. So I can do whatever I enjoy doing, no matter whether it is kitesurfing or working on my business". I thought of the Steve Jobs quote and reminded myself how easy it was for me to get up in the morning. Many of the people I knew hated the life they were living.

He interrupted my thought process: "The reason I am asking you Julian, is because I have a nephew who reminds me of you. He can do whatever he wants, he doesn't have to work an actual job either, similar to you. He has big goals and dreams, and he is going to all these classes and workshops, but eventually he doesn't get anything productive done. He seems to be so committed to his projects, but there are no actual results. So what I am wondering is, maybe you can give him a tip about how to break his inefficiency?" "Ok, so he is asking me an actual question!" I reflected on what he was saying, "Hmmm, I think it is the 100 hours of effort I put in a week?" I replied. It was more of a question than an answer. I did not know what had changed since Cocos. The waitress brought some fresh cheese and we changed the conversation before we could dig deeper.

We continued talking about financial topics like the stock market or the benefits of opening a Spanish company. I did not have a chance to answer his question and after saying "Adios" and going back to my hotel it bothered me, as he had always given so much value and now I could not answer that seemingly simple question. I went to the gym and relaxed in the sauna. I started to ponder about what had given me inspiration and had made the difference after coming back to normal life after ten days of complete disconnection on Cocos. One thing I had changed was I had stopped calling my work "work". Since I loved what I did, I had started calling my "100 hour work weeks" "100 hour chill weeks". Maybe that was the difference? Maybe his nephew should stop calling what he does, "work" and find a better word associated with it? What was his nephew doing? I just knew he was working hard. I paused. "That's it!" I jumped up from the wooden bench in the sauna and rushed into the ice cold shower and (still dripping wet) straight to the elevator. I could not allow myself to lose my string of thought. Back in the room, I opened my laptop and started typing the Subject line of an email to my Spanish friend: "The Power of Daily Routines". I now knew what I had changed. In the sauna it had suddenly popped into my head. Cocos had messed up my habits so much, that when I came back I had started adopting new daily routines. Before Cocos I had been on my computer or phone all the time, but I had dropped that habit on the boat. So when I was back I developed a new approach to when and how to use technology. These new daily patterns made my 100-hour chill weeks so incredibly efficient, that with less energy I achieved an extremely high amount of output. That was what his nephew was missing, and I wanted to outline what I was doing.

I want to share the context I wrote in that email with you in this story, so that you will be able to have the most efficient days of your life. So buckle up and get ready, because we are shifting gears into full speed. Incidentally, it does not matter whether you are still in school or university, or you are employed, self-employed, or even unemployed. The principles are always the same, and while my personal schedule may not fit in with yours, you will be able to adopt the concept and develop your own rhythm. Daily routines are essential, as our brains work best if something has become a habit. Just like driving a car. At the beginning, it is quite tough and exhausting, but at some point you don't even have to think about it anymore; it has become automatic. It is the same with your work schedule – if you follow the same schedule over and over, it gets easier and easier to do. You need less energy for the same task and can increase the workload or as I call it, chill-load. Now don't get me wrong – I do have crazy nights out, but I learned that I should stay on my daily schedule for six days a week. The seventh day is a mess-up day that keeps the fun and diversity without losing productivity. If you have a regular schedule already because you are either studying at school or university, or you are working regular hours, then it will come quite naturally and you just have to add a few additional habits. For those of you that have to either fill your calendar on your own (meaning you have to schedule your day by yourself without a boss) or are employed with erratic work hours, you might not be able to schedule your habits at exactly the same order every day, but you should keep the same groups of activities at around the same time. You will see what I mean. Let's get started.

It may surprise you that I start my daily schedule the evening before, not in the morning. Why is that? If you don't prepare your next day properly ahead of time, it will take you more energy to get active after waking up. I try to get seven to eight hours of sleep. I know some people experiment with cutting sleep to four or five hours per night, but when I tried that a couple of times it really did not suit me. Instead of becoming more effective the opposite happened. So if you can get by with less than seven hours of sleep that is great, just be sure you can still give 100% throughout the day. If you want to determine how much, or how little sleep you need, then try to cut it down by 30 min a day until you reach a point where you are bad tempered and unable to function properly. It might be great to do this with a partner - like a "spotter" on the trampoline. Tell your partner your plan and ask them to tell you when they see a noticeable difference in your mood and productivity. Then you will know how much sleep your body needs and you will be able to calibrate accordingly. Give your body some time to adjust to the new length and also understand that your body needs different amounts of sleep at different times.

If I have an exciting project on hand, I can also get by with less sleep, but normally the seven to eight hours work perfectly for me. Since I want to get up before 6:00 am the next morning, I make sure I get into bed between 10:00 and 11:00pm at night. I always sleep with an alarm, except for on cheat day, where I sleep as long as I want. I use a so-called smart alarm on my phone that is downloadable as a free app. It will wake me up when I am not in a REM sleep phase, which is the deepest sleep possible and therefore not a preferred wakeup time. Why am I rambling on about sleep in your daily pattern? Well, if you are not getting paid to dream, and I have not heard of one person who does, you will not make any money for sleeping. You might be making money while sleeping, but doubtfully not for sleeping. So essentially the more you sleep, the less time you have to be productive. The key is to find the optimal balance between working efficiently without losing too much time lying in bed. Like I said, I get to "chill" 100 hours a week, which means you shouldn't sleep more than seven or eight hours a day. I read stories of Donald Trump only needing three to four hours, but whether that makes sense long term is a discussion in itself. There are various sleep protocols that have been tested, where you sleep a bit shorter during the night but then take a nap in the afternoon. It can get as crazy as applying polyphasic sleep patterns[21], which means you work four hours, then sleep two, then work four hours then sleep for two again and so on. In total, you would still be up for 16 hours and sleep for eight hours in a 24-hour cycle, it is just spread evenly rather than doing it in one go. I actually tried it and it works better than you might imagine. The only real challenge was finding a place to get a good two hours of sleep every six hours, so eventually I went back to the one time seven to eight hour sleep protocol. Try it out and see what works best for you, but of course, keep the people around you in mind so they don't give up on you and have them head for the hills!

Before going to bed I have a few things prepared. Studies show that flossing before going to bed is the most efficient of any time. I do believe in taking certain supplements, even though I have a healthy diet. In the evening I take fish oil, zinc and magnesium. I also drink at least two cups of water before going to bed. Why? Because if I am lucky, my bladder will wake me up even before the alarm does. Whether you shower or take a bath in the evening or not is entirely up to you. Some people cannot sleep for some time after such stimuli, as the adrenaline rises, especially if you have a very hot or cold shower; that's the case for me.

Before actually hopping into bed I prepare my sports clothes for the morning. This makes doing early morning sports a lot easier than if I have to prepare them after waking up. I make sure my plans are set until lunchtime. If you are someone who gets to choose freely what to do, learn to distinguish between important and urgent things. It is a key factor in an efficient daily routine. It took me quite some time to understand which things are actually important and to put those first. Sometimes a message from someone pops in or an email comes up, that asks you for something quite urgently. You move away from your important tasks, such as creating a

---

21 http://www.highexistence.com/alternate-sleep-cycles/

PowerPoint for your next sales presentation, and your entire thought flow is now interrupted. The "urgent" request may be important to the sender, but neither this, nor your reply is actually important to you. "Important" things are only those things that bring you actual results. Your sales PowerPoint presentation may get you more customers, so it is important. Staying in a thought process throughout a key meeting is important; so don't let "urgent" pop-ins occur.

If you are struggling with distinguishing important vs. urgent, then use a method that I employ every evening. I write down five to ten things that I should be doing the next day. The reason why it is five or ten things is because the Pareto Principle[22] states that 20% of these things will bring 80% of your results. This means either one out of five things, or two out of ten, will bring you 80% of your entire results. If you don't believe me, read up on it for yourself, or even better, test it! 20% of your customers will bring 80% of your revenue, 20% of your co-workers will cause 80% of all the trouble and 80% of what you do throughout the day, has pretty much no impact… only 20% of the total. You can apply this Pareto Principle to anything, and because of that you need to use it to your advantage. Write down these five to ten things, and then circle either one or two of them that you personally feel will bring you the most results. The next day, these are the first things you start with and you don't move on to anything else until they are finished. There are even strategies where you never even do the other items, just because their impact on your results is too insignificant. I don't do that myself, but feel free to try it out.

Great, now that I have established these core principles, let me tell you the last thing I do before falling asleep. I open my diary, where I jot down a few things about the day, such as what went well or how I can improve certain things for the next day. I never write down the bad things but always focus

---

22 https://en.wikipedia.org/wiki/Pareto_principle

on positivity. I show gratitude about all the wonderful things in my life. Trust me, even if it seems your life is not going well, you have to pick out those things that are. If you are alive and you feel that is all you have, then be grateful for that. I never let any negativity get close to me after my diary posting, which means no Facebook, no emails, no messaging etc... And of course: No watching the news. I love to watch some YouTube videos about quantum theory, science, entrepreneurship or other value-bringing channels, but no time wasters like movies or shows. Those are for my cheat days only. I either read a book or listen to a podcast. If it is a book, it is normally a light fictional read. Podcasts are great too, because if you listen to them on 1.5x speed they are over after around twenty minutes and you hit dreamland smoothly.

When I get up at around 6:00am, the first thing I do is put cold water on my face to wake me up completely. Since I had prepared everything in the evening, I am quick to rock and the smart alarm wakes me during a good sleep time. I love my morning coffee and have an additional caffeine pill. Yep, I am somewhat of a caffeine-addict – which is a personal preference, and I am not necessarily recommending it to you – this is just what works for me. I don't believe in taking multi-vitamin pills however. Many might scream when reading this, but I have read enough studies showing that high dose vitamin pills, particularly the fat-soluble vitamins, do more harm than good[23]. I then get in front of my computer but since I cannot do creative tasks yet right away, I do my personal and my company's accounting. You know me well enough by now that I am super picky with money and jot down every dollar spent for myself and also within my companies. At some point I need to outsource that, I know, but until then I do it first thing in the morning to have it out of the way. Then I update my name list with all the contacts from the day before and put in some notes. I stay away from consuming social media,

23 http://www.medicinalfoodnews.com/vol04/issue3/toxicity.htm

email or phone messages. The reason I write "consume" is because I use special social media tools where I can prepare pre-written messages to be sent out during the day, without reading at that very moment what junk is happening in the world. Also, since my email is "on manual receive", meaning I only receive emails if I actively press the "receive button" on my email program, I can send emails without getting new ones in. Important is to use a timer for any of these things. Otherwise you spend too much time on some of the tasks and don't focus enough on important things.

By 7:00am I have completed all money related tasks, have updated my name list, sent out emails and prepared all social media updates. Now I am ready for sports. Mostly this is the time when Bettina gets up – so I'll make her a quick cup of coffee as well – relationship work, remember? I haven't received one negative possible input from the outside world up to that point. Also, I am always listening to happy and cheerful music during that first hour. While doing sports I always listen to either an audiobook or a podcast. If you prefer, listen to music. Audios while doing sport are shown to increase performance, so you want to listen to something. If you have to be at work by 7:00am, you just have to shift the entire schedule earlier to make it fit. Try to do it as early as possible however, since you want to start the day at your own rhythm without outside influences interrupting your daily habits. Personally I love to get a lot more accomplished by 10:00am than most others might do in the entire day. Don't overdo the gym. 20 minutes of endurance, for example a run outside, and then 20 minutes of weight- or bodyweight-training are perfect. If I can jump into a pool, I do that. It will wake me up even more. I get into the shower afterwards and use a warm-cold-warm alternating water method to boost my skin's blood circulation and thereby my energy. Many times I just stand in the shower at the end, reflect about how awesome life is and thank the universe for this great start of the day – almost like a meditation. Give gratitude.

After all that I head back to my computer to hit all the happenings (including the negative as well as the positive) of my surroundings for the first time. If you have to go to work or any other place, then this is the time to do so, if possible make sure you have all this done before hand. If that means you need to go to bed earlier, do so. Remember, in my first year of medical university I had to get up at around 4:00am. I went to bed before 9:00pm every night to be sure to get enough sleep. I missed out on a few late night activities, but true success lies in the ability to choose between what you want most in life (for me it was a medical degree) over what you want in that very moment (stay up late). Think about what that means for you and what you have to do in your daily routine to make things happen. If you like a good breakfast, have it now. I love to have a morning protein shake or some good eggs. I switch on my emails and social media sites. I filter out the important messages, reply and push the unimportant ones back. Remember to understand the difference between what's important what is urgent. I use either a Google stopwatch timer or the Pomodoro Technique[24] to keep track of my work. I try as much as possible to stay away from scheduling meetings or calls before lunch, simply because this is when I am the most productive. If you are more creative in the afternoon then arrange your schedule accordingly, but I prefer doing blog posts, writing newsletters, updating websites, or creating PowerPoints in the morning.

My phone is most of the time on mute, so I don't get distracted during work. I want to be in control of where my focus goes without letting other people interrupt me during that time. Normally this keeps me busy for around four hours with a couple of breaks in between. It is now 12:00pm and I get ready for lunch, which I like to spend with the key people of my "Name list for Life". Lunch is normally scheduled until 2:00pm and since I have the luxury of not having to go to an office, I can choose my lunch place freely. I don't know what

---

24 http://www.pomodorotechnique.com/

your lunch opportunities are, but if you can, always do it together with someone. Eating food in a social environment has been important for over 10,000 years, so leverage on that to build meaningful relationships. After lunch is my normal low-energy time. I use the time from 2:00-3:00pm for social media updates, personal phone calls or other less important to-dos. I learned to use the short breaks like when I am on a bus, train, or waiting for something in a productive manner. I jot down a quick update, answer a Whatsapp or make an appointment in my calendar. Be sure to have a list of these things to do, as it will boost your productivity a lot. Otherwise these things turn out to be huge time wasters during times when you should actually be productive. The rest of the afternoon depends on whether I am meeting clients, business partners or no one. If I go to an event or basketball training, it is normally from 7:00-9:00pm. I need to put in some commute time, but it always works out to get me back home in time. I am not a big dinner eater but I like chewing on some nuts for snacks during the day, and have an energy bar in the afternoon. Sometimes I have a small salad in the evening, as I prefer to eat light before bedtime. Again, your individual preferences will dictate what is best for you. And then it is back to the evening where I repeat my daily pattern from the start. I do this for six days a week and on day seven I do what I like, relax, and keep it fun. Most important, my schedule is highly efficient and productive. It makes me focus on the things that bring results and filters out things that seem urgent but are not important.

I hit the "Send Button" and a five-page email went out to help my friend's nephew in Barcelona. Six weeks later I received a Thank-You note by letter from him. It had worked and his results where improving. I just sat there with the letter in my hand, smiling. I had received so much input from him, and now I was able to give back. What a wonderful feeling to know how a few tips can turn it all around. You can and should follow a similar routine too. Trust me, it will be extremely powerful. I laid out my personal plan above. When you focus on scheduling your personal plan, focus on the following three key lessons. First, A daily routine is a must to have great results. It is not optional. Some key performers in our world such as Mark Zuckerberg go so far as to wear the same clothes every day. This is quite extreme, but you get the point. They do it for a reason. If your day is quite different every day, maybe because you travel a lot, then at least try to group certain activities around the same time as much as possible. For example start with physical activity, do mental challenging activities before lunch and do socially engaging things in the afternoon. Second, learn to distinguish between what's urgent and what is actually important. This is the biggest driver to being productive. When making TO-DO lists, circle those 20% that are the most important. According to the Pareto Principle they will get you 80% of your results. Third, start your day in the evening. All the things described above get messed up if you are off for a bad start after waking up. I have learned that for my mornings to be good, I need to have them prepared well the prior evening. If you follow all these principles you will not only get a lot done, but you will also make your week turn from a 100hour-work into a 100 hour-chill week, if that is what you want.

I know there was a lot of content in this story and applying it will be a challenge at the beginning. Over time you will figure it out and it will become easier and easier. Combine your daily patterns with the knowledge of getting a name list for life and you are set for greatness. And, do not forget your health and the people around you. Take a few minutes or even hours now and schedule out your daily routine to have the most efficient days of your life while applying the lessons learnt.

SPACE FOR MY TAKE AWAYS

23.

THE MLM STORY -
WALKING AGAINST THE LINE

Whenever you find yourself on the side of the majority, it is time to pause and reflect. – Mark Twain

In the last two chapters I shared with you about the skills I had to learn to make 2011 such a successful year. Now I want to share with you what I have actually been doing from 2011 up to now. Back then I wanted to know what other successful people had done to make their fortunes and noticed that many of them were building a business. I am not talking about a small- and medium sized one, but a fully independent entity with internal equity value. This is important to understand, and I covered it partly in chapter 17 when I described the difference between scalable and non-scalable income streams. A large business is one of the best ways to earn a scalable and a much higher residual income, which is what I was looking for, and you should be too if you would love to stop exchanging your time for money. Schools don't teach you much about how to start your own big business, as they advise you to take the "safe" route of being either employed or self-employed. That is why I want to dedicate this chapter to how I went against the odds to get involved in my first big business and scaled it into some serious passive income in just around four years. In chapter 25 I will tell you all my income streams that I am having at this very moment, to give you an idea of what might be interesting for you. There are basically four ways to start a big business that can bring you scalable passive income over time. If you remember my tree-story, just like growing a tree, in a business you will not reap many rewards at the beginning. The good thing however is, that all four ways that I will show you in this chapter can be started part-time, so at the start of your big business you can often stay in your regular job or continue your current activities.

Option One is that you have a fantastic idea and are willing to act upon it. Remember, having an idea means nothing. Richard Branson did not manage to shake up the airline industry because of his great idea, but due to his amazing execution compared to other competing airlines. There are very few ideas out there that haven't been thought of by somebody already. No idea, no matter how great or revolutionary, has become a reality without the massive and sustained action and belief of its creator

Option Two is that you know a business partner, and you can join his or her venture by bringing value. The important message here is that you don't join as an employee, but as a true partner or even co-founder with equity in the company. This means that you are holding shares and can participate in the entire company's profits. If you or your business partners know how to raise money, both options don't necessarily require lots of money upfront. But this option requires taking massive action on a great idea. Most people who want to go this route lack money plus action and therefore struggle to do either option. The great part about option one or two is that once the business gets bigger over time and creates massive internal value, one could sell part of the business to outside investors, which is what most successful entrepreneurs do. It gives them their high net value. Mark Zuckerberg and Bill Gates are not rich because of their high salaries, but because they own part of their businesses, which are extremely valuable. Many other entrepreneurs try to follow in their footsteps, which is not easy of course. Back in 2011 neither my friends nor me knew how to raise money. We did have some ideas, but without the ability to persuade other people to buy into our ideas, we did not get very far. Therefore neither one of these two options was feasible for me back then.

Option Three is to acquire a franchise, such as McDonalds, which is a proven system. You buy a license from the host company to be able to use their entire system and logistics. A franchisee does not have to know the right people or have a good idea. The catch however is that most franchise licenses cost north of US$50,000 or even US$500,000, not including staffing and setting up the business itself. At the beginning of 2011 I had just started getting my finances back on track after my disastrous wipeout in Brazil, so this option was also not possible for me.

The last option, **Option Four,** is the most controversial among all these four options. Since the other three options were not feasible and I generally loved to take "the road less travelled", I was open to go for this one. Option Four is to start a "Network Marketing" business. I believe many readers, and therefore also my "younger self", will either get in touch with network marketing at some point in their future or have already experienced it. Since it is a multi-billion dollar industry and growing every day, I feel it is crucial to share my story and the valuable lessons that I have learned so far. I can tell you so much already: My experience was not only successful in terms of income, but also in terms of my skill-set. Since I had no actual business background, network marketing helped me to become a public speaker, presenter, and to improve my sales skills – all things that were new to me back then.

The idea of network marketing is fairly simple but many times misunderstood, and this lack of understanding has helped to give network marketing such an ambivalent reputation. The solution that network marketing tries to bring to the market place is, just as the name suggests, marketing a product or service via a network of people. In traditional business a company pays a marketing or sales team to sell or market its product/s. If team members perform well, they may receive sales bonuses, which is wonderful, but the downside is that when they leave the company, they will not make any more money from any future sales, even though they had created them for their company in the first place. It sounds like a great deal for the employer, but he or she runs the risk of the sales- or marketing-person not generating sufficient revenue, but still taking a salary and/or the employee leaving for better opportunities right after receiving often expensive education from the company. Since it was not always a WIN-WIN for the employer and the employee, other solutions started to be introduced in the hope of providing a better method for marketing and selling. An option to do so is that of "direct sales", either door to door or more often nowadays, through the Internet. Blogs, Facebook, Instagram, Pinterest, and email marketing campaigns allow companies and brands to build an audience and promote their products or services through their network. Included in that is "affiliate marketing", where individuals (the sales- or marketing person) can sign up for free, and receive a commission if they make a sale. Many people who are very successful on social media channels – the so-called "Youtubers", "Instagramers" etc. are using this strategy today to monetize their work. The downside here is that while it provides some sort of flexible income, it requires quite a large audience, as the commissions are not high. Also once you stop promoting a product or service, your income will suffer unless you keep promoting something else.

Huge companies, such as Amway or Tupperware started developing a new strategy. Users of the product or service can sign up to become a distributor and earn money through the sales revenue they generate. They are not employed by the company, but work on their own terms, just like a business owner within a business. This is similar to the direct sales and affiliate model described above and often all these approaches overlap. The big difference is the distributor's opportunity to recruit other distributors to their team. The recruiting distributor will then earn a certain percentage on the sales that their new recruit is making. In return, the new recruit receives training, guidance, and support. This brings scalable income for both distributors and host companies, such as Amway or Tupperware, benefit from the additional revenue. When people hear this explanation, they often confuse legitimate network marketing with illegal "pyramid"- or "Ponzi"[25] schemes. While pyramid and Ponzi schemes are illegal, network marketing is a well-recognized and popular business model that generates billions of dollars in annual revenue, worldwide. It can be difficult to differentiate between an illegal pyramid scheme and a legal network marketing opportunity, especially for someone new to business. To avoid this trap, I suggest you read this clear explanation from the online "Entrepreneur" website[26]. Essentially it comes down to how much focus is on the sale of a product or service versus pure recruitment of other distributors. A legitimate network marketing company will focus on product sales, and use the recruiting of new distributors as a method to gain more market share. Eventually this means that anyone starting as a distributor in a good and healthy network marketing company can earn an income that is commensurate with the effort they put in to sell and market the product or service, as well as expand their market share by teaching other distributors how to grow their own organization the same way. This method is fair for everyone. As would be the case in any other business, in network marketing you will not make a dollar if you do not generate any revenue. This is the benefit for the host company, which does not have to provide unnecessary salaries for people who are not productive. The concept is to pay for performance. Through his educational and inspiring documentary, The Rise of the Entrepreneur, a well-respected entrepreneur, Eric Worre, is showing the world the benefits to everyone of network marketing. This is currently available at: http://www.riseoftheentrepreneur.org/

---

25 http://www.biography.com/people/charles-ponzi-20650909
26 http://www.entrepreneur.com/article/35744

and I highly recommend it for your personal and business growth to educate yourself about this topic.

Since I did not feel I could pursue a business of my own yet, I first had to practice in the environments of the large businesses. Network marketing was a perfect opportunity for that. Good network marketing companies have great training structures with workshops on how to present well, how to develop a business mindset, how to overcome the temptation to give up, how to close deals, how to work with people how to become a leader and most of the times even how to keep a proper namelist. Besides the namelist, that I already had, all skills I wanted to acquire. Up to that point, I had never spoken in front of more than a classroom full of people and I was a lousy presenter. I knew that if I ever wanted to lead a company, I had to become a people's person and a much better speaker. Today I have spoken in front of hundreds, if not thousands of people; all thanks to learning, step by step, how to do it. Before moving forward, I want to be very clear here: I am NOT pushing you to become active in network marketing. Actually, most people will not be any more successful in network marketing than they would in any other business. Also, while writing this book, I am NOT active in any network marketing company, even though I am receiving some serious passive income, which was exactly what I wanted when I started pursuing this industry in 2011. In accordance with the general practice for this type of writing, I will not talk about which company I was working with, but I do want to describe my decision process and what tips I can give you. Before even thinking about it, make sure that you want to invest a couple of hours a week into this business. You don't have to quit your job, you just have to be sure you really want a scalable income. The few hours a week are very hard work, but eventually it will all be worth it. Since network marketing is a people to people business, someone pitching you a business opportunity that they ask you to join will most likely approach you.

While on a kitesurf trip, Michael, a very good friend of mine, asked me if I was open to make some money on the side. Of course I was, and since I knew the basics of network marketing I understood the business model he was pitching. He explained the background of the company first and I still have to smile looking back and thinking of the circles he drew on a piece of paper that would resemble people. If you have ever been in a network marketing presentation you know exactly what I mean. There were the typical words: "All you have to do is use the product and find five people who will do the same. Then these five find 25 and they find 125. Once you know it, you will have thousands of people in your group and you are making passive income!" It sounded intriguing, but I sensed that it would not be all that easy, but more about that later. There are two key factors you have to look at before stepping even one foot forward: Do you like the product or service, and is it well executed? These are probably the two most important questions, because no one will repeat-buy a product that doesn't work or is ridiculously overpriced. Likewise, people will not use a service that proves inadequate or flawed. Many companies already fail at exactly these two points. In fact my company was very competitive when I started, but got worse over time by missing out on many opportunities in the marketplace. This was eventually the reason why, after four years, I decided not to expand the business further. Yet I am still enjoying my residual income from there and have moved on to start my own business.

Really ask yourself when getting in touch with the company: "Would I use the product? Do I like the product? Does it make sense? Is it well priced? Is it well executed? Could I see myself promoting it?" If you can answer these questions with a firm "Yes", you are good to go. Some distributors will tell you things like "Don't worry about the product – we are just here to recruit. You don't have to use the product, it is more important that other people are taking it." And so on. Ask yourself this question: "Do you think Steve Jobs would have sold Apple computers but used Microsoft himself? Heck no.

Do you think Elon Musk, the owner of Tesla Motors, would ever drive a car powered by fuel? Never ever! You have to love the product or service that you are promoting. You need to understand that network marketing is about generating revenue just like any other business, just that you are part of an entire network of self-employed business owners. Another crucial point to consider is whether you feel it will be great to work with the people that are showing you this business. Most of the time you will have a friend showing it to you together with one of his or her business partners. Remember, if you knew it all and had done it all already, you probably would be starting your own business. Chances are you are thinking about joining a network marketing company for the same reasons I did: You want to make some passive income, have some guidance and don't want to leap into starting your own company entirely by yourself. So, if you feel that the people you would be working with cannot give you proper training or guidance, you can stay a user of the product or service but I would not recommend promoting it to others since you do not have enough knowledge to provide them with proper training and support, or maybe you are able to find another person within the company to work with that fulfills your requirements. You will have to go for training to improve your skills. I did seminars with Jordan Belfort (from the "Wolf of Wall Street) about closing deals, took courses from Insurance Agents about how to approach strangers on the street, and did Body Language Training and Public Speaking Seminars. They not only benefited my network marketing business but all aspects of my life, so it was definitely worth it.

When someone tells you that making thousands of dollars a month with just a few hours a week will be easy, you should take their claims with a large pinch of salt. Michael did not tell me that, but he thought that all he or I needed was five other people each. In network marketing the Pareto Principle comes into play once again. For you to have five people that build the business together with you, you need to have 20 others who are interested initially, but eventually do not build the business with you. The principle of 20/80 is always the same. Jump back to the chapter 22, in case you forgot how it works. In order to have 25 people from whom only five are actually building with you, you need to talk to at least five times that amount. So you can imagine what a turn-off it is to speak to over a hundred people and have 95% of them telling you that you are an idiot for believing that you will ever make money "doing this". My "namelist for life" allowed to me to reach out to all the key people I would need to build a global business. Everyone I spoke to advised me not to do it and I faced some of the toughest rejections of my life. Dozens of people told me "No" or "Don't talk to me about that" and so on. I knew that any entrepreneur undergoes the same process when trying to start something new, but actually being in it myself was one of the most humiliating experiences ever. Many of my friends and family members believed this was just a phase and that I would get back to "my senses" soon. Many did not understand why I, being a well-respected and successful person, would go into this industry. The "hard-sell" recruiting tactics of some other companies had scared many people off and many "scam" companies had caused people to lose thousands of dollars. It was the left-sided thinking (Cashflow Quadrant-wise) that had people scared of moving to the right quadrant side. I learned however, that the only way to find out something for myself, was to actually do it myself, while learning about the mistakes other people made doing what I was about to do. There was no value in listening to people who had made a mistake and then tried to tell me not to do something. They never learned what they should have done differently or better.

My friend Michael did not manage to overcome the rejections eventually, and so after a few months I connected with a few other entrepreneurs in our company to get help and guidance from them along the way. The law of big numbers played in my favor and after six months of non-stop resistance I had finally built up my core team in Europe. My training and reading was paying off and with my strict time management regimen I could work through my schedule ten times more efficient than most other people who had a lot more knowledge or experience. I then learned the different phases that the people underwent, who I talked to, but who were not interested to work with me. First was the "Having no clue about anything but having an opinion on everything phase". They either tried to show me all the reasons why it would not work or how I was doing it wrong. They had no clue. I learned earlier in my life only to listen to people who had success in what I was about to do and that was what I did. Next was the phase when I was having some small successes. People started making excuses as to why it was possible for me, but not for them. They claimed it was because I did not have to work, or it was because I was a medical doctor, or because I didn't have children. It did not matter what it was, it was only excuses why people would not want to pursue their goals in life. It had nothing to do with this business actually. However I pushed through that phase as well, and after a couple of trial and error phases in Europe I made the decision in mid-2012 to move to Hong Kong and take it to the next level. I will talk in detail about that move in the next chapter, but what was mind blowing was all the fear that people tried to instill in me. "You will fail, you will not make it… bla, bla, bla, bla!" I could not bear it anymore. My true break-through happened in Asia, as it was a brand new market and I could translate all the skills I had learned in Europe to build up a mind-blowing organization of over 27,000 people to date. Think about it – 27,000 people (mostly in Asia), most of whom I could not even communicate with directly. And you know how the people responded now? Depending on the different type there was a super small percentage of people who were proud of me and told me "Great Job!" A larger percentage would tell me "Oh, I always knew you would do it – but for me this would not have been possible; you were lucky being in the right place the right time." Nonsense! Anyone could have done exactly the same thing, had they put their mind to it.

And then there was yet another group of people. I had had some experience with them previously (especially at the beginning of my kitesurfing experiences), but never to the extent where they almost "broke my neck" (figuratively speaking). These were the "haters". What I experienced during the years of 2013 and onwards was such an incredibly tough experience for me that it took me a long time to recover. It felt like walking against the longest line of my life, where every person in there told me I was walking the wrong way. Haters are people who do nothing else other than "hate". It does not matter whether or not they agree with you, or if what you are doing actually makes sense; these people just choose to hate you. Since I had never previously experienced such an intense level of adversity it almost knocked me out of my shoes, the first time I received a Facebook Post about what a "Liar and loser I was." Through hard work I had made over US$ 50,000 in my first year and together with all my other income streams I had my first year of over US$100,000 or 6 figures in 2011. I was incredibly proud of achieving my goal for that year. I was not someone to show off, but if you are used to making 20% of that money and suddenly through lots of hard work you can make five times that much, you can treat yourself to some nice things, such as an Audi A7 sports version or nice new clothes. I never bragged about it, I was just proud to show the results that hard work can bring. Obviously, some people did not agree with me. They thought my success in Europe and Asia was not deserved and literally demanded for me to step down and "go back to where I came from".

After I started removing their Facebook or Twitter posts, they even wrote an entire blog posts about me, where they ridiculed my work ethic and put my medical license in question. I did not understand it at all. I could not believe there were people out there who would try to push someone down who was working so hard. I started to feel insecure for the first time in my life and actually became quiet and not as hard working for some time. 2014 was not a peak performance year for that reason. Even though I tried, my focus was no longer so clear. There was too much noise and I was walking against the line, thinking about joining the line. For the first time ever. Why would these people that I had never met and probably never will, try to bring me down? Why would they want to hurt me? I had done nothing to them, nor had I ever had the chance to confront them about their hurtful claims. I could not find any answers to these questions, so the only option I had was to start reading and learning about these haters. From where did they appear? Why did they do what they were doing? How could I deal with them? It took me all of 2014 to answer these questions and shake off their hatred, and by doing so, I was now able to make 2015 powerful and leapfrog year that I described earlier. Haters are people who actually hate themselves for not having the courage to do what other people (in this case me) dare to do. But instead of being honest and working on themselves they start blaming everyone else around them for their lack of achievement. It is easier to point the finger, but remember, the other three fingers always point back to you.

Throughout 2014 I was trying to learn from others how to deal with these haters. I read autobiographies of people who had lots of haters, watched YouTube videos about this topic, and eventually I realized that the only way to manage them was to face them, and to be stronger. The way to deal with haters is to be thankful to them, because once you have haters it also means that you are doing something worthwhile. No one will hate you if you are just this average person, because you are simply no threat to anyone else. So, **Step one:** Be thankful that you have haters. **Step two:** Ignore them, and block out the noise. Focus and keep going because nothing you say or do will change a thing. Do not react to anything they say or do at all. It will actually only add salt to your wounds. **Step three:** Increase the intensity, push through and go further, so that the haters give up and go away. To quote Winston Churchill again, "Never give up, never give in!" At the end of 2014 and all through 2015 I started sending my own social media blast out to show everyone I was back. Today I look for the haters and I am thankful every time someone writes something negative to try to put me down. I know it is exactly then, that I get the extra respect that I was probably looking for, for all the hard work I had been putting in.

I truly believe that you should try to build your own business. Nothing in life will teach you more about life itself than either pursuing your own idea or working with a network marketing company. Building a business is the best way to start earning scalable income. This is your first take-away lesson from this story. The second lesson is that just like in anything else, to be successful in business is 20% knowledge and 80% experience. You will not get rich from just reading books. You have to take action and learn by doing. It does help to learn from the right sources, but once you step into the game, you will see how it is actually played. Learning from the right sources means to listen to successful people and ignore the opinions of people who have failed in what you are about to do. Which brings me to the third lesson: By building a business you are willing to do what other people are not, so that you are able to obtain what these people cannot. It is a powerful statement, because what will inevitably happen is that these people will not want you to become successful after all and will try to push you down. Don't let them take away your dreams. There were many times in those four years that I was not sure whether I was doing the right thing. I made my share of mistakes, but if I had not made them then, I would be making them now! There is no express elevator to success; you have to climb the stairs one by one. Being in network marketing was the best business school I could have ever attended and the people I met, the relationships I built and the skills I learned are the reason I am where I am today. And that is a place most people will never visit, simply because they are not willing to go through what I went through.

Before talking about my huge move to Asia in 2012, let me challenge you to walk against the line yourself. This can be any time when other people disagree with you, but you know that you are doing the right thing. If you want, start your own business, no matter whether it is your own idea, a franchise or Network Marketing. Get educated, and learn the skills to drive a company forward. Understand that you are succeeding when other people are talking about you; whether it is good or bad, to your face, or behind your back – they are talking about you! You need that, as it is the only way for you to see that you are walking against the line, doing something that others are not capable of doing. Push through and go to greatness. Take action now.

SPACE FOR MY TAKE AWAYS

24.

THE ASIA STORY -
GOING ALL-IN

"You may say I'm a dreamer, but I'm not the only one. I hope someday you'll join us. And the world will live as one." – John Lennon

In the last chapter I shared how I started in a business that required me to move against the "crowd", and how I proved to the naysayers around me that I could succeed where they expected me to fail. While I was building that business, I realized that I would need to get into a market that represented the future. A market with a lot of people and lots of consumption. There is no market larger than Asia, considering that with India, China, Indonesia, and Japan, almost two-thirds of the world is living there. I had travelled to Asia often for kitesurfing, but I had never actually lived or done business there and I knew that many things were different from "Western" countries. I spoke to my girlfriend, family and friends about quitting everything in Europe and transitioning completely to Hong Kong. With its great balance of the Chinese and Western culture I regard Hong Kong as the capital of Asia. They reminded me of how I had previously tried to expand my business to the US and Spain, and had failed miserably. I knew if I wanted to make it, I had to commit and step out of my comfort zone. It was going to be daunting to move into a new city where, although the official languages are Mandarin Chinese and English, the spoken language is mostly Cantonese. And I literally knew just a few people. I spoke to my kitesurfing buddy Jerome, who agreed to let me stay at his place in Hong Kong for the first couple of months, which would help to give me a smooth transition. Without him, I would have never managed to make it. I was scared witless, but I had learned one thing from my basketball idol, Michael Jordan: "You miss 100% of the shots you don't take!"

So, if you are reading this and thinking: "Well, that is great Julian, kudos to you for being so courageous, but what am I supposed to do if I am too scared to step out of my comfort zone?" Let me tell you the secret, and I know it, because I was not courageous enough either. I know that I just told you that I had moved out of my comfort zone, but I didn't tell you how hard it was for me to do it. It took all my courage and strength to bury the fear and force myself onto that airplane and not to get right back on when I reached Hong Kong. Let me explain: I am no super-hero, who can do what others can't. It is actually the exact opposite, but I learned to develop simple and easy skills to overcome that insecurity. What I did that would force me to move out of my comfort zone was to "burn my boats". It is not a tactic that I would apply in every aspect of my life, but I will advise you when and when not to do it.

There is a story about Cortes, the Spanish explorer, who is widely credited with discovering the "New World" of the Americas. When he arrived in the new world in the 1500s, he wanted to conquer the Aztec empire, but wasn't sure his men would be determined enough to do so. They might think about surrendering and stepping back. So what did Cortes do? He burned their boats. He literally set fire to them (or ordered someone else to do it). There was no way out and the men had to fight and win in order to survive. And so they did. See, most people would never burn their boats. They would always leave an option B, maybe even options C or D or E open. So if one thing seems to not be working out, which often happens if you are not committed enough, you move on to the next thing and end up not succeeding at anything.

I had failed in my previous trips to Spain and the U.S. exactly because I did not "burn my boats". Since I wanted to succeed in Hong Kong, I had to step up my game. So, how did I "burn my boats"? Simple: I sold my car in Europe, booked only a one-way flight to Hong Kong, packed up my old apartment in Austria, and even signed the papers to be officially a non-resident in Austria. Could I still go back? Of course, but I had made it a lot harder to actually do it, since I had given up everything there. What would most people have done? Just as I had done for Spain and the US previously, and not given up anything in Austria, keeping an apartment, car, and thereby a backup plan, so as soon as an obstacle appeared, they could move back to their safe and familiar life.

In my first couple of months in Hong Kong, not being able to speak a word of Chinese, it was a constant struggle: a stream of turndowns, rejections and ridicule. Everyone told me I would never be able to succeed. I felt like quitting and going back to Austria, where I spoke the language and was familiar and comfortable with the environment. But that would have meant that I had to book a new expensive flight, look for a rental car and find a place to stay. Eventually I came to the conclusion that whenever I was in self-doubt, that it would be ten times easier to just stay in Hong Kong and stick it through. Had I not put myself with "my back against the wall" with any other option than succeeding, I would have just gone back. The fascinating thing about constantly pushing my own limits was similar to when you train a muscle. I adapted to the challenge until it was not a challenge anymore, but rather became daily business. I had forgotten that the reason I liked Europe so much was because I was used to what was happening there. Hong Kong was a new struggle and initially it was uncomfortable. After a few months in Hong Kong, it was normal and I could not have imagined it any other way.

After around 9 months (it was now almost mid-2013) I managed to achieve mediocre traction for the first time for our business after hustling non-stop. We had built a great and motivated team, even though it was still rather small. Since Hong Kong had some momentum, we now started to expand to other Asian countries: The Philippines, Thailand, Macau, and even New Zealand. When I came to Hong Kong, one of the main answers I got from people about literally anything, no matter whether it was about food, religion, social media, technology, apps or business was: "Sorry Julian, you don't understand, but your way does not work here. Here we are different than what you are used to!" "Julian, Hong Kong is different!" Have you ever said something similar or had that thought when you heard about something new or different that would have forced you to get out of the comfort zone? Well, let me tell you this, I experienced the same reaction in my home country Austria, Germany, US, Dubai, South America, and everywhere I visited in Asia. It didn't matter which topic. I showed people a smartphone and our new app, and the reaction was that people here are not so good with smartphones. We were talking about new technologies and the reply was that these technologies would not get adopted here until around 15 years down the line. Think about yourself, if I ask you the questions above about how advanced your environment is for new things. How good is your country with new apps? How advanced do you think your country is in technology? Is it quite open minded? Want to know something? Whoever you ask these questions, most people will tell you they are not open minded, not "fast adopters" and not good with tech. However, they will tell you that other countries are for sure better than them. It is only them who are so slow. Why is that?

Most people prefer to make excuses about "their" region or country being special, just so they have a good reason to hide behind not having to move out of their comfort zone. I still remember my parents refusing to be on social media, simply because, they claimed, at their age they don't need it. *Right*, and today if I email them I don't get a reply, but if I make a Facebook status update they are the first to comment or like it. You don't have to be the first person jumping on something new, but believe me it will help you big time if you learn to become an early adopter of new technologies and ideas, because they will dominate the world. The time of the "industrial age" ended in the 1980s; we are now in the "information age". Accept it, or become extinct like the dinosaurs or the fax machine. It is not my intention to scare you here, but I have received so much rejection about new concepts and ideas over the last couple of years, that it is hard to put it into words. It was either because people would not accept upcoming changes or they tried to push me down, just because they were scared that I could actually make it happen and they would miss out. Some people who did not even know me slandered me behind my back! Many of these attempts almost worked and would have made me give up on my dreams to create something in Asia. While my story is about building a business, your story could be about something else, such as pursuing a musical career or starting an art collection. You do not get out of your comfort zone, just because it is too cozy in there, and when you get out, you move back too quickly, simply because you can. Learn to resist the lure of your comfort zone and use the tools of burning your boats whenever possible, to let your comfort zone catch up with you, just as mine caught up with me. I learned to deal with all the obstacles over time until I could overcome them with ease.

By 2014 we had massive traction all over Asia and we built a network of far over 20,000 active people being connected through a common meaning. I had overcome the initial resistance and learned to deal with the people's excuses that were basically the same the world over. While some people preferred the wave of change to pass by without them, some stepped up and embraced it. It is amazing to see what one person is capable of achieving with the right mind-set and determination. Whenever you feel like a seemingly insurmountable obstacle is in front of you, remember: A huge wildfire starts with a single flame." You can do anything you set your mind to. Don't make excuses; take action and give it all you've got. Avoid moving back to your comfort zone, and never give in. I probably would have never stayed that long in Hong Kong, had there not been many people around me who wanted to see me fail, but at the same time others who wanted me to succeed. I had to prove the naysayers that I could do it, and I could not disappoint those who believed in me. Moving to a new region can sometimes be very scary, but if you manage to overcome your fears, you will experience a wonderful new world. After my success, many other people tried to get traction within our business as well in Asia. None of them made it. The wave had passed. When I came to Hong Kong, I was facing a lot of rejection because I brought a new idea. It is the only way, however, to create new business. You cannot make a new business on an old idea, you need it to be "new". Those people that stepped up and caught the wave won, the ones that waited will now have to wait for the next wave.

Now in 2015, Bettina and I are facing a similar decision again. Stay in Hong Kong or move away? We have been living here now for over 3 years, although I have been travelling all over Asia non-stop. But now I am looking for a new challenge. I feel that my job is done. I lit the flame and now the fire should burn by itself. That is the idea of residual and scalable income. My network of 27,000 people worldwide needs someone to look up to, and of course, I will not just disappear into thin air, but slowly shift my focus. The interesting thing that I experienced at that moment was that the one single thing that was originally so far outside of my comfort zone, had now become my actual comfort zone, and now I am moving on to something new, outside of my "new" comfort zone. The human body is able to quite quickly adapt to new challenges, but it's more difficult for our minds to accept change. It's so easy for people to fall into a "holding pattern" or as I like to call it, the lazy mode. Today I have been going through the same steps of rejection, adversity, misunderstanding, and sometimes even hatred, as I did back in 2011 when I moved into the business that I am about to step away from now. How strange, no? Actually, it is quite normal. Back in 2011 it was a change to which some people did not want to adapt. Change is never easy, not for anyone. Neither for me, nor for the best entrepreneurs or change-lovers out there. However, some people learn to deal with it, while others get stuck. Adaptability to change is something anyone can learn, just like a language. I had built a business to earn residual income, not to work in it for the rest of my life. I achieved that goal, and now I receive monthly payments, even though I am no longer actively pursuing that business. I can focus on this book, coaching, and consulting, and I am looking into starting my own big business in new areas. In the end, that is what life is all about: having a plan, executing it, no matter what, until the goal is achieved. I have achieved my goal of passive income and that is why it is the right step for me to move on to something new. Never do the same things over and over again and expect different results.

So, should you also change everything you are doing and go all-in? Deciding to "burn your boats" doesn't mean you should also "burn your bridges". Don't burn the connections (bridges) to your friends or family. Yes, you should stay away from people that put you down, but that does not mean you have to ignore all of them completely; you decide what works best for you. This also means, you should not give up your main income-providing job (bridge) while you are preparing to "burn the boats". Most businesses can be started part-time, and only later will you actually need to take a true leap of faith and go "all in". There are some entrepreneurial risk takers like Elon Musk (CEO of Tesla Motors and Space-X) who risked every dime he and his family had on his success. He was as close to total bankruptcy as one could possibly be, but he actually pushed through and made it. He is the exception to the rule. I am by no means advising you to play it safe – au contraire! I think you should just take many calculated risks in life, but you should maintain the connections that matter to you. I hope the difference makes sense to you. Whether you are planning a big move yourself or just want some inspiration for you own story, take away these three massive lessons from my time when I moved to Hong Kong. First, understand that those who prefer to stay in their own comfort zone will use every possible excuse to explain why they should stay there, and thereby keep you there with them. If they have children, they will use their children as an excuse, while the children should actually be the reason to strive for greatness. This is just one excuse of many. The end result is always the same. It did not matter whether I spoke to people in Austria, Germany, the U.S., Spain, or Hong Kong. It was always their "region" that was special compared to all the others. People love to use "others", which means to make them special or outstanding. In the end, people all over the world in my opinion want to have similar things: People want to be happy, they want to feel safe, they want to be around people who respect them and they don't like change. I hope you realize this for yourself the next time you fall into this trap as well. The comfort zone is cozy, but the magic is happening outside!

I sometimes feel exhausted from pushing myself outside, and the only way I manage to do it, just like coming to Asia, is to "burn the boats". This is the second lesson to take away from this story. It means that I took away what kept me in Austria, so that for me to move back became harder and harder. Then, to actually move outside the comfort zone becomes the easier path, and that is why I not only moved to Hong Kong but also stayed there. I forced myself to accept the fact that I would be uncomfortable for some time in a new environment. Within just a few weeks however, the uncomfortable became comfortable. You will experience the same thing if you leave your "safe haven". Remember however, burn boats, do not burn bridges. With bridges I mean the connections that you are using regularly, for example, friendships and networks. Even though I burnt my boats, making it hard to move back to Europe, I stayed in touch with friends and family to keep the relationships alive. If they had become a reason why I should move back, I would have cut the communication so I wasn't tempted. Also, I was making enough money to be sure

I could survive, even though I initially struggled financially in Hong Kong. So even though it was a new environment, I did not endanger the people I love or myself. I firmly believe that most people struggle with new environments and change, but it is the tools we use to deal with them that separate those who thrive from those that are crushed under the weight of change. The reason I am pointing this out again is that many people believe that the great achievers are somewhat special, but it is only the tools they use to handle the pressure and change that are special, not the actually people themselves.

The third and last lesson is to put yourself ahead of the wave if you want to be successful in business. Just as you would do in basketball or any ball sport, you want to run to where the ball is going to be, and not where it is now. If you run where the ball is already, it will bounce away to somewhere else and you will be too late. In surfing, it is exactly the same phenomenon. The good surfers position themselves ahead of the waves, and not behind. I am telling you this because I see so many people and companies who are falling behind trends and are running to catch up after they have "missed the wave" Many people fail to embrace new technologies and do not understand that apps and mobile data devices are the future. I have been fortunate to work with so many cultures and backgrounds that it was amazing to see how people or companies tend to wait to see what happens, without preparing for it, so they can benefit from the new trends. Steve Jobs once said: "Once you understand that the world we live in was created by people that are no smarter than you, so for you to predict the future, the best way is to create it yourself!" I hope you take this third lesson, to start to anticipate where a market or trend is heading. My move to Asia was my business break-through, but not because there was so much already in place, but because I created it together with an amazing team. Today I am looking for the next wave. This is what true entrepreneurs do. Learn to read trends, embrace change, and never consider your region being unique in a certain field for business.

You can apply this to anything else you are doing or planning on doing. My move to Asia might have been an easy challenge for someone else, but it was extremely tough for me. It was so far outside of my comfort zone that it gave me nightmares. I had been travelling my entire adult life, but I always went home at some point. That is exactly what I forgot about many times while in Asia – I could have gone home any time had I truly wanted. So, are you on the verge of doing something, but are scared to take the "risk" of moving out of your comfort zone? Let me challenge you: be honest with yourself, and admit that you could step back in any time. You could go back. Be honest with yourself! So, take up the challenge, and take the leap of faith! Boats look beautiful in the harbor, but that is not what they are made for; they are made for sailing. So now it's your time to go "all in", burn your boats and launch into a new challenge, ahead of the crowd.

SPACE FOR MY TAKE AWAYS

25.

THE FINAL STORY -
BEING FINANCIALLY FREE

"We are never in lack of money. We are in lack of people with big dreams who would die for them to become reality!" – Jack Ma, Founder of Alibaba

The past 24 stories were memories from the times in my life from age five to 29. This last story is about what is going on in my life right now and the lessons to take away for the future. So far I have been describing lessons for the right mindset, health, productivity, relationships, and business. I have covered financial topics briefly, but I want to get into more detail in this last chapter, as it is affecting me a lot at the moment, in a good way. I talked briefly about the Cashflow Quadrant in the Cashflow Story, which is story seventeen. Looking back at Kiyosaki's book, there is a lot of theory in it, which is mind-blowing and great, but it is lacking the clear guidelines on how to actually move to the right side of the quadrant. I know I am repeating myself by saying knowledge is not worth much, if you don't act upon it. Eventually I have gained that knowledge myself through meeting some extremely smart people at conferences, workshops and seminars; and from all the information I have gathered, I was able to develop seven income streams for myself that will make me a USD millionaire before the age of 30. If you are reading this and thinking, "I don't care about becoming a millionaire", then keep reading anyway for some hands-on tips that you can easily use, even if you just want to make a little bit of money on the side. Remember, the goal isn't to give up work, but to be able to spend the time and energy on your true passions. Whether this is collecting stamps, playing golf, travelling, staying in your job, or doing something completely different that interests you, it does not matter. Money does not buy happiness, but it gives you options. And by using these options wisely, you can become incredibly happy and satisfied.

My goal since early in life was to be financially free; that means I could live my life without having to worry about money. What was important for me to understand was that becoming financially free did not necessarily mean that I had to earn a lot of money, but rather that I was able to keep a lot. This is an important concept, because many people earn a lot, but also spend a lot and can therefore never achieve financial freedom. So, before I go into the income side of the equation, I want to talk about your expenses. You have to cut down on them as much as possible, which will allow you to invest the leftover money in the various income streams described in this chapter. I shared with you in my Saving-Story (Story Number Six) how playing Monopoly taught me to put aside as much money as possible at the beginning of a month. I have kept increasing that percentage over time, and today I am trying to put aside 50% of any money coming in, so that I can invest it into new income streams. You don't have to start with 50%, but start with 10%. You just have to try it out by putting the money aside as soon as it comes in, and not waiting until the end. This might mean that I cannot visit coffee shops, or that I won't eat out as often, but being financially free is extremely important to me and it starts with controlling my expenses. Re-visit story number six [The Savings Story] to remind yourself that you have to accept to make sacrifices in the short run. The next way to cut down costs is to get rid of bad debt that has high interest rates. In general, this is credit card debt, consumer loans, or other payments that you only make for consumption. Do you remember when I almost went bankrupt having to take out a huge loan from the bank to cover my financial losses in Brazil? I paid off that loan as soon as possible and thereby avoided paying out high interest. The two biggest expense factors are uncontrolled daily expenses and high interest rates on consumer loans. Make sure you are in control of both. I learned that at the age of 24 and within a couple of years I had mastered them. If I can do it, you can probably do it ten times faster! The trick of paying down a big loan is the same as you would eat a big meal: one piece at a time. This means, if you owe US$10,000, then don't wait until you have saved up the entire amount, but pay off (for example) US$100 a month, consistently.

Now I will talk about the most exciting part, which is where your income can and should be coming from. I talked briefly about this in story 17 (The Cashflow Story) already, so go back to that if you want to freshen up on it. I will now share my personal experiences with all the income streams that I have created for myself since then. As mentioned above, I learned to use them from other very successful people, seminars and workshops. You might have your own examples and stories, but I hope that by sharing mine, I might inspire you to consider new or other options. I have learned that, generally speaking, all possible incomes can be summarized in seven different streams.

Income stream one is the only active one, where you exchange time for money, and is on the left side of the Cashflow Quadrant – all the others will be on the right side, and thereby scalable. I talked about income stream one in the Cashflow Story already, so I will only scratch the surface here to avoid repetition. Up to the age of 24, 100% of my income came from income stream one, but today my income from this stream is a tiny percentage of my entire income, and comes from my coaching and consulting activities. It took me close to five years to shift my income entirely, but it is achievable for anyone and should be your goal as well because it opens up completely new avenues of freedom for what to do with your time. You can start building the other income streams step by step, and at some point you no longer need income stream one. For example I used the money I earned from kitesurfing to invest into other projects that built my scalable income side of the other quadrants over time. As long as you watch your expenses, and keep investing as much money as possible from income stream one into the other income streams you can follow the same blueprint. Income streams two, three, four and five are in the Investor Quadrant, and Income streams six and seven are the Business Quadrant.

Income stream two is interest income. This is the scalable income that most of us either know of, or have experienced already, simply because banks tell us about it. I wonder why? Putting my money in the bank when I was less than ten years old taught me the power of interest, but back then the interest rates were still quite high. Today, interest is close to zero, so it will make a tiny fraction of your income, but actually a lot of profit for the bank... ah right, that is why they tell us about it! The reason why I believe it is still important and it does make sense to put back-up money into a savings account, is that I try to keep six months worth of expenses in there in case anything goes wrong and I need a back-up, I have access to it quickly and it gives me peace of mind. In return I have to accept to have low interest, however with online banking there are quite a few banks offering fair deals even in low interest times. There are ways to spike up your interest income however. When I was kitesurfing in Venezuela a few years ago, I met an early investor of a peer-to-peer lending platform in the U.S. He showed me the future of money lending and I was amazed. The concept is simple, as I will now demonstrate in this example. You lend US$1,000 to someone, but you split it up between 100 different people. Each borrower then receives US$10 from you. Other lenders do the same and so any borrower will receive US$1,000 in total, not from one person, but split up between various people. The borrower pays the lenders fair interest in return and since risks are shared over a group, it is very unlikely that all US$1,000 is ever at risk. These P2P lending platforms are becoming very popular all over the world, and I am using them in Europe as well as in Hong Kong. I get close to 20% return per year on my capital with an acceptable amount of downside risk, which is excellent. What you could do for example is to add US$100 a month to such an account (for example from the money that you save from income stream one). After a year that would be a total of US$1,200. 20% interest income from that is US$240 a year, or US$20 a month. Over time this amount builds up and your scalable and residual income out of stream two will rise considerably.

A Note of Caution: As with any financial undertaking, there are always risks. Carry out your own research and don't rely on the word of others, even me. My personal sharing of what I do to optimize my interest income is not an instruction. Never invest into anything without knowing what you are actually doing.

Income stream three comes by way of dividends. The first time I heard about dividends was when I read a book by J.D. Rockefeller, who said: "Do you know the only thing that gives me true pleasure? It is to see the dividends coming in!" Since this came from one of the richest men who have lived on our planet, this fired my curiosity to find out more. Simply put, dividends are paid by companies to the companies' owners. The easiest way to own an entire or part of a company is to own stocks. You might be reading this thinking: "No way, stocks are so risky and you also lost money in stocks Julian!" This is not entirely correct. You can minimize your risks in stocks by obtaining knowledge about them. That was exactly the reason why I had lost so much money before. I had no clue what I was doing back then. Most people buy stocks and hope for them to increase in value. This is a pure gamble. I used to buy stocks like that too. But when I was 26 years old I went to a great investing seminar in Zurich, and the speaker there showed us what, in his opinion, was the "best way" to invest in stocks. It was to go for yield, rather than speculating on appreciation. Yield is basically dividends, even though there are other strategies as well. You can read about it on

Investopedia or other financial websites. The idea is to buy stocks of a great company that has a history of paying regular dividends every year and to buy them at a good price. Some companies increase those dividends over time, which is even better. After I buy the stocks, I do not care about whether the price goes up or down, but I "get pleasure from the dividends coming in". If you have never bought stocks before, then do NOT run out blindly to do so. Consult an expert (or even several experts) and never get into something where you do not understand the risks. I hope you have learned that by now.

I want to tell you in even more in detail what I am doing, and again, please do not take this as instruction. It is for you, and you alone, to decide what works for you. I buy stocks of dividend paying companies, mainly from the Dividend Aristocrat[27] list, and keep them for a long time. This is basically a collection of companies that have a great track record for paying dividends. I will only ever sell the stock if the company stops paying dividends; otherwise I plan on keeping them for years. If the stock market goes down, and stocks get cheaper, I buy more. I try to get dividend yields of around 3-4%, which is not always easy to find. But for example in 2011, or now in the summer of 2015, there are so many great companies that are available at good prices. What you can do as a newbie, is first of all to learn about how stock trading works (read books or go to a seminar), and then ease into the market by investing a little bit of your income every month into various stocks over time. This is called dollar cost averaging. For example you could start with US$100 a month and buy an ETF[28] of dividend paying companies (for example SDY[29]). Over time you will build a very nice group of stocks that pay you money almost every month. The stocks' prices might go up or down, but you will still get dividend payments

---

27 http://www.dividend.com/dividend-stocks/25-year-dividend-increasing-stocks.php

28 Exchange Traded Fund

29 https://www.spdrs.com/product/fund.seam?ticker=sdy

guaranteed. As previously stated, please make sure that you are fully informed before plunging in, and do not just act on other peoples' say-so (including mine!). Remember Warren Buffet's words: "Be greedy when others are fearful, but fearful when others are greedy!" From time to time I get a "good tip" from a friend or the newspaper, which I rarely follow, simply because my own rules seem to pay off a lot more. Many times I am sitting for hours doing research on the financial products. I use http://finance.yahoo.com and www.seekingalpha.com but you might find your own tools. Always be careful, whom you listen to; everyone has an agenda, and that may or may not be to your benefit.

Income stream four is the income of "buy and sell". It is one of the most powerful investment incomes possible, because of its extreme scalability. Just think about all the money that is made from import and export, which is entirely buy and sell profits. I got into buying and selling very early in my life, and the two main lessons I want to share with you are: be an expert in the field where you want to trade, and make the money in the "buy". It is important to understand it is never guaranteed that you can sell anything at a higher price than you bought it. Someone might tell you that a wine will appreciate or gold will always go up. This is simply not true. You might want to make money selling stamps, shoes, diamonds, bitcoin, stocks, real estate, or anything else. Only get into a field where you consider that you know more than 99% of the other participants. Remember the story when I was in basketball and I bought and sold basketball gear to make good profits? I was well versed in prices and the sport, and it was the same again when I was in frequent flying or in kitesurfing. Each time I considered myself to be an expert in these areas and there were not many others who knew more than me about which flights or kitesurf gear. So, if you bought an apartment or a stock, in hope that prices would increase, or you bought gold or rare wine for that matter, let me tell you who the experts are on these things: THE EXPERTS! You may be very knowledgeable but ask yourself seriously, "Am I an expert?" There are very few people who make consistent profits with trading wine, and I have not met one person who made consistent money with trading gold. The best banks in the world lose money on these things because it is impossible to predict where the market is heading. So go into a field, where you consider yourself an expert, and then read the three top books in that field, to strengthen your knowledge.

The second important lesson on income stream four is to make the money on the "buy". If you want to invest in wine, you need to be close to 100% sure that the price you are buying it at is the lowest in the market. The same is true for stocks, stamps, or diamonds. When I bought the basketball gear in Germany, I knew that very few people could get the same price. There is legal insider trading in any industry, and it is always the people who make the money on the "buy" who will win in the long term. Everything else is gambling and not sustainable. For example I have a friend from Switzerland who constantly tells me how much money he just made on a Penny-Stock,[30] or on a gambling-scheme. But this only works until his luck swings the other way; then all his money is gone again and he starts from scratch. It happens every year, but he never learns his lesson. In basketball or flying or kitesurfing I still consider myself to have expert knowledge, and so I can buy and sell with significant profits in these niche markets. I do not gamble on hopes for price appreciations. I know I will buy at a price that I can always beat when I sell. The richest people or the largest companies in the world do the same thing, just at a larger scale. They buy in China and sell in Europe or the U.S. It is almost impossible for them to lose money as long as people in Europe or America cannot buy these things themselves in China. You have to find your own niche, study it, and build your income stream four successfully!

Income stream five is real estate, which has become one of my favorite income streams, especially in the past

---

30 A stock with very low price, sometimes just a few cents, with extreme fluctuations in price

year. It is very powerful, but also time-consuming, looking at new deals, sourcing new options and making phone calls. Without my dad, who is helping me on this big time, I could never do it. Just as I described in income stream four, do not buy real estate in the hope of appreciation, but buy it for the rental yield. It takes time to become an expert in that field, but it can be a great niche, especially in your designated area, which is where you should start. Do not buy your first property far away. I bought my first one right next to where I grew up. I also bought a lot of books about this subject and went to real estate seminars. I had learned from my mistakes in Brazil, where I had lost all my money due to lack of understanding. I have given you clear guidelines so far for all the income streams and I want to do the same here. At some point however, you have to gain actual experience, and with that, you will make some mistakes. That is normal. Do not be discouraged, rather learn from your mistakes and keep going. Since income streams two to five are part of the I-Investor quadrant and I always go for yield, my goal in any of these investments is to have a 20% per year return on my own capital. I can do this in P2P lending and I can do this with dividends if I get a good price on a great company. It is my minimum return as well in "buy and sell" and it is also the return I want on my own money in real estate. So, when I buy a potential property, I want to buy a property where I see a positive market tendency, but moreover where I can make around 20% annual return on the money that I invest. Let's say I invest US$100,000 of my own money, then my target is to generate around US$20,000 a year from that. These deals are not easy to find, but who said it was easy? I just said they were straightforward guidelines. Imagine having saved up US$100,000 and you generate US$20,000 a year from that using these guidelines. Most people could live on that. That is why I explain it step by step here so it becomes achievable for anyone. Again, don't follow blindly. These are just the personal experiences that are working for me after several others, less successful attempts. Income streams two to five can either be funded with the money you earn from income stream one or from the yield generated within these incomes. It is called compounding, and so the earlier you start doing it, the faster you will accrue a sizeable income. Being young does have some advantages here, but I found that the older you are, the better and calmer you become, especially in the "buy and sell" income. For example more senior investors have experienced typical market cycles, and do not get thrown off too quickly if things seem not to be going their way. They stay calm, and wait for the "right" moment, which they have learned through prior mistakes, and they use the knowledge they have gained from these experiences.

One of the skills I have learned over the past years and it is a skill that you should also learn, is the ability to raise money for such investments. It will really increase your earning possibilities because you can leverage on these incomes even though you don't have much money yourself yet. Imagine buying an apartment for US$ 1 million, without you having to put up any money of your own. You manage to raise it from someone else, with you putting in the sweat-equity. To summarize: Income stream one is based on time (the more time you spend doing work, the more you get paid) and income streams two to five are based on the money that is part of the play (the more apartments or stocks you own, the higher the potential returns). The last two income streams (six and seven) are based on how much value is served to how many people. They are the incomes of the Big Business Quadrant, which is the most powerful and exciting of all. I talked about it in the last couple of chapters and I would say that most millionaires and probably all billionaires made their fortunes in this quadrant through these income streams. Once they have made their fortunes, they most likely keep their money in income streams two to five, because this is where money works to generate more money. The concept is simple, but again, not easy. To earn money from a business you need to create something that brings as much value as possible to as many other people as possible. You do not necessarily need a lot of money to get started, but the more value you can give and the more people you can reach, the more money you will get in return. Most of the time you don't even need a new idea. You just need to see a need for something in the market place and then take massive action with great execution.

Income stream six is Royalties and Licenses, the category into which my kitesurfing book falls, for example. It was not an amazing idea and there are other people offering kitesurfing books as well, but it was the great teamwork and execution of how the book was put together that made it successful. We are selling thousands of books a year, giving great value to kitesurfers all over the world. And in return I am paid a royalty every month – the more people I reach, the more value I give, the more royalties I make. Famous singers or authors make so much money because they use a network of distributors, publishers and marketers to get their service or product out to millions of people. Back in 2011 income stream six was my first real step over to the right side of the Cashflow Quadrant. If you want to benefit from this income stream, think of a topic to write about, just as I have done in kitesurfing and again with this book. Anyone can do it, but it is just about actually doing it. Having the book finished is maybe 10% of the work. Now it is about using distribution services, publishers, and other marketers to get the book into the hands of the readers. Or if you are a singer, the same applies and you need to use label companies or YouTube to get your voice heard. Maybe you have an idea for a great patent, and you can license that to another company. In general, the more experience you have, the better are your chances with this income. It is good if you start investing into incomes two to five while you are younger, as time is working against the compounding effect the older you get. In income stream six use your knowledge, create something the world needs, find a problem you can solve and get it out there. It has taken me a lot of time while I was writing this book, but the good thing is, it is scalable and I can earn residual income afterwards. I did not need much money to write my book, rather a lot of sweat equity and knowledge. It means anyone who would also want to do that as well, can do it, and believe me: Income stream six is what you want as a big part of your total income.

Income stream seven is building a business with equity that you could later have the option to sell to other investors. It is what I described in stories 23 and 24 and it is the most powerful income of all, but also the hardest to achieve. It is the income that allows people like Elon Musk or Mark Zuckerberg to become billionaires, starting from literally no money at all. If you want to build your own successful big business, you need to learn three major skills. First, you need to learn how to raise money. Even if you already are a millionaire, you will need to convince other people to invest into your business so it can scale and grow even faster. Secondly, you need to learn how to attract other great and talented people to work with you. You might be a genius, but you cannot do it all and your company is only as strong as its weakest link. For example Steve Jobs, who was a great entrepreneur and marketer, managed to have Steve Wozniak as his engineer or Jony Ive as his designer. He could have never made Apple great without them. These are just a few examples of the importance of this skill. I used to work with a company where the founder was excellent in raising capital, but could neither manage to recruit nor keep talented people. What happened was that the company was constantly struggling, as it never produced innovative products and that is not what I want to happen to you. The third skill is that you need to be a relentless, hard-worker who never gives up. Building your own big business is difficult and only those that push through hard will succeed. Income stream seven will be where I will be spending most of my time after this book is finished. It will take me 100 hours a week and I won't get paid straight away, but consistently over time and it will be all worth it.

Here I have laid out the seven income streams with guidelines that anyone can follow! If you want to make US$1 million a year you have to make US$2,740 a day, or around US$115 every hour. To quote Steve Jobs; "Stay hungry – Stay foolish". In six months I am turning 30 years old, and one of my 2015 new year's goals was to become a US$ millionaire before my 30th birthday. I still have some time to go and even though it is a huge goal and I am not sure if I will achieve it, I am striving hard to get there. I calculated that anyone who puts their mind to it could become a millionaire within ten years by working with these seven income streams. Shoot for the stars and reach the moon. Since my income is sufficient for my needs now, why not quit everything and travel to "live life". It is no longer about the money; it is about a deeper meaning, which is something everybody needs. Residual income allows everyone to pursue his or her passions to a deeper extent. I had studied medicine to help other people. Although I am not practicing actively as a medical doctor I do want to help others by paying it forward with this book. I want to give back some of the knowledge and tips that I have received from other people. Chances are that you have completely different ideas for your own meaning for life, and I want to emphasize one thing to take to heart: When you are on your death bed, you will not care one little bit about how much money you have, you will only care about the impact your life has had on others. So don't waste your time running after money, but use it to build residual income so you can focus on important things with meaning.

Take away the three most important lessons from this chapter: First, stop trading "time for dollars" as soon as you can. You need to develop the mindset of your time being the most valuable asset in your life and learn to generate money, either from money or by giving value to other people. Lesson two: Learn to use the seven streams of income that I described above. Use only one or two to start, but try to use as many as you can over time. It might take a while for you master them, but once you do, you will rock your life. The third key lesson is to leave the past behind, and focus on the future. Have dreams and set goals. This gets harder as you get older, but this is when it is the most important. Know where you are going; otherwise you will end up lost.

I hope that these 25 stories have taught you some valuable lessons that will help you to look forward and build your future. So my wish would be that whoever reads this book can be motivated to grow. If I can do it, so can you. So please go out and help to make the world a better place. My last call for action is that if you find this book helpful, pass it on to just one other person to help them change their life forever as well. The more you give to others, the more you get back.

Let's go and tell the world.

SPACE FOR MY TAKE AWAYS

WHAT IS NEXT?

"In any moment of decision, the best thing you can do is the right thing, the next best thing is the wrong thing, and the worst thing you can do is nothing." – Theodore Roosevelt

I started this book at the beginning of 2015 while I was on holiday in Phuket, Thailand. It was on my To-Do list for this year as a goal that I had always wanted to achieve. Now, as I am writing this chapter it is the end of September, so it took me roughly nine months to complete it. While writing, many people asked me how I will publish it, or who would buy such a book. You know what? Say "Yes", tell the world, and figure the details out later. Even though I have finished writing, I have no idea yet about the next steps. I have written this book out of a passion to leave a legacy, a tool that my children might be able to pick up, and learn 75 valuable lessons from 25 stories that will boost their lives in ways that they could not have done without. You might think that I am nuts to start writing without actually having a plan. I have to admit, you are probably right, but I had a clear goal and that was to publish this book within one year, by the end of 2015, and as you are either holding this book in your hands or reading it as an eBook I have achieved that goal.

Looking back, the first couple of chapters were easy to write, as I was really motivated when I got started. As with anything, after a while it became a routine and the excitement dropped off. I began thinking that I should change the title of the book to "10 Stories I would tell my Younger Self". I kept coming up with excuses why ten stories would be enough. But actually, it was just because I wanted to give myself a let-out clause! I am quite a slow writer and if I wrote two pages a day that was good progress. So what was the solution? I burnt my boats. I went out and told all my close friends that I was going to write 25 stories. So they all knew and I could not cut the number of stories down. Remember, we all have the same struggles - the difference is just how we deal with them. I am not naturally good at this, but I learned how to overcome it, and I have passed them on to you in this book. For my kitesurfing book I had a partner who did the illustrations and publishing, so now it was a whole new ball game finding someone to proof-read, draw the illustrations, design a good cover, and roll out the publishing. Without Bettina none of that would have actually been possible. Even when the book was finished, I wanted to cut the physical part and just leave it as an e-book. But guess what I had done already? I had told everyone that they could read a hard copy, so I had to deliver. I had set my goals, and I worked out the plan along the way, using the same trick to stay committed, as I had done so many times before. If you are not 100% sure about something that you want to do, you will come up with excuses and you surly won't commit to it. 100%. I know every time that I will probably try to chicken out, so I simply have to take precautionary measures. For me this is telling the world, for you it might be something else. Whatever it is, use it if you want to get something done.

It was an amazing journey throughout this book while travelling through dozens of different countries and three different continents. Sometimes I was flying in Economy Class from Bangkok to Chiang Mai and other times it was on a business class flight from Zurich to Hong Kong. On a trip to Europe I had some melancholy thoughts, and then I wrote the sad chapters. Other times I just came home from a great basketball match or kitesurfing session and wrote the happy chapters. Sometimes I wrote in utter silence, while other times I listened to classical music. Authors say that when you write you find yourself, and I have to admit it is almost like meditation when clicking the keyboard and seeing the words appear on the laptop screen. This is my second book, and even though I am sure it will not be my last, it is especially important to me, as it allowed me to express my deepest life lessons that I would love to pass on to the world. Many times people read success stories and books that focus mostly on a person's current achievements, but most people reading the book are still on their initial steps of a long journey. I know how hard it is to go against the odds and even more, your family, friends, or today, social media, who tell you that you won't make it. You might have already taken the first step on a new venture, but you get stuck with the fear of what these other people think of you, which paralyses you and stops you from raising your voice or letting your light shine, out of fear of what others may think. Remember, it is not about what others think; people will think what they want, irrespective of what you do. Be a person of virtue, and others will buy into you no matter what. There is no other way to overcome that initial fear other than to accept that it exists and carry on, anyway and to refuse to be defined by the voices in other people's heads. I know it is hard, but just like anything else that is hard, it is totally worth it.

If you have read this book from the start, by now you should have made your long term, mid-term and short-term goals. You should have written a daily To-Do list and have a good routine. No matter whether you are rich or poor, have a college degree or not, are popular or not, all the steps can be followed with little to no money. People don't become big achievers because of the great help they receive, but rather because they remain motivated, take a firm decision, and work hard to overcome large obstacles. Maybe your obstacle is that you have too much help around you. Focus on your essential income producing activities in life and push your life to the next level. Imagine how awesome it will be, when you are financially free, or time free or are free to choose whenever and wherever, you will travel. To which person, or people, have you always wanted to prove that you are capable of more? All these factors should motivate you to take action based on the lessons from these 25 stories. I re-read them every single time I have doubts myself. 2016 will be a powerful year and if you set goals or have dreams, make them huge – it costs the same energy as setting small ones, so you might as well make your goals big!

Will I be staying in Hong Kong in 2016? I don't know. Bettina and I will go where the biggest opportunities are calling us. Neither one of us is scared to try new things. Yes, we might fail in these new ventures, but with every failure lessons are learned, and these lessons will boost our knowledge and skills for new projects in the future. What matters is the action you take based on what happens to you. Some people learn to make the best out of every situation and my goal was to show you that I was an average child who took "the road less travelled" many times to produce extraordinary results, whether it was in choosing not to pursue a career in medicine or leaving Austria and moving abroad. Many people won't make decisions like that because such decisions have never been a part of the lives of the people they know. I hope that these stories will inspire others to brave and make the decisions that matter to them. Today's business environment, with social media and online businesses allows everyone to start a business from scratch for just a few hundred dollars that literally has the potential to earn millions of dollars in the future. So use these opportunities when you see them.

I want to thank once again all the people who made this book possible, especially:

- Most of all, I want to thank once again my partner Bettina, as without her, this book would have never been possible. Taking care of all those areas related to actually getting the book published, such as sourcing vendors, talking to suppliers, and dealing with the logistics, would have been impossible without her.

- Gillian Kew for editing and checking the final version, and giving me valuable feedback on the style.

- Terry Teemley for editing the first draft.

- Also, I would like to shout out a big thank you to all the podcasters, bloggers and marketers who helped me get the word out, so that people (maybe even you) get to know about this book

- And of course all the other people who gave me feedback on the title, cover and layout. There are so many, I cannot name them all here.

If you reach out to me on social media, let me know what you liked best about the book. Which story inspired you the most? Is there anything that you would have loved to hear more about? I would love to get YOUR success story when reading these 25 stories – nothing would make me happier than hearing how this book helped you.

If you want to meet me in person, you will find me either on the beach, on the basketball court, or on my next venture in shorts and t-shirt working hard for the next start-up to change the world and leave a legacy.

Knowing is nothing – Execution and Action are everything!

Yours,

Julian

About the Author

Dr. Julian Hosp is an author, entrepreneur, and leapfrog high performer. Julian was born in 1986 in Austria. In his teens he played professional basketball in Austria and then went on to become a professional kitesurfer for almost ten years. There he wrote his first book, "Kitesurfing Tricktionary". He graduated from Innsbruck Medical University in 2011, but later he decided to employ his hard-earned skills and discipline in the business world, rather than in medicine. Looking back, he describes that decision as one of the hardest ones in his life, as both his family and friends expected him to develop a career as a medical doctor. In 2012 Julian moved to Hong Kong, together with his partner Bettina, to expand his business ventures in Asia. Today he is not only a successful author and entrepreneur, but has become a much sought-after public speaker, coach, and social-media-strategist for individuals and companies all over the world. His life motto is "work-life-balance is all about doing that one thing 100%" and his favorite food is the fastest food available to save time. At the time of writing of this book, Julian is still living in Hong Kong and when not pursuing his next venture is out playing basketball or rocking the waves, kitesurfing.

The best ways to connect with Julian are:

www.25stories.org
www.facebook.com/25stories
www.twitter.com/25_stories
www.instagram.com/25stories

CPSIA information can be obtained
at www.ICGtesting.com
Printed in the USA
FSOW02n1945211216
28760FS

9 789881 485007